Archibald Duff

Old Testament Theology

The History of Hebrew Religion from the Year 800 B.C. to Josiah 640 B.C.

Archibald Duff

Old Testament Theology
The History of Hebrew Religion from the Year 800 B.C. to Josiah 640 B.C.

ISBN/EAN: 9783337416836

Printed in Europe, USA, Canada, Australia, Japan

Cover: Foto ©Lupo / pixelio.de

More available books at **www.hansebooks.com**

OLD TESTAMENT THEOLOGY

OR

THE HISTORY OF HEBREW RELIGION
FROM THE YEAR 800 B.C.

BY

ARCHIBALD DUFF, M.A., LL.D.
PROFESSOR OF OLD TESTAMENT THEOLOGY IN THE YORKSHIRE
UNITED INDEPENDENT COLLEGE, BRADFORD

FROM 800 B.C. TO JOSIAH 640 B.C.

LONDON & EDINBURGH
ADAM & CHARLES BLACK
1891

Begun on the Eve of my Father's Birthday in 1889.

To his Memory

BE INSCRIBED ALL THAT I WRITE;

FOR HIS DEVOUTNESS AND HIS DEVOTION

TO WHATEVER WAS HIGHEST HAVE BEEN TO ME THE

INSPIRING WORD OF THE ETERNAL.

A. D.

July 9, 1891.

PREFACE.

The attempt is here made to write the history of Hebrew beliefs from the year 800 B.C., as these are preserved for us in the Old Testament, to delineate the personality of each contributor to them, and to estimate the place of each in the onward movement. The time seems ripe for such a work.

The appearance of treatises on related topics, literary and historical, in the field of Old Testament study, and the demand for these, imply the further need for a constructive account of Hebrew religion as a living growth in history. Two works have just appeared which may well be said to mark an epoch in Biblical study in this country, viz., Professor Cheyne's Bampton Lectures for 1889, on "The Origin of the Psalter," and Professor Driver's "Introduction to the Literature of the Old Testament." Let me here thank Professor Cheyne for his magnificent work, so eloquent and so rich in stores of learning. By it he renders signal service to all thoughtful religious teachers, and through them to the whole kingdom of God. It has been a deep pleasure to me to see that method of work with Old Testament documents which I have contended for in this volume so clearly laid down and so strictly followed by Professor Cheyne in his handling of the Psalms. He begins his work by exposition of those psalms about whose date there is little or no controversy, and thence proceeds to give judgments, thus made possible and reliable, concerning the controverted writings; and his aim, above all, is to construct the story of religious life and faith manifested in that poetry. I may borrow from Professor Cheyne his words on p. 124, and apply them to my own work and to my conviction of its correctness in principle; as he says, "Our conception of the range of Bible-history, and of the extent and methods of inspiration, has already, I trust, begun to widen. The opening words of Heb. i. 1 ($\pi o \lambda \nu \mu \epsilon \rho \hat{\omega} s$ καὶ πολυτρόπως) should already be acquiring a richer and more satisfying significance."

Professor Driver's admirable work is a new departure altogether in English literature. I am very fortunate in having been able to consult it while reading the proofs of the following pages. The appearance of such works means that our Christian teachers are turning with a new devotion to the Old Testament, and are demanding all possible aid in its study, and in the investigation of the arena on which Christianity appeared. The present volume aims to serve this study by a constructive view of the facts of Hebrew religious life.

Another ground for publication is, that many men in the ministry urge that they ought to be allowed to share in the joy which students in class testify they find in this investigation. For some sixteen years I have been lecturing, in the Congregational College and in the University in Montreal, and in Airedale College and the United College here, on the whole course of the history of Hebrew religious faiths down to the end of the first Christian century. To Professor

Duhm, now of Basel, and to his *Theologie der Propheten*, published in 1875, I owe deep gratitude for early guidance by that pioneer work in this direction. The pleasure which the men of my classes have received has been evidently deep. I have myself been surprised, and made more glad than I had dreamed I should be, by their enthusiastic and lasting devotion to the Old Testament, as it has constantly arisen. Many have begun the work with a prejudice against the Book, produced by want of acquaintance with it. For this want of acquaintance the treatment of the precious records as a mere canon or rule and liturgy is largely to blame. An unhistorical method kills interest in the records of life: "The letter killeth, but the spirit giveth life" (2 Cor. iii. 6). Let me here say how my students have made my classwork a constant delight, even while sorrow has been my companion; and let me thank the whole loved brotherhood of fellow-workers who have gone out from the classroom to tell widely of the beauty and blessing in the Old Testament.

For, all about me near and far, here and over the sea, pastors have urged that the method and results so interesting to students should be laid before men who are already beyond class-days. Hitherto much difficulty has lain across the way, but now the demand has made the answer possible.

The origin of the following discussions as class-instruction explains much of their form, and may let me anticipate some criticisms. Perhaps I preach too much in these pages. But I am called in my life-work to teach men to preach; and I can never forget this. Rather have I both preached regularly to my classes to show them how to use the Old

Testament for the people, and to this end I have devoted a large share of my time to preaching to missionary congregations up and down the country; and no doubt I have thus taken on the preacher's habit. But I am comforted by remembering that the greatest teachers I have known—my beloved master and dear friend, Professor Park, as also the late Professor Phelps, and Professor E. C. Smythe of Andover, and again Tholuck, my almost more than father, and Ritschl, both saintly and now sainted men, and even Lagarde, my inspiration, so also younger men of singular teaching power, Haupt of Halle and Herrmann of Marburg,—all have seemed to me to preach to their classes as they taught. It is no doubt right thus to rouse enthusiasm.

Perhaps I have deviated from strict historical exposition more than some would have done to say things which belong rather to Prolegomena on the one hand, and to the Christological section of modern dogmatics on the other. These excursive passages have had their rise also in my class-room habits; and the habits have grown by necessity. Constant questioning on the part of the student is the true way to learning, and it is certain that just such questions will be put as might be discussed with fitness among Prolegomena or in Christological study. I feel, however, that the questions of the student will prove to have been a good guide in meeting the anxieties of the reader; and I think I have not gone beyond justifiable limits.

My method of frequent recapitulations has arisen also in the exigencies of the class-room, and will perhaps prove to be of good service in aiding students outside of the class.

The present rapid increase of study of all phases of religious life has made the Old Testament peculiarly a centre of scientific interest and research; but the work done has been thus far chiefly analytic. Large stores of accurately tested material are now lying ready for the synthetic workman who shall build together in complete historical statement these separate results of analysis and criticism. The appearance of the unbuilt material, and the apparent negations which analytic and critical operations necessitate, have caused uneasiness to the timid and to the mere onlooker. But the constructive work was sure to follow; it follows by the very nature of processes of thought, for the mind questions only in order that it may obtain answers, and criticises in order to have a rightly adjusted system of positive truth. The effort is made in the following pages to give in constructive historical form the results of such research in the special field of Hebrew religion.

This volume covers a period of nearly two centuries, and, it is hoped, will be duly followed by exposition of the succeeding periods. The whole of the documents of the Old Testament will thus be used, and also that extra-Biblical religious literature which arose among the Jews in the later centuries before Christ or during the early Christian generations. The aim is, indeed, to give the story of the Faiths of the Hebrews; but this is to be watched as it appears in the course of the Biblical and other Hebrew religious records. The whole work will thus be at once a History of Hebrew Religion, and a Guide for the Christian Teacher in the Use of the Bible. May it help to lead to a closer study of the precious Records, and to an ever stronger, calmer, and more joyous proclamation of the Love of God as it is manifest in the Son of Man, our Lord and Saviour Jesus Christ.

I have acknowledged help from my students, who, let me add, have done most of the work in making my Index; and I have now named several eminent teachers whom I follow gratefully, as I shall name others in the body of my work. One guide and friend has done for me in these latter months more than I can ever tell or reward. Rev. James Fotheringham, author of "Studies in the Poetry of Robert Browning," has most carefully read all my proofs, and given me the great aid of his profound philosophic insight, his fine literary judgment, and his close acquaintance with the history of the rise of our Christian Religion. I record his goodness here, although I can never repay it. To other kind friends also, I am indebted for constant counsel and aid during the preparation of this volume. May the loving help of all find some reward in aid which the book may bring to others.

A. D.

The United College, Bradford,
    Oct. 15, 1891.

CONTENTS.

BOOK I.

INTRODUCTORY STUDIES—THE PENTATEUCH AND THE STUDENT.

CHAP.	PAGE
I. INTRODUCTORY	3
§ 1. The Pentateuch stands first in the Canon . .	3
§ 2. Our problem is theological	3
§ 3. Pentateuch investigation cannot be accomplished first	4
§ 4. The method of procedure	5
II. UNSATISFACTORY METHODS	7
§ 1. The Pentateuch cannot be its own standard . .	7
§ 2. In the end the Pentateuch will give confirmatory evidence	9
§ 3. The study of literary and linguistic differences in the Pentateuch cannot be the test . . .	10
§ 4. The claim that there is a religious test . .	11
§ 5. The demand for an infallible guide . . .	11
§ 6. Of the test, "What does God say?" . . .	14
III. THE CONSTRUCTION OF THE REAL STANDARD AND TEST .	16
§ 1. The pleasure it will give	16
§ 2. The autograph records of Hebrew religious life for eight centuries	16
§ 3. These give the history of the people . . .	20
IV. ILLUSTRATIONS OF THE RESULTS	23
§ 1. Necessary counsels	23
§ 2. General remarks on the Pentateuch—(a) law of Moses; (b) the New Testament use of "law;" (c) the supposed forgery	23
§ 3. Illustrations—(a) concerning Deuteronomy; (b) concerning Elohist and Jehovist; (c) concerning Levitical ceremonial; (d) concerning the narratives; (e) concerning the editor	27

BOOK II.

HEBREW RELIGION FROM AMOS TO JOSIAH,
OR FROM 800 TO 640 B.C.

PART I.—THE RELIGION OF AMOS.

CHAP.		PAGE
I. ANALYSIS OF THE BOOK		35
§ 1. Of its literary history		35
§ 2. The analysis into nine paragraphs		36
II. THE MAN AMOS		41
§ 1. Our need of him		41
§ 2. His inspiration		42
§ 3. The scene of Amos's preaching		44
§ 4. The age of Amos and its wide activity		49
III. THE ANTECEDENTS OF THE AMOS AGE		56
§ 1. The meaning of the question		56
§ 2. The faith of Amos in a Davidic age		56
§ 3. It is common to the prophets		57
§ 4. What this faith meant		57
§ 5. The work of David		58
§ 6. The rise of world-monarchies		61
§ 7. The name "Jehovah of Hosts"		63
§ 8. The sum of the argument; the nature of the David-revelation		64
IV. THE AMOS-REVELATION		66
§ 1. It comes amid wrestlings—(*a*) thoroughly human; (*b*) in company with God; (*c*) wrestling with God; (*d*) wrestling with men; (*e*) wrestling in argument		66
§ 2. His revelation was breadth and keenness of conscience—(*a*) the tribal conscience; (*b*) the first writing prophet is the prophet of conscience; (*c*) Amos's demand is righteousness; (*d*) the wrongs of his time		70
§ 3. His conception of man		76
§ 4. Amos's view of the ways of revelation		81
§ 5. His view of the nature of God		85
§ 6. The problems he left unsolved		87

Part II.—THE RELIGION OF HOSEA.

CHAP.		PAGE
I.	GENERAL CHARACTER OF HIS BOOK; ITS CONNECTING THREADS	90
	§ 1. Chronology	90
	§ 2. The perplexities of the book; in text, &c.	91
	§ 3. The unchaste society	92
	§ 4. His general idea of Jehovah and Israel	93
	§ 5. His political knowledge	96
	§ 6. His love and esteem for men	99
II.	ANALYSIS OF THE BOOK OF HOSEA	105
	A. Chapters i.–iii. in three sections	105
	B. Chapters iv.–xii. in nine sections	105
III.	THE MAN HOSEA	111
	§ 1. His home	111
	§ 2. His rank	114
	§ 3. His personal story	115
	§ 4. His mind and way of thinking	117
	§ 5. His heart and feeling	118
	§ 6. His inner soul	119
IV.	HOSEA'S RELIGIOUS OPINIONS GENETICALLY CONSIDERED	120
	§ 1. The kernel of his thinking	122
	§ 2. What he inherited from others	123
	§ 3. What was new in him	123
	§ 4. His doctrine of men	129
	§ 5. His idea of God	134
V.	THE ADVANCE MADE AND TO BE MADE	144
	§ 1. The material pathway for this	144
	§ 2. The advance made by Hosea	146
	§ 3. The advance still needed	148

Part III.—THE RELIGION OF ISAIAH.

I.	A SKETCH OF THE WHOLE COURSE OF THE DEVELOPMENT OF HIS THOUGHT, AS MANIFESTED IN HIS RELATION TO ZION	150
	§ 1. Perspective in history	150
	§ 2. The faiths before Isaiah concerning Zion	151
	§ 3. His own experience in Zion	155
	§ 4. Zion in the early discourses	166
	§ 5. The hour of change	168
	§ 6. The growth of the new faith	173
	§ 7. The changed faith at the fall of Samaria	175
	§ 8. Thence to the end	176

CONTENTS.

CHAP.	PAGE
II. ANALYSIS OF THE ORACLES IN CHRONOLOGICAL ORDER	181
§ 1. The Assyrian canon	182
§ 2. Chronological outline	184
§ 3. The analysis proper, in outline.—I. The Oracles of Judgment; II. The Oracles of Grace under Ahaz and Hezekiah	189
§ 4. Description by paraphrase of the substance of Isaiah's preaching, following the analysis given	196
III. A SYSTEMATIC VIEW OF ISAIAH'S FAITHS, GENETICALLY CONSIDERED	227
§ 1. The kernel of his character	227
§ 2. A scheme of his thinking	233
§ 3. His faith in the overlordship of Jehovah	234
§ 4. His faith that the earth must be cleansed	242
§ 5. His grasp of the grace of God	254
§ 6. His rise to faith in regeneration	259
§ 7. His thought on three fundamental questions—God, Man, Perfection	265
IV. ISAIAH'S PLACE IN HEBREW RELIGIOUS HISTORY	285
§ 1. Advance in conception of God	286
§ 2. Advance in understanding man's nature and value	288
§ 3. In estimate of religious relations	290
§ 4. In comprehension of the future	291
§ 5. The problems he started and left unsettled	291
§ 6. His limit of Divine presence and salvation	292
§ 7. His hope for material prosperity	292
§ 8. Of the expected Prince	293

PART IV.—RELIGION IN JUDAH FROM ISAIAH TO JOSIAH.

I. PRELIMINARY	295
II. THE ANALYSIS OF MICAH	299
III. THE RELIGION OF MICAH AND HIS TIMES	305
§ 1. Its general characteristics	305
§ 2. The mind of these times concerning religious forms	310
§ 3. Their estimate of the soul	315
§ 4. Their fundamental faith	323
§ 5. Their relation to the Pentateuch	328
IV. CONCLUSION	330
INDEX	333

BOOK I.

INTRODUCTORY STUDIES—THE PENTATEUCH AND THE STUDENT.

OLD TESTAMENT THEOLOGY.

CHAPTER I.

INTRODUCTORY.

§ 1. *The Pentateuch stands first in the Canon.*

THE narrative books of Hebrew Scripture are all placed first in the Christian Old Testament. Therefore, the very first question the Bible student asks must be, how he can understand and use these books. In other words, how may we sit with Christlike reverence at the feet of these Jewish teachers in the Moses-Torah? How shall we exalt the Pentateuch and its continuations in Kings, and the parallel work called by us "The Chronicles," to the high honour they deserve, bidding them tell us the deep inspiration and Divinely-given faith of their writers and their heroes?

§ 2. *Our problem is theological.*

We have here little to do with a purely literary problem. Our business must be distinctly religious, theological, and aimed directly to bring spiritual blessing to men to-day. We are to study something more precious than the history of documents and scribes, or of wars and kings, for we have to ask, "What is God?" Our special task is to trace the footprints of God along Hebrew pathways, and to read the meaning of His voice in His ceaseless communings with Hebrew souls. We are to ask, "What was the ever-living Word of God before He became flesh in Bethlehem?" Forasmuch as the great Triune God liveth eternally, and the Father eternally sendeth forth His Son, ordained for ever to give light to the world, anointed ever to give life and power to trusting souls, we ask what was the Son, what were the manifestations, revelations, inspirations of God among the Hebrew people before the birth of Jesus? What was the pre-existent Christ in Israel? What is the story of Revelation or of Inspiration which we may gather from the Hebrew Scriptures? We ask, therefore, naturally first, what the Pentateuch with its continuations tells us of the course of God's inspiration of men? But the answer here, at this stage of our work, must be indirect.

§ 3. *Pentateuch investigation cannot be accomplished first.*

All direct results of Pentateuch investigation must be deferred until another problem is solved; for the very first result of any thoughtful reading in it is the discovery of remarkable art in its construction, and therefore of need for corresponding skill in handling it. It is at once strikingly poetical and also decidedly philosophical. Speedily it becomes an exceedingly complicated structure. The criticism of it is no task for beginners. It is a common axiom that wherever much controversy gathers, centres, and abides, there must be a difficult problem, and one demanding reverent skill. Here is a work that has started fresh debates in every meeting-place of thoughtful men, and at every new dawning of mental strength. Its problems must therefore be beyond the tyro's skill; and the wondrous old fabric, pricelessly precious, forbids in venerable solemnity the rude touch of the ignorant. The august persons of this world-drama of religion will be silent as the Sphinx to all who have not sat long bowed over the alphabet of their profound speech.

§ 4. *The method of procedure.*

Our first discovery, then, on opening the books of Genesis, is not a final result but a Method. The Method is simply that, in coming to analysis of any controverted records of the religious life of a people, we must bring to the task an advanced knowledge of the people. Study of the Pentateuch demands preliminary knowledge independently gained of the main course of the history of the Hebrew people's religious life. To value truly such an intricate record of God's speech to man, and man's recognition of God's character, we must first qualify our hand and eye and judgment for the task by gaining from some independent sources a general outline of the history of that Divine speech to men and that human recognition of this speech. Need it be said that here is no pre-judgment of the controverted records? The preliminary acquisition of skill and careful judgment can never make an early record into a late one, or make venerable treasure worthless. Nay, rather, only such acquisition of skill will preserve the treasure from any tarnishing touch, and the record from careless displacement. Truly indeed will the student himself be prejudged by this demand for preliminary acquisition of skill. But the true student will be content to be prejudged and sternly tested ere he begins to utter judgments or to trust his own judgment on such difficult problems. The finest mark of the worthy scholar is his abiding humility before the great monuments which he seeks lovingly and fearlessly to decipher. It is only his perfect love and reverence that cast out all fear.

In coming, then, to the Pentateuch controversy, we must first learn all the story of religious life in Israel that can be learnt from sources independent of the Pentateuch. This done, we may then proceed to an examination of the Pentateuch, and to the discovery of the place or places in the course of history to which it belongs. We can learn thus whether it must be placed as a whole before the beginning of the story already gained from independent sources, or whether it falls in as a whole at any one point in the course of that story. We shall learn whether perhaps one part falls into one niche in time, and another part into another. Such work will be actual analysis of the book, and will justify us in counting it either homogeneous on the one hand, or, on the other hand, a composite of many elements and origins and dates.

CHAPTER II.

UNSATISFACTORY METHODS.

ERE we proceed to define closely the sources of the historic test which we must construct and apply, and to give introductory outlines of the independent course of Hebrew religious history which we seek, let us note some of the inadequate tests usually applied to the Pentateuch and the allied historical books.

§ 1. *The Pentateuch cannot be its own standard.*

First, it is sometimes said that the Pentateuch ought to be its own standard. It ought to be allowed to settle by its own statements the controversy concerning its own date. This means, in other words, there ought to be no controversy. But there is controversy. The controversy is not indeed whether the Pentateuch is or is not a splendid literary fact, a magnificent literary structure, a finely fascinating literary work. All agree that it is all of this; the man who has not read it is the only doubter here. Again, the controversy is not whether the Pentateuch be or be not a great series of scenes in religious life. No one doubts this who ponders over its every paragraph. No reader doubts that the books give singularly great, and profoundly impressive exhibitions of religious life. The same impression is produced upon the reader as upon him who stands before a great painter's canvas or a great sculptor's stone. You enter that hall in Dresden galleries of art, where all alone in majesty, unique and glorious, solemn and beautiful, the Sistine Madonna shines. You are silent, bowed, reverent before the monument of mighty genius; you are conscious that here is overwhelming power. You stand, a puny man, on the floor of the tremendous Coliseum in the Eternal Rome, and you know that here great minds planned and great power built. You stand beneath the beetling mountain limestone crag; you climb far above and trace the print of fern-leaf on the huge sandstone sheet; you rise past layer after layer written full with the hieroglyphic speech of fossil life, and you bend astounded, cognisant of the enormous forces that have worked all this. Great it is; and behind it all, beside it all, is the Creator. But now you begin to ask when God wrought all this, and what are the successive methods of His operation? There are geological controversies concerning the age of rocks, their relative age, and the agency of one vast layer in the formation of another. What standards shall decide the controversies? You must first study the places where there is no controversy and construct from them your standard. There are keen controversies touching the age of great works of art. How were they produced? Great they are; that we know. But what were the great factors in them? At what periods of the painter's history did he use his pencil with such skill? Knowledge gained outside the picture must largely decide. If the artist have failed to write his name upon his canvas, who was the artist? These questions can be answered only by him who has made abundant previous study of all the uncontroverted certainties in the field; and he will apply to the solution of difficult problems some test constructed by independent study of uncontroverted facts.

For every analysis there must be some external test,

and for every criticism there must be some external canon or standard. In solving a problem we refer to axioms and fundamental propositions; when a judgment is to be given we must refer to independent law and evidence. If, therefore, you would lay a measuring-line on the Pentateuch, that measuring-line cannot be the book itself. The very task which is proposed by every Pentateuch student, whether he lean to the composite theory or to the homogeneous, is that he shall discover where the place is in history, or where the places are, into which the Pentateuch or its portions do exactly fit. The Pentateuch must be held apart, meanwhile, until we have learned the events of history independently of this source. The Pentateuch may not be its own test.

§ 2. *In the end the Pentateuch will give confirmatory evidence.*

Undoubtedly in the end the Pentateuch will throw back confirmatory evidence on the investigations and on the standard. The niche or niches whereinto the work fits will be themselves illuminated afresh by what thus fits into them. Certainly, while we are testing a mass of keys to see what locks and treasures they will open, we simply pass along the line of locks trying in turn each key in every lock, and so we learn to which each belongs. But then these keys, entering their own wards and unlocking their own doors, let fall floods of light upon themselves as well as upon the treasures within. A series of new fossils, all unarranged, is placed in a geologist's hands for arrangement in proper chronological classification. His previous knowledge of the geologic ages enables him ere long to classify the fossils satisfactorily. Then these fossils, thus perfectly arranged, throw a whole flood of new light back upon the previously known history of rocks and history of life. So the Pentateuch will in the end make all Hebrew religious history brilliantly, gloriously vivid.

§ 3. *The study of literary and linguistic differences in the Pentateuch cannot be the test.*

Again, the existence of literary variety and linguistic differences in the Pentateuch cannot furnish the sufficient clue for criticism. If we do find distinctly dissimilar styles as we read the Hebrew from page to page, and note philological gaps between line and line, who shall tell us the order in which the various shades of the language arose? We must appeal to the history of the literature and the language, as gained from other and quite independent documents whose dates we know. If once a false order be assumed, the consequence must be distortion in every sense. If the philological standard put effect for cause, and branch for root, chaos will come again at the end as in the beginning. The historian will grow confused at every line, no thinker will remain for sheer weariness, and common men will turn away carelessly. It may be said that it will be sufficient to discover philological variety without discovering any order of sequence in the dates of the component parts. This is impossible; but were it possible, what good would it bring us? It is not mere literary curiosity or aimless wordplay that lies before us. We yearn to know God's face, and the ever-gracious disclosures thereof, as He has given—first to the fathers, then to the children—the ever deeper and deeper treasures of His love. What are the highest heights of revelation? What are the first faint springs of infant thoughts of God? Tell us not of mere multiplicity of revelations, for that wearies into terror. Tell us of the order of God through the ages eternally rolling onwards, which is itself the great infinite fact of God, the same yesterday, to-day, and for ever.

§ 4. *The claim that there is a religious test.*

Again, there is a test much in the mind of many persons in a somewhat undefined fashion, yet not at all indefinable. This test is suggested by the troubled complaint we hear of want of reverence, want of delicacy, want of satisfactory completeness in the work of analysis. The complainers prophesy, indeed, with a pleasant sharing of the scientific attitude, that certainly there will be plenty of work for good analysts to do a hundred years hence, even were all analysts now and onward perfect masters of their task. But then the complaint awakes again that the work of all the analysts so far is not satisfactory. It is not complained by the timid for one moment that scientific Hebraists and Old Testament theologians are bad, idle, lazy, superficial, "scamping" workmen, or unsatisfactory in any of these senses. None of the complainers would make any such charge against Old Testament students. It is not, then, of scientific unsatisfactoriness or incompleteness that complaint is made, for this incompleteness and unsatisfactoriness are acknowledged by even the timid complainers to be the true, essential, desirable quality of scientific work. Scientific workmen must never claim to have reached a *ne plus ultra*. Next century there must necessarily be plenty more to do. The complaint is not against scientific unsatisfactoriness; it is a complaint against *religious* unsatisfactoriness.

§ 5. *The demand for an infallible guide.*

The complaint takes another form, which shall help to define this undefined test. It takes the form of a cry for some certain and infallible propositions by which men, minds, souls may hold firmly amid the darkness of life. There is a cry for some historical facts to which the soul may easily point in time of need, sure that these facts of history guarantee God's character and purpose. But the very search for such a guarantee of character drives the soul to seek more than mere events. Character is sought, and character implies a Person. The cries of the timid are for a personal authority, an infallible person, who shall be absolutely known, and who shall assure us how God will act. We do need some knowledge of God which shall be absolutely comprehensible by us in a personal Revelation. We must have a Word of God in flesh. The cry is most legitimate; the timid are quite right. We must see God; and we believe we do see Him in Christ Jesus. Here then is a test: What does Jesus say of the Old Testament and the Pentateuch? or, what was believed concerning the Pentateuch in the first Christian century? Observe that the second of these two questions is really always put forward in place of the first. We have not Jesus' words, but we have the records of men round Him as to what He said. We take their words as His. Why is this in any sense right? Why should opinions of men standing round Jesus, some nearer, some farther, be taken as His even on questions of intense importance, such as: What is God? What is His character? What will He do? And also on questions of only less importance: What has God done? What was the past? What was Israel? What is the Pentateuch?

The common answer is: Those men were filled with His Spirit. He was present in them; and it will be generally allowed that we are at no disadvantage in lacking writings from our Lord's own hand, although our knowledge of His opinions is thus thoroughly moulded by the subjective peculiarities of the New Testament writers, their times, abodes, and audiences. The Spirit of God was present with those writers, the Spirit of Christ was speaking in them and through them. The speech of that Spirit through them was not a speaking "in spite of" their local or subjective peculiarities, but it was speech of God in their peculiarities. We do not say that Jesus was the Word of God "in spite of" His flesh; the Word of God was made flesh. Likewise the Spirit of Jesus was made flesh after His resurrection, and the New Testament gives us all we possess of that Word of God from those early days after the crucifixion.

But the Spirit of God has not ceased to dwell in men. The Spirit of Christ has not ceased to speak through the subjective or local peculiarities of men to-day. Not one living soul to-day could by any possibility put on the subjective local peculiarities of the first century. Not one could put off now his own subjective quality, gained from the present century, and from last century, and from the Reformation, the Renaissance, the Schoolmen, the Dark Ages, the later Roman Empire, and all the past. Our Lord Jesus, the Christ in the first century, spoke the language of the first century. He did not speak at all in the language of the nineteenth. So the present Christ, the Word of God, ever living and speaking in the nineteenth century, does not speak altogether in the language of the first. He does speak altogether in the language of the nineteenth, including in that language and speech all the fruit of the nineteen centuries since the first. What follows? Clearly that we learn the opinion of the present Christ on every question now from the thoughtful voice of His Present Body, wherein He is made flesh to-day. Christ liveth to-day in us; we are to-day partakers of the Divine nature. The mind of our Lord Jesus Christ, concerning especially the Pentateuch, is to be learned in the thoughtful mind of Christians now; and, as of old, he that will do the will of God shall know of the doctrine whether it be of God. In simple words, he that will seek shall find knowledge. Such seekers may speak in the name of God—nay, they must speak, for they have the mind of Christ. Like Jesus, they must bear the burdens of others. Some can hardly learn, for they have been prevented by the various misfortunes of society; but their listening trust in the seekers who preach God is to them life everlasting.

In conclusion, two things must be said: first, let it be plainly understood that only the man who reads the Bible has the authority of Jesus to say what is in the Bible.

In the second place, let there be absolute denial of the cry that the analysts of the Bible are not godly men. It were presumption to write certificates of Christian character for scholars in Old and New Testament theology; but let it be recorded here as an honour to this page that increasing personal acquaintance with these men, the oft-named men and the little-known investigators, always reveals them, man by man, to be the very embodiment of saintly spirituality, eager missionary activity, apostolic fervour, and Christ-likeness.

§ 6. *Of the test, " What does God say?"*

The test, "What does God say?" is profoundly important; and it is perfectly answered in the words of the Gospel, "The Word became flesh." The meaning which these words conveyed in the first century depended on two things: (1) What was it to utter God, God's Spirit, God's heart, God's unchanging love? The answer was found in "The Death on the Cross." (2) But what was it for this Love to be flesh in the first century? The answer must be found in the special customs and possibilities of that century. But it is not possible for us to-day and here to think according to those customs. The literary possibilities of the first century are not possibilities for us. This is the doing of Providence. It is not of chance, it is of God. Therefore the question of profoundest importance rises again, "What does God say in the nineteenth century?" The answer is as before, "The Word became flesh;" and, as before, we look for the present revealed God, and we find Him in His children, in those men who are one with God, who utter God's Spirit and God's love. We find the Christ and the voice of the Christ to-day in those men who are new creatures in Christ Jesus, in whom Christ is formed, who are reconciled to God by the blood of His Cross, and who are found in Christ, risen with Him, striving to attain unto the resurrection of Christ. God is in these men; He works in them, thinks in them, speaks in them. What He says of the Pentateuch is heard in the souls of those of His children who work devotedly at this subject. That is the common faith of both conservative and advancing men. If it were not the faith of conservative Christians, no one of these would dare to write or speak one word on the subject, for to them all that dare be said would be already said. Even were they to copy biblical passages which they believed to be suitable, here again the copying and choosing hands would sin, being guided by the judgments of to-day. But thanks be to God! we can hear His mind to-day only in the thinking minds of to-day. Such listening is profoundest reverence.

CHAPTER III.

THE CONSTRUCTION OF THE REAL STANDARD AND TEST.

§ 1. *The pleasure it will give.*

THE study of this last test leads us thus to the historic test suggested above. The mind of Christ confirms the historical method, demands the historical method, and condemns the unhistorical as wrong. The task of the student grows heavier indeed, but the attraction grows also, and the burden becomes light. To the faithful historical reader the Bible is no longer a dust-covered relic, but a treasure-house bringing raptures of delight. Unhistoric method has closed the Bible, and must keep it closed. The faith that the thought of to-day may not test those records bears its fruit in neglected Bibles, in Christians who do not know its story, its lives, its loves, its beauty, and in many a Christian teacher who is ready to acknowledge that he has not read it all. But insistance on historic investigation is introducing us to acquaintance with the great souls of Hebrew days and of the first Christian age as new, rare friends. The pleasure of friendship, of human fellowship, is kindling round the old volumes. They are proving to be full of human attractiveness, love, and beauty.

§ 2. *The autograph records of Hebrew religious life for eight centuries.*

How then does this method proceed to discover the real course of knowledge of God among the Hebrews? How shall we construct this history, at first independently of the Pentateuch, in order that we may next lay the independent standard upon the Pentateuch, measure it and analyse it thereby, and finally weave all the Pentateuch material into its true place in the great plan first wrought out by God's finger and now traced out after Him by us?

The answer is that we possess a series of autograph records of Hebrew religious life running through all the eight centuries before our Lord's day. For we have the long series of words and prophesyings, burdens and promises, by which the men of God in all these centuries strove to rouse and win their fellows to righteousness and rest. They prophesied—they preached, and their Gospel was God. Soul struggled with soul; living men, they wrestled with living men in keenest conflict of will with will, of purpose with inclination, of thought with thought, of vision with imagination, that by all means they might save Israel. It was God, loved in their hearts, known in their souls, that kindled and moved their flaming words. God, and no other, created them; God gave them life, home, and heart. God, and no other, whispered their hope and faith; God breathed in their song and speech. How much God gives! How much He gave them! He disclosed His character to them. He told them His cares, His love, Himself, until they loved Him and all His ways. Out of that love came their evangel of wisdom, of righteousness, of hope, of truth. They saw and spoke, seeing one after the other deeper and ever deeper truths. When we read to-day we start at their insight; we bow, and kiss the page, saying with reverent voice, "This is the Word of God."

Do we doubt whether the visions of God that such seers saw may be exalted as the highest religious characteristics of their times? Do we read Amos and Hosea, Isaiah and Jeremiah, and rise thinking it probable that there have ever been men more truly men of God than these men were? Do we insist, like the Rabbis of the early Christian centuries, that the fellowship of God with these men was of a lower sort than His fellowship with Moses? Were the efforts of these prophets to save their fellow-men less good, less holy, less divine than the efforts of Moses? If any men nowadays relegate them to a farther distance from God than they allow to Moses, shall we do so? Does God do so? Are they not peers of the great realm? Who will venture to say it is a dishonour to the 12th chapter of Deuteronomy to compare it with the 5th chapter of Amos, or the 7th chapter of Jeremiah, or the 33rd or 53rd chapter of Isaiah? Is it not reverence for that Deuteronomic discourse to ask whether it belongs to the same category of religious exaltation with any of these prophetic passages? Who will shrink from considering the question whether Deuteronomy belongs to the same stage of bold, sublime, sacred advance, or to a time of quieter, reflective, sacred consolidation? And if the date of the composition of Deuteronomy xii. be in the crucible of controversy, who ventures to charge with irreverence a high trial of that chapter by the standard of a chapter in Amos? Indeed, such comparison has been steadily practised by both conservative and advancing Christian men for centuries past. And the Lord Jesus has been with them all, as they have been fain to acknowledge of one another, when days of special conflict have gone by.

Come then, let us read the words of these seekers and seers into God's heart. In vain should we stay to define their inspiration, and to argue that they had it, if we did not first read their words, all their words—in the light of their historical setting, and grasping the meaning of the hearts of the men and a vision of themselves as they stand in their own place in the noble line. Let us not argue concerning inspiration, but go read to men the great mastering truths—soul truths that an AMOS wrote—

> "Seek good, and ye shall find God."
> "All the sinners shall be cut off with the sword."

Or those of the answering HOSEA :—

> "I am God, and not man; I am Israel's lover."
> "I will not return to destroy."

Read the oracles of the son of these fathers, the sublime ISAIAH, who had no hesitation about his relation and even his children's relation to his God: but how shall we quote Isaiah?

> "God touched my unclean lips, and cleansed them."
> "God is Immanuel."
> "The sinners are afraid."

But—

> "They that dwell in Zion shall be forgiven."

Then tell men the tale of the simpler MICAH, who sang :—

> "When I sit in darkness my God shall be light about me."

Who has fully read the depths of brave JEREMIAH's soul and words?—

> "Lo! I am with *thee* to deliver thee."
> "I will give *them* a new heart of flesh, that they may know me."

Have we felt EZEKIEL's faith in a resurrection that might repeople the empty Palestine? Recall the more miraculous faith uttered by an ISAIAH to the exiles :—

> "Go ye forth from Babylon!"
> "When the poor and needy seek water, I Jehovah will not forsake them."

Do we teach our children that story of the desert, and with it the faith of that preacher?

"Even though Israel be not gathered, yet . . ."
"We may be God's salvation unto the ends of the earth."

Have those scenes and words been recalled to re-inspire our missionaries and their upholders? Handel has taught men to sing part of Isaiah liii.; and when preachers tell men to-day the story of its first utterance, their wondering audiences shall melt in tearful cry, "God be merciful to us!" Men are weary to hear from us the story of these inspirations.

Such are but glimpses of the story of two whole centuries, that are full to dazzling brightness of such words. The whole eight centuries from Amos, or nine centuries from Elijah to our Lord, can be illustrated almost as fully as those first two of them may from which the utterances above are taken. In some cases the material is still more abundant.

§ 3. *These give the history of the people.*

So much for illustration of the religious counsels that were moving men then. But in these we have more than a history of the preachers of the times. The history of sermons is also the history of audiences. The sermons of a preacher tell far more than his own knowledge of God; they tell more, indeed, than a tale of his own spiritual or mental growth. They tell of the soil on which he grew, and that in a more important sense than does a tree tell of the nature of the ground beneath it, its dryness or moisture, its alpine height or its marshy luxuriance. The sermon tells what home experiences God used in making the preacher; it tells also what sort of homes and experiences the preacher is trying to mould. In the prophecies you may see the people to whom they were preached. In the speaker's words the hearers are all plainly pictured. Those comforting words tell of the longings they cherished and he strove to soothe; those arguments tell the difficulties, hard and real, which they felt and raised, and which he felt and strove to overcome. Those great faiths of his echo great faiths of theirs; those approvals and commands tell what righteousness could be or was in the people; those condemnations mark out the well-known sin. Those hopes and warnings and eschatological visions of the prophet tell what the people could expect for their own future.

Yonder, then, in the four or five preachers of the brilliant eighth century; in as many of the seventh, that reflective age; in the sublime supernaturalism on one hand, and miraculous missionary grasp on the other among the masters of the sixth century, and amid its exile; then, after the return, in the darkened yet saintly souls that have left us their words from that same century; on again, in the elaborate plannings and dreamings through Ezra's days and onward till Alexander's, when finest fingers wove fairest lacework of earthly glory, in song and form, about the earthly temple; on still through apocalyptic seers' highest hopes, that, soaring into the invisible, amid the martyr-fires of Antiochus pictured beforehand the very man and Christ of God that should be; in the more comfortable ecclesiasticism and Scripture-worship of both Palestinian and Alexandrian commentators; and finally in the philosophic writers, who were certainly "not far from the kingdom of God"—in all these sermons, preachers, recorders, and records there is imbedded for us a rich, almost a complete story of the successive thoughts of God which Israel and Judah, people and prophets, had through well-nigh a thousand years.

The material is abundant, the work is fascinating. Let

a man first master this succession of religious life, as furnished by these well-known data; then he will be able to undertake Pentateuch analysis, and his judgment concerning the historical books—from Pentateuch on to Chronicles—their contents, their meaning, their inspiration, will be trustworthy and life-giving.

CHAPTER IV.

ILLUSTRATIONS OF THE RESULTS.

WHAT will be the result of such work? It is only fair to ask and to give some illustration.

§ 1. *Necessary counsels.*

But first let some necessary counsels be remembered. Since the possession of the standard we have described is indispensable to complete historical reliability, therefore it is hazardous to risk here any illustrations of future results. Still let there be the attempt, lest the way seem too long at the outset; and in the confidence that even adverse criticism, if genuine, will be based on a preliminary construction of the standard described, and is therefore desirable.

Another counsel is, that unnecessary pain to students, teachers, and people must be avoided. This is indeed one of the primary aims of this method of studying first the uncontroverted writings.

By this method may be avoided very materially that frequent painful experience of the sudden discovery of startling discrepancy between traditional and scientific opinions. It is right to avoid such pain, and therefore we may not justly say much in detail here of results.

§ 2. *General remarks on the Pentateuch—(a) law of Moses; (b) the New Testament use of " law ;" (c) the supposed forgery.*

There are one or two somewhat general remarks suitable before giving a few special illustrations of the results.

(a) The expression translated "law of Moses" (תּוֹרַת מֹשֶׁה) is somewhat misunderstood for want of careful regard for the nature of Hebrew speech. The word "Torah" does not mean "law." It means "instruction." It is a prefix-noun describing concrete action, and is derived from a verb (יָרָה) meaning "he pointed," or "he taught." The noun is frequently used; and in the unquestioned cases, which are abundant, it means that instruction which a prophet or a priest or any teacher might give by way of information as to the past, warning and counsel for the present, and expectation concerning the future. Therefore we might expect that the Torah, which we English folk style the Pentateuch, would contain narrative, direction, and promise. And so it does. It is not a book of law, although laws are of course an element in it. It is not even specially a book of law; laws are comparatively a minor part of it. It is essentially an instruction concerning the ways of God toward the Hebrews. So it tells a long history of His creation of them, and includes in this an account of the way He wishes them to take and the hopes He sets before them.

But again, the second word in the expression, "Torath-Mosheh," has been understood as if it were a genitive of the author. It is a wonder that this theory has not been criticised. Recently even conservative opinion has moved steadily toward acknowledgment of various origins for the materials of the work. It is commonly said that, whoever wrote the Pentateuch in its final form, that final writer must have collected documents from earlier hands, and incorporated these in his book. Thus the explanation of the title "Torah-of-Moses," as meaning "Torah, whose author was Moses," has practically passed out of use. And the change is grammatically perfectly correct. A Hebrew, reading the words "Torath-Mosheh," would have understood them to mean "The Deliverer-Torah," or "The Divine instruction concerning deliverance." The word "Mosheh" is here used in an adjective or attributive descriptive sense. The whole work, therefore, ending at Deuteronomy, or, it may be, at Joshua, or even at 2 Kings, is an instruction concerning God's way in creating, saving—that is, delivering His people Israel. It is the story especially how He brought them up out of Egypt, with all the previous blessings, and all the requirements, and all the later hopes included in that picture of God's way. This was "The Torah of the Deliverer."

(b) Now, since this was the very charter of those Hebrews who possessed it, we can easily understand the reverence it received. This reverence ought naturally to appear in the New Testament literature and life. And no doubt it does. There of course the word Torah cannot occur, but the word which takes its place is "Nomos," and this is a not altogether unsuitable substitute. When, then, we find Paul distinguishing between "salvation by faith in Jesus" and "salvation by the Nomos-works" (the works of the law, as we render it), or simply "salvation by the Torah," it is quite possible that he did not mean to distinguish between salvation by faith and salvation by works, whether of a ceremonial law or of a moral law. He meant most likely to distinguish between salvation on the one hand as a simple human soul by trust in God present with man as man, and on the other hand salvation as a true Hebrew, proved by his birth and ways to be a son of Abraham, and so claiming all the privileges of salvation that were ensured to Hebrews in their great charter, the "Deliverer-Torah." The whole matter is one for careful inquiry by New Testament theologians.[1]

---

[1] A similar misunderstanding of such a title has taken place in the case of the *Institutio* of Calvin, which has been so persistently called "The Institutes of Calvin." Calvin probably thought of giving simply a theory of Christianity; most men have supposed he gave laws by which the elect must be governed.

This reminds us that the whole fallacy concerning the elect was based upon Pauline language. There was certainly a Jewish doctrine of the elect; Judaism was just that doctrine. When men began to theologise concerning Paulinism and Christianity, it was very natural to preserve the formal notion concerning *an* elect, with simple alteration of the qualifications of that elect. Thus the persistence in Christian theology of a doctrine of the elect helps to confirm the opinion that Paul's polemic was not so much against works, deeds, duty, as against the essential fact of Judaism, the theory of a chosen few elected according to the great charter of the people, the "Deliverer-Torah."

(*c*) Once more, let us anticipate an exposition to be given in a future volume of this work. It is often said that if Moses did not write Deuteronomy, the actual writer forged Moses' name by imputing the work to Moses. The charge becomes a real charge, and does not remain a mere hypothesis, when we find the Revised Version saying that the writer of Deuteronomy lived on the west side of Jordan, where Moses never was (Deut. i. 1; iv. 46, &c.)

Now, the writer of the book takes care not to say that Moses was the writer. He is careful also to give his authority for his own work of narration of what he believes Moses did and said. He gives in Deuteronomy v. Moses' authority for what he the Deliverer did and said, and in chap. xviii., resuming the subject, he gives the similar authority by which a later man may do similar work, and learn, know, and describe what Moses had done. We may almost say that the writer of Deuteronomy gives his own sign manual in Deut. xviii. 18 *ff*. He is no impostor. He declares that he himself has God's authority for writing.

§ 3. *Illustrations*—(*a*) *concerning Deuteronomy;* (*b*) *concerning Elohist and Jehovist;* (*c*) *concerning Levitical ceremonial;* (*d*) *concerning the narratives;* (*e*) *concerning the editor.*

We proceed now to a few brief illustrations of the results of Pentateuch analysis.

(*a*) In meeting the question, "When did Israel become able to understand or use the Book of Deuteronomy?" the test described has long been used by men of both the critical schools. Conservative men have held that its use earlier than 800 B.C. is proved by certain allusions in Amos to the religious uses of leavened and unleavened bread, and to the payment of tithes at certain threefold divisions of time. Another class of students have compared Deuteronomy with the story of the Josian Reformation, and think that then was the period when all Judah solemnly recognised the Deuteronomic principles as the rule for the kingdom.

This leaves of course undecided the date and person of the writer; but here again there has been singular unanimity in appealing to the standard we have described, although the results of the appeal have not been in full agreement. According to some, the generations shortly preceding Josiah might have furnished, in the order of Providence, just that reflective and argumentative kind of religious faith which records itself in Deuteronomy, and it is held that therefore Deuteronomy was written then. Others agree that the style of the book suits that age. But they hold that the real author may have lived several centuries earlier, and may have been enabled of God to write as if he were living in the later age. Just such a case of authorship was once held by Dr. Delitzsch to have occurred in the case of Isaiah xl.–lxvi. (Comm. Isaiah, 2nd ed. p. 410). Dr. Delitzsch said there, "We have granted that the author of chaps. xl.–lxvi. keeps to the Exile as his fixed standpoint through all the twenty-seven chapters, moving his position only as one in the Exile would be always moving nearer to the Emancipation; and nowhere does he betray that his actual position or environment is different from this his ideal position." Dr. Delitzsch believed that the writer, living in say 725 B.C., was divinely and extraordinarily enabled to think and write exactly as if he were among the exiles in Babylon in 675 B.C. The extraordinary or miraculous character of such authorship Dr. Delitzsch held to be nothing impossible. And no one can prove the impossibility of it. Others hold that the early writer did indeed thus project himself into a time several centuries after his own time; but they add to this the opinion that an audience also actually surrounding the early speaker heard him and thought with him as if they were all living, not in their own time and environment, but in the later time of Uzziah, Hezekiah, and Josiah. While Dr. Delitzsch believed such a vision or transposition in the plan of the prophetic writer of Isaiah xl.–lxvi., some would hold that in the case of Deuteronomy such a transposition took place in the minds of both writer and audience. They consider that the audience who adopted the Deuteronomic teaching under Josiah were a second audience. Of course in this case, as well as in the others, the Book of Deuteronomy, even on such a theory of it, will give us a correct picture of the popular state of mind under Josiah, which is the most valuable matter in view of our effort to construct the history of religion in Israel.

Finally, some think that the book did indeed suit exactly the people who adopted it in Josiah's day, and does reflect their religious character; but they hold that it fitted with equal exactness the men of the Exodus in Moab. This view of course supposes a fixed religious character, continuing from the Exodus to Josiah's day, say seven hundred years, without change. The important fact for our present purpose is the general agreement that Deuteronomy, whensoever written, corresponds in religious standpoint with Josiah's time, and furnishes most valuable material for the history of religion at that time. Thus the value of our method of work is confirmed by all.

(*b*) Our standard has been generally acknowledged to be the correct one by all classes of investigators of the problem whether the so-called Elohistic, methodical passages, running from Genesis to Kings, are of an earlier or a later date than the so-called Jehovistic and popular passages in the same books. Very few teachers of any shade of opinion have refrained from applying to this matter the test which we have proposed. Many who are strongly conservative in their results have firmly and nobly opened the way for continued thorough application of our test. The results are not complete, but as they near completion they add intense and constantly increasing interest to the study, and to the parts of the Bible which are thus studied.

(*c*) The test may be applied again to the many collections of ceremonial regulations contained in the Pentateuch. When it is so applied there is discovered in these successive sets of regulations a striking series of parallels to the prophetic processes of deeper and ever deeper search into the character of God, as the previous independent study of religious history in the prophets reveals these. The fancy that theology is a dry study vanishes like a dream, forgotten in the hearty pleasure such earnest Bible study gives; and the steady growth of this research is convincing thoughtful men that the study of religious phenomena is no more a dilettante's trifle. One rises, for example, from careful analysis of the Book of Leviticus saying, "Never was there a more fascinating story of life," so intensely interesting is the evident progress of reflection, of wonder, of a very agony of striving after peace in the soul. And a higher result still comes to the historical student of these laws, for he is confirmed in faith in the Great Spirit's unfailing presence in all the simplest ways of men. Those anxious estimations in Leviticus of the value of anointings with oil and burnings with fire, of apportionings of sacrificial flesh, and of cutting and adorning of fit garments, of preservation of genealogies and of gradations of rank, those analyses of guilt values and of the vital function of blood and its symbolic spiritual significance—all these have wearied many readers of the Bible, and have been left unread as purely local and trivial phenomena. But they came into being in the order of Providence, and the worshippers who practised them tried them one after the other in earnest reflection how they could be perfect before God. So they moved on in wonderfully advancing refinement of these regulations, and this means that God did indeed care to have men reflect thus, and grow by such reflection. He inspired their desires, their struggles, their faith; He was present there. The historical reader rises believing, "Surely this presence of God amid such weary ritual struggles proves that He is never far away from us also!"

(*d*) The narratives of the Pentateuch and the succeeding books are at times popular, homely, of the fireside or the noontide resting hour. They are then poetry of the rarest sort, the songful communings of a nation's days of childhood, the strong excitement and eager demand for righteousness that marks the healthy youth of a nation. Comparing these with the history constructed already by independent study of the prophets, one hears the very voices of these men echoed again. You hear at one point the quick lyric measure and the overflowing joy and passion of the earliest prophets. You recognise then the voice of an age that had not lost the power to weave in finest nature-parable the facts of men's earliest life. Again you are in the atmosphere of the simplicity, boldness, and sorrow of the *Nahash-David*, first soul to burst away from the Eden-home, and from laws of childhood, into the daring and suffering of maturity. Then further on you read terrible denunciations poured out on the wrongdoer and his wrong deed, with no discrimination, and with little thought of mercy. They could frame their home-like pictures round with a dark border, and write thereon the dread Amosian penalty, "All the sinners of my people shall die by the sword;" "The soul that sinneth, it shall die;" "In the day of disobedience thou shalt surely die."

At other times those Pentateuch narratives are philosophical or philosophico-poetical. We hear in them a very sound of solemn psalm and stately chant. We shall recall, as we read, the periods in which our previous study of history shall have revealed the rise of careful reflection on creation, on the meaning of God's name, on the dark problems of life, on the facts of Providence in the past and on the troubled hopes concerning Providence in the future.

But whether the narratives are of one sort or the other, and whether they shall prove to be like to the people of one age or of another, the hands that wove them together were moved by a faith minded above all things to exhibit in the story of "a little one among the nations" something of the great control of God over all.

(c) To end these illustrations, we may observe that there is a rather scholastic classification of kinds of inspiration that ends by finding the climax of all inspirations, and indeed almost the only real or infallible inspiration, in the final editors of the Pentateuch. Such a fancy is like the refinements of the ritualist, and may make the serious student smile. But this is certainly true: that subordinate as editors must always be, those Pentateuch editors—to avoid the outlandish word "redactor"—were men of sublime faith, of fearless grasp, selecting, moulding, fitting, even rejecting very precious things; and they remain men of grand religious power to this day.

We leave now the questions of the Pentateuch, to construct the history of this Hebrew religion from the materials given in uncontroverted sources. Only complete study of these will entitle us to return to the Pentateuch as men fairly skilled for its analysis. But, from the beginning and henceforward and at the end, the best, highest, latest and only true study of the Bible must be that which finds there the story of God talking with men and therefore reads it to see God and to reveal Him. God needs man's every hour to tell man all the love of God. The history we now begin is the story of God, of the God-man, of God's Christ, of God's life given to men, to Hebrews, to Christians, for all men, the same yesterday, to-day, for ever.

BOOK II.

HEBREW RELIGION FROM AMOS TO JOSIAH,
OR FROM 800 to 640 B.C.

PART I.

THE RELIGION OF AMOS (CIRCA 775 B.C.).

CHAPTER I.

ANALYSIS OF THE BOOK.

§ 1. *Of its literary history.*

THE earliest of the virtually uncontroverted monuments of Hebrew religion is the little book of the prophet or preacher AMOS. In our work with this book, and with each book we may have to discuss, we must take as substantially completed for us by other specialist hands all the exegetical and literary historical work that ought to lie completed before us as preliminary to our own special task. It is not necessary to load these pages with the bibliography of those literary and exegetical departments. Lists of works and teachers that the student must consult may be found in works on theological encyclopædia. But the student cannot afford to pass unheard any teacher in the Old Testament department of theology; and study of those teachers' published work can but inadequately make up for lack of personal acquaintance and direct pupilship.

Let the writer add to such general acknowledgment of unspeakable indebtedness the glad testimony of his deepest reverence, and in some cases close personal affection for the masters he has followed in Old Testament study: Drs.

Riehm, De Lagarde, Duhm, Wellhausen, Stade, Delitzsch, Kautzsch, Guthe, Smend, Kuenen, Rénan, Cheyne, Davidson, W. R. Smith, Carpenter, Driver, Cave, Whitehouse, Meade, Curtiss, Briggs, Bissell. Where these men have published their results of investigation, there is not very much that a well-informed studious man could find fault with, either in the completeness of their investigation or in the strict correctness of their method.

§ 2. *The analysis into nine paragraphs.*

The Book of Amos is virtually the earliest certain autograph of a Hebrew religious life. It carries a characteristic title, "The Utterances of Burden-Bearing;" for the author's name had that sad solemn significance, and all his utterances have that same sad, solemn tone. Whether the name was given him by his fathers, or by his followers, is an interesting question; if by the latter, then his warning influence found quick response, whereas if by the former, we have all the more certainly in the boy and man and prophet a picture of the solemnity and character and religion of his whole time and generation.

The Oracles may be read through at a sitting, for they make only nine short chapters. Their contents may be easily divided into nine paragraphs, nearly coterminous with the chapters, as follow:—

¶ 1, chap. i. 1–ii. 5.—A song of seven stanzas, with regular refrain, chanting (Jahweh's) Jehovah's lordship over all the nations that lie around the horizon of central Israel. That Overlord's care is chiefly first to condemn wrongs that men, or rather tribes of men, do to their neighbours, hurting especially the body and liberty, but also the sense of honour. And secondly, the Overlord's care is to declare that the course of coming Providence shall be all retribution for these wrongs. With this claim and description of over-lordship the oracle turns from the circling peoples to strike henceforth only the central Israel.

¶ 2, chap. ii. 6–end.—The chant goes on, but soon sways into less stanzaic form, declaring that all Israel's doings have been cruel, lustful, greedy, and ungrateful. All has been disregard of Jehovah, who is Providence, Creator, true Receiver of Divine honour, and whose whole desire is for kindness, honesty, purity, faithfulness among His own loved tribes. For these wrongs He will make all coming Providence a retribution.

¶ 3, chap. iii.—Tells of Jehovah's need of personal friendship, and of His plan to have it with one people, Israel. But He has been bitterly disappointed, for the inhumanity of Israel is intolerable to Him. Therefore retribution shall fill all His future Providence.

¶ 4, chap. iv. is in three subdivisions. First, the retribution is declared certain upon the court harem and other persons of high rank for the cruelty, selfish and sensual, of the harem ladies. Secondly, a taunt is flung at the religiosity of the day; for abundant religious observance, and thoroughly pleasurable religious observance too, are quite consistent with immorality. Thirdly, in continuation of the second subdivision, the providences of Jehovah are declared to be the true occasions for actual contact with Him, vision of Him, humble intercourse with Him. This view of them has been utterly disregarded. Therefore Amos solemnly proclaims Jehovah's creatorship of all nature, and His sole rule and real presence therein; and he bids Israel now at last know this, and think and act in such real consciousness, and begin thereby a real worship of God.

¶ 5, chap. v. may be called a dialogue, where the words of the answering hearer may be easily supplied from the words of the preacher:—

"Ye die," cries he; "Providence is against you."

"How then shall we live?" is the implied answer.

"Seek the Life-giver, the Creator, Jehovah, who 'causeth to be,' for such is He by very name, as by very nature."

"But," they say again, "Jehovah is with us in the many sanctuaries—Gilgal, Bethel, Mizpeh, Beersheba, where He chose to show Himself to our fathers, Samuel, Moses, Jacob, Abraham. Our venerable faith is this: wherever He has showed His face there will He be again, and there shall we stay and eat the feast of sacrifice to Him. He *is* here; we shall then live."

"No, no," cries the preacher; "seek not sanctuaries, but seek the Life-giver. Believe no more in safety in that venerable faith," cries this first of the long line of Hebrew iconoclasts. "Seek not places, but seek Jehovah."

"Why? How," they answer, "can He be away from these?" Note that both preacher and hearers of this first great doctrine of revelation believed not in one revelation once for all, but in an ever-possible, ever-new revelation.

The answer comes, fearless and dread, "Your sin, your multitude of dishonest deeds, your cruel silencing of honest speech, your slanders uttered from the very judge's seat against the petitioner whose rights cross your wishes—these all drive God away from you. He is not in all the courts, homes, hearts where you do these things."

"Imprudent man," they shout; "thou art a fool who speakest thus. Thy place, thy bread, all oughtest thou to lose for such words—ay, thy life. Hush! Keep silence! Prudence bids thee."

The imprudent preacher only sounds again aloud his cry, "Seek good, seek good. When ye find good, and possess it and dwell in it, then Jehovah, that God who abides with good, shall abide with you. Ye say He is with you now; He shall really be with you then."

But this gospel of life is hopeless, because unused. The hearers persist in worship, feast, song, sacrifice, which are godless, untrue, hateful. Therefore retributive providence is the only outlook; dangers, horrors, slavery, wailing, death shall come. Thus shall the presence of Jehovah be felt indeed, but not as a life-giving presence. For He causes all things, death as well as life; and the coming great " Day of Jehovah," the day of His manifest presence, shall be a day of death.

¶ 6, chap. vi.—A more pointed condemnation. The highest authorities—officers, chairmen, committee-men—are the worst men. They cause most mischief, and are most careless about it. Therefore plague shall ravage, and every providence shall be retribution, until in terror men shall grow superstitious towards Jehovah. They shall grow terrified to speak His name, and so at length it shall cease to be desecrated.

¶ 7, chap. vii.—Parables, possibly for the simpler folk. Amos tells how he once tried to believe in forgiveness, and more than once prayed for mercy on Israel. And Jehovah listened. Again and again Amos felt an assurance they should be forgiven. But now they have gone too far to be forgiven again. His great grace is exhausted. No wonder, for the chief man charged with leading Israel to God and speaking Jehovah's mind to Israel is the very chiefest despiser of the godlike heart and word of Amos. The prophet declares how unselfish his own aim had been. For no price, or honour, or self-satisfaction had he spoken, but only to utter Jehovah's own mind against badness and for goodness. But for these godlike things there was no sympathy in the Bethel-priest, Amaziah. Therefore the priest and his people must suffer a pollution which they can feel—visible, tangible—a horrible outlawry from Jehovah's home.

¶ 8, chap. viii. 1–ix. 10.—Once more a parable of death for the text, and then a sermon that gathers together all the dread oracle sentences from the past paragraphs or sermons, until the most terrible of all is added, "For the sinner there can be no forgiveness."

"All the sinners shall die by the sword." Down to Sheol they shall go in pollution, and there they shall be for ever bitten with torment.

¶ 9, chap. ix. 11–end.—In the world thus cleansed Jehovah shall dwell, the glorious God, at home in the land that shines with pristine glory. The golden age shall dawn again—that is, the David-days shall come once more, and shall endure for ever. Wide rule over all known nations, wealth, health, peace, power and prosperity in field, in vineyard, and in hall, shall be for ever through all the coming ages the glad portion of Israel with his God Jehovah.

CHAPTER II.

THE MAN AMOS.

§ 1. *Our need of him.*

THE question will often rise, But what have we to do with this man, and with any of these far-away people? Let us say a word in answer. We are certainly not constructing here the history of mankind in general, wherein no doubt this man Amos and his fellows would have their place like others. We are investigating religious history, where Amos certainly has an interesting and prominent position. But further, our aim is not the mere knowledge of religious phenomena. Our impulse is an eager thirst to know what our own religion is, and has been, and may be. Ours is like the very practical desire of the mariner on the wide ocean, whose first daily inquiry is, Where am I? and How must I move now? Here then lies our reason for reading Amos. We know what Christ is to us to-day, but we would know what He was yesterday in order that we may certainly know Him to-morrow. Peace for us lies herein. We seek assurance of more than our present living being, out, as it were, upon the wide ocean of time. Our life insists on widening its grasp and including in our personal possession the whole story of our past and the promise of all the future. Here lies a constant characteristic feature of the soul's life. The real self yearns for larger and larger life—in fact, the living soul must have some share in the infinite life.

Therefore the story of Christ is of personal interest to us, and the story of His coming is indispensable to the growing soul. Truly has He created life in us, and He is, therefore, the first revelation we have of God. He is "Son of God" by His power over us; or, as the Hebrews understood these words, He is to us "Very Divine Being." We fall before Him with humble gladness, crying, "My Lord and my God." But none the less is He "Son of Man," and, again, as the Hebrews understood these words, "Very human Being." As such He became, He was born, He had ancestors physical and mental; and knowledge of Him means knowledge of His physical and mental genesis.

Amos is a marked feature in that genesis. His words stand like brilliant gems in the treasure-house of records of the story of Christ. Those oracles are part of Christ's story, and so part of Himself. In this sense, as Amos is a part of Him who is to us "The Word of God," he is a part of the Word of God. Indeed, his story is not merely a part of the story of the coming of Jesus, Son of Man, but Amos himself is also a part of the unfolding of the Divine revelation which culminated on the Cross. Therefore Amos's words, life, self are part of the story of the Son of God. It is no wonder that this conclusion agrees thoroughly with the strange experience we have as we read Amos's words. Again and again we bow and say, "Surely this is the voice of God."

§ 2. *His inspiration.*

We need, therefore, no preliminary apologetic to prove the inspiration of Amos before we read his words as living food for our very souls. When we have read his words we recognise his inspiration, and then only. All argumentation *à priori* that he is inspired, *i.e.*, argument that he is in the canon, and that, because the canon is all inspired, therefore he is inspired, and will therefore furnish spiritual food, and therefore is to be read—all this is superfluous, and waste of precious time. It may be interesting scholasticism and traditional dogmatic method, but it is not vital.

But Amos makes a constant claim that he is uttering the utterances of God. Does not such claim seem blasphemy, unless we have good reason on other grounds for believing that he had a right to speak thus? What right had Amos to use such language? Must we not hold either that this language marks him as a trifler, and shuts him out from all religious respect, or that his very claim and unhesitating practice may indicate the presence of a religious power which we must at least face and investigate? Now comes to every mind the fact that we too hear a voice of whose utterances we are ready at once to say, "Thus saith the Lord." There lives not a soul which lacks utterly convictions of various sorts. The final authority for these and their ultimate source must unquestionably be the same as the final and supreme source of all things. Further, we cannot get away from the controlling sense of some of our convictions. Some of them are by no means mere opinions. Mathematical demonstrations are surely the mind of God. But we have besides these other convictions, whose hold we cannot by any means escape. We are sure that "we ought to do right." That "duty to do right" may be hard to prove, and sometimes we may be tempted to ask whether this sense of it is not a mere custom, a result of ages of practice; nevertheless we do know that we ought to do right, and nothing can convince us that we ought to do wrong. Nay, more, there are comparatively few persons who are always in uncertainty what particular things are the right things which they ought to do. We can go further, for a great host of living men are convinced that they are children of God, doubly dear to Him, forgiven sinners, born again into a new, strong, glad, godly course of life in which God will help them to abide. They trust, as many, many more in the past have trusted, that the Spirit of God speaks to them, bearing witness with their spirits that they are God's children. In such faith they lay hold of their callings, they train up their offspring, and they step forward through this life into the world beyond. In all these things they believe they know and obey the very voice of God whispering to them. They can say, like Amos, " Thus saith the Lord."

There is therefore nothing unexpected in Amos's faith—on the contrary, we expect just such faith in every true man. We understand his claim of oneness with God's mind, for we make it ourselves.

§ 3. *The scene of Amos's preaching.*

This scene and his position in history go far to give reality and value to his words, and to create the keenness of our interest in his words to-day. Come back and look.

It is evening, and the sun's level beams are striking across the western hills, gilding with fairest beauty the domes and pinnacles, the wall-tops and feathery palms of the queenly Samaria. She rests there like a golden crown on that proud head, that lordly hill rising in the midst of the fat valley. Fat, rich valley indeed it is, whose circling slopes, sweeping round this central hill, are all hidden beneath the veil of vines. On the bottom of the vale perhaps corn is waving, but up on the rocky central height the vines spread again about the jutting cottages of the vine-keepers until the hill seems like the face of some revelling youth garlanded with vine-leaves and purpling grape-clusters. Twice happy Samaria, planted amid such gardens, and exalted high on rocky height, inaccessible if guarded well;

by nature and by name thou art "The Keep." Great city too! Thy royal courts gather a host within thy walls, and attract from far the merchant, the herdsman, the husbandman with grain and fruits and cattle and wares of every sort. Plenty of fortune-seekers are there—the man of pleasure, the skilful player on string and pipe, the low and the high, the lord and the lady, the master with his slave, the subtle or the bold evil-doer, as well as the princes, the judges, and good men too of every calling—all are there.

It is even, and on the broad "Rehoboth" squares, where market has surged the whole long day, the night-fires are smoking. Round them are ranged the herds, that are bleating less now, and settling to their rest. Nearer, close circling by the fitful blaze, the motley groups of men, sellers and buyers, strangers and townsmen, chaffer over their trade, their purposes, the little world they know, or the wider world that some far-travelled ones can tell of. The piper pipes and the singer croons his lay of home, or of desert, or of sea. The enthusiast lifts his voice over his theme, and the gay, the careless, the simple, the superstitious, the devout, listen with common interest.

Hark! one voice sounds shrill and strong, although not so loud. What is this man's power, thus to silence and to hold all others? Perhaps we have sat upon some house-top bordering hard upon the square, as we have watched and listened; but now let us come down, and from the house-court thread the narrow lane out to the gathering congregation of this solemn herdsman-preacher.

He is a striking figure, as some men turn out to be who at first sight have seemed ordinary—plain-spoken, homespun folk. This very plainness makes the impression all the deeper when we see the calm depth of the eye, the quivering firmness of the mouth, the alert readiness of the whole frame. The late Mr. Green quotes Sir Philip Warwick's picture of Cromwell thus: "I came into the House one morning well clad, and perceived a gentleman speaking whom I knew not, very ordinarily apparelled, for it was a plain cloth suit, which seemed to have been made by an ill country tailor. His linen was plain, and not very clean, and I remember a speck or two of blood upon his little band, which was not much larger than his collar. His hat was without a hatband. His stature was of a good size; his sword stuck close to his side; his countenance swollen and reddish; his voice sharp and untunable, and his eloquence full of fervour" (Short Hist., p. 554). That picture of Cromwell is almost a picture of Amos. His eloquence was full of fervour. Resting one arm upon his shepherd's crook, he sways the other high, and it falls full of threatening solemnity. He is dark with the southern sun, and his rough-spun garments are somewhat hidden by the hairy leathern cloak that tells of the wild storms he has often faced alone with his flock on the mountains of Judah. Far up on those southern slopes is his native town, nestling indeed beneath the higher mountain wall, yet well seen from far. It is well known as the "Beacon" hamlet; its fit name is Tekoa, "Place of Trumpet-stroke;" and when from its walls the watching trumpeter strikes an alarm-blast, his warning is heard afar, far away in Bethlehem and even by Jerusalem's gates. But it is a sunny place as well; the burning sun ripens the grape-clusters round and ruddy there, for near it lies Beth-haccerem, "The home beside the most excellent vines," the southern Carmel. So the life of Amos was spent in part among gardens, vines, fields, and groves of sycamores, whose quiet, delicious luxuriance fed rich imaginative thoughts, and led to graceful clear utterance; another part was full of following the flock on the mountain pasture, or over the stern pass, or down through the deep gorge, that valley of the shadow, where sunlight beamed at noon-time only, and gloom hid the ravenous beast's crouching or the horrid snake's coil. Up yonder on the sullen mountainside Amos had stood guarding his sheep, while the thunder rolled and the terrible lightning darted across the blackness. He had thought there, like a true Semite, of the Being that was behind the storm; and his lonely cherished thought had deepened into a very speech of God to him. He felt he had talked and walked with his God. No doubt the twain had been agreed. Gazing across the wide horizon, he had listened to the thunder-tread upon the mountaintops; round the whole heavens he had seen One lead the winds. He felt Jehovah moving his soul within him, giving to him his thought. Down into the gloomy glen he had peered and stalked, listening for the horrid roar or hiss, yet girding his heart with brave faith in Jehovah's power to control the lion, the serpent, the nations, all things. There was a third portion of his life. His business led him at times away north to the market-towns, especially to the greater city Samaria. The new sanctuary in Jerusalem was already sacred with the traditions of the glorious David-age, a centre whence Jehovah's oracles ought to sound out over all Israel as well as Judah, but it was not yet the only place for intercourse with Jehovah, exclusive of all others. Amos knew that Jehovah was with him wherever he went; he had walked in friendship and truest worship beside his God on mountain and meadow, in orchard path or city street. He honoured the sanctuary of Jerusalem, indeed, but he gave it few words and few thoughts; and when he denounced other sanctuaries, and bade men seek not these but seek Jehovah, he never told them that Jerusalem was a place where they might find Him.

It is in Samaria we find him setting up his Divine oracle, with a faith apparently far, far before its time.

It was this faith, so absorbing, and so perfectly exhibited by his personality, that arrested all hearers, silenced and drew together all other talkers, stole through streets and halls like the dawn, held the city listening, brought the foremost priest of the chief Israelite house of God to the spot to hear for himself and to condemn.

Here is a problem of the very hardest sort—How does one man, conscious of a purpose to be godly, and acquainted with the Divine purpose to bless his people, nevertheless strike to death a fellow-man who is conscious of the same things and who is aiming to accomplish their realisation? It is a common experience to-day; it was the fact of the Cross; it was the experience of Amos at the hands of Amaziah; it is the inexplicable fact of sin. As the rabbis who caused the crucifixion were preachers of almost the identical faith that Jesus proclaimed, viz., the abode of God in and with every soul that truly seeks Him, so always those who know best, and who might do best, and who indeed at times actually do best deeds, may prove the very deadliest evil-doers, and may crucify one another. As the *odium theologicum* to-day is the most odious unholiness, so Amaziah, a servant of Jehovah, would have struck Amos dumb, the man who also knew himself to be a servant of Jehovah and commissioned by Him.

What cause could there be for the antagonism? Amos may have seen in Jehovah some part of the great God's immense character which Amaziah did not see. The cause of antagonism must lie in the limited vision which the one soul has, but which to him is all Divine and even all he thinks can be Divine; while the other soul receives a farther vision necessarily altogether new, and therefore apparently excluded by the former. All along man's story there has been this struggle of souls to claim each for itself an utter oneness with God, a knowledge of Him which excludes all further knowledge. It is a splendid struggle and claim; it marks human nature as partaker of the Divine nature. Yet in reality just this very certain share by one soul in the Divine nature gives every other soul an equal claim. One soul's fellowship with God implies God's fellowship with the whole family; and therefore the vision of God must be ever growing greater, ever, ever new, for ever and for ever opening new pages of the infinite Word of God.

We have therefore to ask what Amos brought which Amaziah had not. What was the new revelation in this new man of God? Consider then, first, that the age of Amos was one of remarkable activity in the development of mankind at large.

§ 4. *The age of Amos, and its wide activity.*

It is difficult to say that Providence purposed some particular developments in this or that period. Our knowledge of the cycles of Providence is far too small for such easy assertion. But our tendency to such assertion is another token of our inborn struggle for oneness with God. It is also the singular instinctive impulse in us towards ceaseless investigation. Unwearied we ask what is in this world about us; what has produced it, and what will it produce?

In spite of the difficulty of mapping the plans of Providence, we can certainly fix great era points in the mighty evolution. The faith in Christianity is a faith that for one definite date in human story we do know utterly the mind of God. On Calvary God's whole mind was revealed, grasped in human soul, and recorded in human history. Remarkably like that era are the years 800 to 750 B.C. Manifestly in that half century the great Creator-Spirit's ceaseless work was for a while extraordinary. Some scholars think that the philosophic poem of earth's creation recorded in Genesis i. was first sung soon after this era, and under its influence. However that may be, it is certain that then thoughtful men of God must have heard with devout awe the very present tread and voice of the Almighty Creator. The Spirit brooded upon the face of the deep, and brought forth light. Look west or east, south or north, and the muttering thunder-throes of the birth of a new age are there.

Far east, on Tigris' and Euphrates' banks, those years saw the intense mental activity that piled the huge stone libraries we are just unearthing, to find, to our bewilderment, disclosures of wondrous scientific skill, literary keenness, depth and beauty, economic care and civil order, with a religious yearning—ay, and grasp—that have seldom been far surpassed. Then the librarians cared to store not their own age's wealth of thoughtful words alone, but they had a care for the past that we might well copy, for they gathered and re-wrote and preserved the lore of the whole thousand years that had gone before them.

And this thoughtful power within was fellow to their power for action without. Earlier struggles for world-empire there may have been, but then first the Assyrian empire began the splendid series of mighty monarchies that has included the Babylonian, the Persian, the Greek, the Roman and its more modern Titanic sons. Egypt has been almost all along the rival of all these, always giving cause to look to the south-east corner of the Levant, always keeping that the arena of war and of wonder.

For a moment look at the west during Amos's day. In 776 B.C., while he preached in Samaria, Greece was rising up into full consciousness, and learning to count her own years and tell her own tale. The first Olympiad began in that year. A dozen years later, in 753 B.C., was the first hour of the common reckoning of the age of the city of Rome. Whether that year saw much masonry rise on the Seven Hills or not may be uncertain, but something held the gaze of all later Romans fixed on that age as the birth-time of the life of their nation. In all these lands the Cause of all causes was quickening life greatly.

So too it was in Israel and Judah. Then lived a whole galaxy of thoughtful men, whose deeds the world has never since let die. Perhaps we may not infer great political prosperity from the long reigns of fifty years each which are attributed to the two kings or sheikhs, Jeroboam II. of Israel and Uzziah of Judah, who ruled in the beginning of the century. The records of length of reigns in those days were subject to the feeling of the recorder. But this feeling evidently made great men of these two rulers—Jeroboam, whose name means "Let the nation increase," and Uzziah, "Strength gotten from Jehovah." Ahaz, the grandson of Uzziah, was a heartbreak to Isaiah, but more because of his cold, hard, philosophic scepticism than for any weakness in him. He was certainly a thoughtful man, a leader among astronomers, and not careless of other physical investigations; while he was far from being irreligious, but rather, like the Athenians, eager to know all about all sorts of gods. His son, Isaiah's pupil Hezekiah, was at the least a remarkable man, playing a great part in the story that we shall have to tell. All the various Israelite rulers after Jeroboam II. gave the great Assyrian commanders a hard task ere they could overthrow Samaria and master Palestine.

But all these were only the lesser stars of a great constellation of genius. Call it only genius, and it is unsurpassed. Here on the world's arena a band of men stood forth and wrote themselves on its records in words which the world has not once in these nearly 3000 years let die—words, we may safely say, that it never will forget. Leave it to later pages to tell how those writers have moulded by their work the whole fellowship of men in ever-widening circles since they lived. To-day their thoughts and words make up very much of the foundations and pillars of the Christian religion; they make up the carving and the inscriptions, the tracery and the colour, the great depths of shadow and the golden wealth of adornment, spiritual and even material, in the vast fabric where our souls meet God. They have done this, Amos and his fellows and peers have done this; and they have done it, as who denies, and who would not expect, by splendid personal qualities. Scholars they were, in that they were men of hard work at their calling, their line of investigation, their effort to produce. They studied not indeed history; neither did they write of earth or of mankind. They studied not law; neither did they write laws of ethics or the laws of matter. They were not poets, wrestling with utterance until they could compel it to imprison the fleeting visions of their souls. They used indeed something of all these, as masters use all things for their service; but their method was another, their aim was another, and their subject was far, far higher. These men were souls struggling with souls, laying hold on very God that they might exhibit Him as motive to move their hearers, to the end that they might win, might hold and weld their fellow-countrymen into oneness with their God. The task of those preachers, who were indeed prophets, is the very highest task on earth. The forces among which they operated were the greatest; those forces were God and the souls of men. The matter they set forth in discourse was the greatest; it was God. But it was not a philosophy of God, and not the mere physical nature of God, so to speak—it was the heart of God, God's will, God's very soul that they declared. It is much to study the laws of gravitation, of light, of electricity, of animal evolution, for these are all God's movements. The laws of those movements tell much of what God has done in the past. But what will God do henceforth? How can we know that, how can we handle that? What is the Will that set in being all those forces of gravitation and of light? Who is it that follows those force-laws as His modes of action? And what is He working out? It is after all a simple question, and the answer is a simple one to the soul that willingly follows those laws. Such a soul knows that it is right to follow them, and in its knowledge and conduct it has perfect peace. We do not say that such souls have always had perfect peace, but they have entered into peace. What is that peace but a state of atonement with the heart of all things? We may turn this into another expression. Such souls believe that the great Cause of all forces will always do right. They circle about Jesus as their Head and Lord because He is the Declarer of that faith even in death. He is thus the centre of the whole family of such believers. He is by the fact and nature and triumph of His death the very atonement between them and the cause of death. By His being such a Person He is the very Revelation or Word of God: He is the very Fact of God revealed. He is the essential Son of God, because Sonship and Fatherhood alone adequately express the relation of such living Revelation and such a Revealed One. We say then that such trustful, dutiful souls gazing ever on this centre of their life and faith do taste and share the Divine nature. They know God's heart, and are one with it, and reveal it.

This brief recital of such great faiths illustrates the height of the matter which the true preacher or prophet has to set forth. Amos did not indeed use such language as we have just used. Our words have, however, sought to express the legitimate culmination of the faith of Amos, as of every man of God.

The unique value of the preacher's task lies thus in the transcendent theme of his utterances. But it lies also in his method, for this is a wrestling of one mind with another. It is no mere description of things which, if a correct description, is an end in itself; for the preacher fails if he has no hearer. It contains descriptions indeed, but these are so couched that they may catch and hold the ear and heart even of the listless. It is not mere poetry where the singer is perfectly satisfied to imprison in measured words the rapture of his own vision. It contains poetry certainly, but that must be the song of the wooer that brings equal rapture to the wooed. It is not philosophic argument, where mind reasons to satisfy itself; but it contains the very highest philosophy, tested by the hold the argument has on the speaker's whole audience. So the prophetic books of that far-off simple Hebrew folk are profound with a strangely masterful philosophy that seems written for eternity. Magnificently beautiful they are with poetry that has never been surpassed, and still steals in upon the hour of sorrow or floats through the days of gladness as the very utterance of the reader's own joy or pain to-day. The true preacher's song is sung for all ages, and the enduring quality of that Hebrew literature marks it as true prophecy and literature of the very highest order. It is of the finest sort of utterance that the Creator has ordained. Its method is Divine.

But if subject and method give such value to these utterances, so does their aim add a transcendent value. They speak with men of God, to the end that they may make men and God one. Such a purpose makes even the narrow formalist who cherishes it a great man. Misguided as his means may be, and foolish as may be his fancy as to what sort of a being God is, yet he is a controller of gods and men. He would bind these together. He struggles to hold them breast to breast by his own clasping arms. This struggle is itself a Divine thing; feeblest men show hereby their birthright. Men were created to be children of God; their nature asserts itself. The Creator surely meant to satisfy the claim which we find so persistent in us. And the preacher or prophet is the great assertor of this birthright, by the high aim of his prophecy. Here he holds indeed the highest function man ever can hold.

It was a succession of such preachers arising in that eighth century before Christ in the Hebrew land that made the age so notable. Another question springs at once. How did their writings or words win such respect and preservation, whilst the prophesyings of earlier prophets were lost? Great preachers, such as Elijah, had risen before, but with all the sharp impression that Elijah made, and with all the care men took to tell how great his character was, they did not preserve any book of his utterances. The question will probably be best answered along with the corresponding one, Why did the eighth century prophets arise, and work so greatly? We turn therefore more directly to Amos himself, to find in him a clue to his genesis.

CHAPTER III.

THE ANTECEDENTS OF THE AMOS AGE.

§ 1. *The meaning of the question.*

WHAT was God's process in His bringing to the birth that age and His inspired prophets therein? If we can trace God's processes in inspiration, may we not hope that by falling ever into line with these we may find His inspiration coming amongst us now, to kindle and bless our souls, and to quicken the whole people about us? Surely this is the task proper of the student of religion, the theologian, to inquire diligently and search what and what manner of times the Spirit of God in us signifies in His revelation to us of the salvation and glory that He works to establish among us. In this quest we are in fellowship with all the prophets before and since Calvary.

Amos and his successors were then no mere men of an hour, no flitting dreams, no gourdlike mushroom growth. Note the evidence in themselves.

§ 2. *The faith of Amos in a Davidic age.*

Amos's closing words tell of his dearest, highest hope by striking a rich and old chord, pregnant with the whole music of centuries past. He sings exultant in hope of a cleansed, clean land, with no sinners and no sin upon it; and he cries "Then the David days shall come again." What was the meaning of this "David day" faith? To

Amos the coming golden age is to be a revival of the
golden age that had been, for the golden days of the
Hebrew past were the days of David. Perhaps they did
not think that the original, pure, unsullied state of men,
fresh from the hand of the Creator, had existed under
David; but then, they certainly believed, was the perfect
culmination of all their national life.

§ 3. *It is common to the prophets.*

Amos is not alone in this faith. All the prophets of
his century declare it with solemn gladness; and in later
centuries it is the faith and oracle of one great prophet after
another.

Hosea hopes for the union again of Israel and Judah
under one head, when the children of Israel shall seek at
once Jehovah as their God and David as their king.

Isaiah laments the separation of Israel and Judah as
the saddest deed that story ever told; and his picture of
a coming perfect day is a vision of the time when "the
scion of Jesse shall rule" in "the city where David dwelt."

So we might quote Micah. "From Bethlehem," David's
birthplace, "shall he that is to be ruler of Israel go forth,
whose goings forth have been from of old." Jeremiah a
hundred years later cries, "David shall never want a man
to sit upon the throne of Israel," and he sings a panegyric
on the great hero king. So Ezekiel, and so the oracles
sent to the exiles in Babylon.

§ 4. *What this faith meant.*

What did this mean in these men's inmost souls; and
to what does it point in their secret trust toward God?
Was God's purpose bound up in their minds with mani-

festations of destiny which had come to them in David; and did these men look back to such a manifestation as one of their dearest spiritual possessions? In other words, let us inquire, first, what Divine revelation came in David? and secondly, what new inspiration came to Amos from that revelation?[1]

Here is the doorway into the very heart of the Hebrews. This point where we stand is the gate to enter into as we prepare to preach from the Old Testament. No mere tale of dates, or of kings, or of ritual, no reading in of modern ideas, nor reading reality out and away from those people, is worthy of a preacher. The real study of the Old Testament consists in learning how men then thought of God, and how by God's providence they moved on to know Him better; and real preaching on the basis of this will consist in declaring how the character of God has been revealed in all, so that men may trust Him.

We ask, then, what Divine revelation came in David? What religious feelings, thoughts, deeds centred providentially in David, and especially what current of religious experience seems connected with him as with a central, abundant wellspring?

§ 5. *The work of David.*

There is no doubt that the possession of Jerusalem by Hebrews dates from the days and work of David. There

---

[1] A prominent physiologist's recent attempt to trace the "Jahweh" religion to fancies such as the witch of Endor story pays no regard to the date from which that story comes to us, and no regard to the much earlier and much more reliable Amos-phenomena. *Ne sutor ultra crepidam.* There is need to say that students had better not credit a most able physiologist with a complete equipment and ability on every point outside his department. The strangest blunders in Chinese philology, in political economy, and in religious and theological history, may be perpetrated by our most valued, honestly admired masters of theoretical and practical physiological science.

was another fact allied to this which gave to Jerusalem its great worth. That city was the seal and symbol of the unification of the Hebrew tribes. David first welded the settled tribes into a kingdom, made them into one ordered people and one organic working whole. He created the nation; and not only so, he spread its rule to distant borders on north, south, and east. On the west lay the Mediterranean Sea; its distant islanders learned to know him and to serve under him.

His kingdom stretched, it seems, from the isthmus of Suez up through all Palestine, over all the mountain-land in the north, away across the desert and the slowly sinking slopes of the immense Euphrates valley till it stopped at the bank of the river itself. Alike wide was his rule from west to east. Here was, in a sense, the first in the great series of world empires. We hardly count hoary old Egypt of earliest days, with its primeval thrones, in the world-monarchy annals, mighty though the Egyptian dynasties were. We begin usually with Assyria in its later glory. But David was before later Assyria. David was the first forerunner of imperial Cæsar; he may almost be called the first world-monarch of later well-known history. The rough tradition, that was long the only guide to men curious over the past, knew with singular correctness that there were three ruling factors in history, Rome, Greece, Judea. Historians are now confirming the correctness of this opinion by showing us that our so-called formal Christian Church has been, almost until to-day, the Roman empire prolonged, and that our so-called formal Christian doctrine has been pre-Christian Aristotle and Plato all too long. And the prophets' doctrine concerning David has had a singular control of the East, and of the West no less. Renan's pointed satire, *Teste David cum Sybilla* (Hist. of Isr. i. 451), points to a great fact. We have a great deal to do with the Jews, and light on many a difficulty comes to us as we face the fact. Thus far we are certain that to the mind of the prophets the David age of the Hebrews was a time of great religious revelation. What that revelation was we must define more exactly.

We have more light to guide us touching David's story, and the Amos-faith touching him. Our records concerning his work have been often attributed to contemporaries of Isaiah and of Jeremiah; and even these prophets themselves have been counted authors of much of the four books of Kings. Some good men have supposed that Samuel must have written the two books that sometimes bear his name; but they will find Samuel's death described when the author is only beginning the last quarter of the first book of "Samuel." We may learn something from our early Greek and Roman and African fellow-Christians, who spoke, we may say, always of "the first, second, third, and fourth books of Kings." We may learn also from the Jews themselves, whose Bible calls Joshua, Judges, 1st and 2nd Samuel, 1st and 2nd Kings, respectively "the six prior prophetical books," imputing to them authorship by prophets. There were many prophets before Isaiah and Jeremiah; but it is remarkable that Amos and his contemporaries were the first who seem to have written down their own oracles and exhortations. Again, the coincidence of Jeremiah's life with the latest events recorded in Kings makes it certain that the writer who finished the book lived no earlier than Jeremiah. Between Amos's day and Jeremiah's, therefore, we must look for what we may call the first clearly uttered recognition we possess of the David-revelation. In a very deep sense we must count that the very age of this revelation. We say rightly that the age when men become conscious of a revelation is the real date of God's giving that revelation. Doubtless earlier records were used by the writer and collector of the books of Kings, in the days of Jeremiah, for as soon as events happen the record of them begins in some way to be formed, whether it be only in memory or in some written sort. But in any case the prevailing character of our records concerning David is due to the times of Jeremiah and to the generations just preceding him. Later serious modifications of details might well happen when the Exile had blurred the past, as we know it did in the mind of Malachi, who, although a singularly devout soul, was yet utterly ignorant of the gospel of Isaiah liii. But the ground-lines of the picture given in those narrative books of David as world-monarch were evidently drawn by one who lived between Amos's and Jeremiah's days. This conclusion will lead us on now to one more important fact concerning what God was doing in those ages.

§ 6. *The rise of world-monarchies.*

The writers, the quiet thinkers, and all men in those two hundred years, lived amid providences very terrible to the smaller peoples of the time.

It was the day of Assyria's march toward world-empire; it was the day of terror for every smaller state, and of subjugation for many; it was the day of Egypt's steady resistance and rivalry; it was the day of Assyria's final crashing overthrow by the hand of her own mother-state, Babylon, that had been long a vassal or slave of her own daughter. Those tremendous invasions, enslavings, catastrophes, thus briefly enumerated, are the chief matter of discussion in all the prophets from Amos to the Exile; they were "the work of God" to every thoughtful Hebrew; the meaning of all these things was the very word of God to them. The Semite—or let us be distinct, the Hebrew—

was more sensitive to the transcendent voice of God than Englishmen are. We are ready to say nature speaks; they knew that God speaks.

Now, just in the movements and thoughts in that Amos age lies one of the quick and clear recognitions of God, or steadily invading and overwhelming convictions of Him, which produced the monotheistic faith. We may view it thus. In a time when each nation cared for itself alone, each nation claimed absolute possession of all its appurtenances, even including God. Each learned to think of a Divine Being exactly fitted to itself, and devoted to itself— "its own Holy One," as the Hebrew would say. They thought that for many nations there must be many Gods; and thus tribalism and extreme nationalism established an actually polytheistic faith. Parallel, however, to this desolating belief there was that touching faith, visible in Amos's thinking as elsewhere, that a god cannot live without a people. The wars of the peoples were the very wars of their gods, and the victory of one god over many was the establishment of a divine over-lordship. Such an establishment had taken place under the hand of David; the recognition of it was the David-revelation. In the prophets' souls there dawned at the very midnight of imperial enslavings the morning of conviction that there must be one Over-Lord over all gods and all peoples, because there could be one nation ruling over all nations. But who should be this Over-Lord? The answer of the prophets sprang at once from their view of the past. There was a day, they cried, when the Lord of Judah had joined all the Hebrew tribes that owned Jehovah under His sole rule; surely that lord David was the man after Jehovah's own heart. His very name signified "The uniquely-beloved." But more, far more. Had not that David made himself lord over many nations far and near? As the Assyrians were now thinking to do, so had Zion's king surely done long before. David's throne had swayed many peoples. Therefore, glorious oracle! David's God Jehovah was Over-Lord over all those gods.

§ 7. *The name "Jehovah of Hosts."*

This faith is matter of history; this singular conviction is recorded in the very features of speech due to those times as well as in the declarations of the prophets. It is worded in the very language of the people, for it is well known that the expression "Jehovah of hosts," the Lord of hosts, Jahweh Sebaoth, יְהוָה צְבָאוֹת, comes into use in and just after the David days, and is most remarkably characteristic of the men who had to do with the construction of the four books of Kings. A few figures will help the judgment.

The expression does not occur in the Pentateuch, Joshua, or Judges. Amos is the oldest document which has it; he has it nine times in nine chapters. Hosea uses it once in fourteen chapters; but Hosea was probably a north-kingdom man, one of those least likely to glorify a Judah king. Micah has it once in seven chapters; Isaiah fifty-four times in the thirty-nine chapters, mostly addressed to Hezekiah's days; Nahum, *circa* 630 B.C., once in three chapters; Zephaniah, 630 B.C., twice in three chapters; Jeremiah, 620–600 B.C., seventy-nine times in fifty-two chapters; Habakkuk, 610 B.C., once in three chapters; the Isaian oracles for the Exile, *i.e.* for 600–540 B.C., six times in twenty-seven chapters; Ezekiel, never; Haggai, 520 B.C., fourteen times in two chapters; Zechariah, fifty-four times in fourteen chapters, of which five chapters with nine occurrences may have been pre-Exilic, the rest of date *circa* 520 B.C.; Malachi has it twenty-four times in four chapters. It occurs fourteen times in the four books of Kings, of probable date 600 B.C.;

and three times in Chronicles, of date say 300 B.C.; and it stands sixteen times in the Psalms.

In brief, the title is a favourite with the prophets, and specially with those who speak much of the David days, and who write the story of them. Those men who arose to preach amid the convulsions of the first wars for world-monarchy, and who called their God the Lord of all Hosts, declared thereby their fundamental faith.

§ 8. *The sum of the argument; the nature of the David-revelation.*

The sum of our argument is this. The David-revelation was, Jehovah is Supreme Lord over all other gods, powers, and nations. This is what we may call the religious antecedent of the Amos age, as it is to be gathered from Amos and contemporary prophets. It is that faith which we find the prophets derive from the period just preceding their own day; and we learn that it is so from consideration of the words of the prophets themselves. Their favourite name for their God, "Jehovah of hosts," is their formula for this faith and doctrine; and their common hope for the return of the Davidic golden age tells us how the great faith which they inherited from the past seemed to them to spring from David's days and from the experiences that circled round him. What we know of David we learn partly from the prophets and partly from narratives collected together under their influence, and all agree to exalt his singular power in unifying the divided tribes of his own people, and in extending their sway over others. To David and to his age, therefore, they looked as the time of Jehovah's manifestation of His power to overcome all other gods. We call it an inherited faith, and yet we call it also their own faith. It sprung in their own souls because of the circumstances in which they lived, that is, the clash of strife for world-empire; but that need drove them to find rest in the meaning of the long-past David events. The revelation which they saw in David gave them life for their own times, just as the revelation which we see in Jesus gives us life amid the needs of to-day. The prophets themselves being witnesses, we learn that the David-revelation was "Jehovah is Over-Lord, He is the Lord of hosts." We must proceed now to discover what was the next stage of insight into the character of God, the stage in which they themselves were the direct original searchers and discoverers. We do not, surely, need to reassert the fact that, whoever be the learner, the searcher, the preacher, it is God, the great Giver of their thoughts to men, who gives the increase, the light, the knowledge.

It is interesting to observe, ere we leave this place, that perhaps we have lighted upon one important cause of the commencement of the use of writing by the prophets at this time. If the preachers were surrounded by danger from the wars and intrigues for world power, danger of cruelty from foreign soldiery and from domestic spies, it was very wise and natural to write the oracles for the most part, and let them reach their audience silently. This was probably one cause of the new method; we shall discover another ere long.

CHAPTER IV.

THE AMOS-REVELATION.

§ 1. *It comes amid wrestlings—(a) thoroughly human; (b) in company with God; (c) wrestling with God; (d) wrestling with men; (e) wrestling in argument.*

This comes amid the wrestlings of his soul. Amos is no mere vessel to be filled with something poured into him and through him, nor pen unconscious held by an invisible writer, nor phonographic mouthpiece uttering another's soul. He wrestles with men whom he would check and change. When they oppose objections he stands at times perplexed for a moment by the difficulty; but then, gathering all the light he possesses on the matter, gathering in solid strength all the reasoning powers he has for the question's solution, with a great struggle he throws the hindrance from before him, and unveils the positive answer that objector and prophet equally need. This wrestling with man is on another side of it a wrestling with God. Never staying to wonder whether God is with him, or has perchance moved away far from him, he turns to the fountains opened for him, and follows the methods God has taught him; then he utters with childlike faith his sublime valuation of his conclusions, "Thus hath Jehovah said." This is inspiration indeed; this is belief in God. Would that some timid men to-day could understand how the day of objectors and objections, the age of opposers and oppositions, is the very day of living revelation from God. In the perplexities come the answers, and in the wrestlings of the reasoning soul compelled by the very keenness of the opponent to straightforward integrity of reply, God's own messages come. The Word of God was from the beginning; they beheld indeed His glory in Galilee, but He lived and spoke in the days of Amos also. The Christ is the same yesterday, to-day, and for ever. Let us watch the soul of Amos actually at work.

(*a*) He is so thoroughly human! The lone mountain shepherd, he stands on the market-place as if he were on his own lofty mountain-side pasture. That look of his comes from acquaintance with every flock, every sheep, every glen below, every cloudy sign above, and all his wide nature-home. And he seems conscious too of having a thorough knowledge of men. He gives his counsel unhesitatingly; his opinions on many things he gives you as very gold; his healthy self-confidence impresses itself deeply upon you, and you obey him. He is indeed so thoroughly his own vivid self, that you feel something of God in him. All he had and gave he had gained by his own strong personality. He was a real man, and just therefore he was a man of God.

(*b*) It is such a man who can speak of God and men as having companionship. You listen as to the story of a personal experience as he tells of the "two who must be agreed if they are to work together." You are ready to believe it is an experience that both the companions, the man and God, have enjoyed. But the honest dignity of the man never lessens but ever exalts the transcendent dignity of the companion God. So he says of that illustrious Friend, "It is He who giveth to man his thought." In that wondrous communion the great Jehovah had doubtless satisfied some mysterious yearning of His own high soul which only fellowship with a man could satisfy. But the man went out from that converse conscious that, for his part, he had there received all that he possessed. For God had there "given to the man his thought." Such a man was Amos.

(c) He wrestled with God. Such a conception is well known to be a Hebrew one. Amos does not himself say that he wrestled; but he tells us of some scenes in his life, and then we say " he wrestled with God." One part of his book is less grand than others, because it is more childlike in style. There in parables he tells of his wrestling, although there also he suffers a tenderness to appear which elsewhere he resolutely excludes. The parables in chapter vii. are tales of his pleading with God to forgive the wrong-doings of Israel. A plague of grasshoppers was likely to come, and Amos says he besought God to avert the scourge, and God heard and did. He wrestled till he prevailed. Again another scourge—this time a fiery destruction—was averted: Amos had rushed in to the rescue, struggling with the God of fire till he prevailed. A third time he strove, but this time in vain. The conclusion he reached was, that God's forgivenesses were a store of good that could be exhausted. The whole position is that of a man in intensely keen action, never allowing for one moment that he knows all of God's revelations until he has searched, tried, and exhausted all the alternative possibilities. So came Amos's revelations to him.

(d) Following those parables in the seventh chapter comes another tale of struggle. To the outer eye it was with a man, Amaziah, the chief priest of Bethel; but it was a struggle with God. Was not this a priest of the God of Israel in the Bethel that Abraham loved and Jacob revered, and where Samuel and Elijah worshipped? What outward sign of Divine commission could Amos have that might set aside this priest's Divine authority? One can feel the fear and sharp uncertain pain in the prophet's heart: one almost hears his silent cry, "My God, hast Thou not bidden me?" If any one doubts the utterly human condition of Amos in that hour, let him read the speedily following words that call any other soil than Palestine's "a polluted land." Amos was a Jew indeed, he was very human in that hour; he was sure to tremble before such an opponent as a great priest. But in weakness arose perfect strength. He dashed aside all official authority which this great priest had; he looked into the sanctuary of his own soul, and there he saw God, heard God, felt God. Forward then he flew to the charge: "Jehovah called me, said to me, says to me, Go prophesy. I tell thee, in His name, thou withstandest Him." It may be hard for some to-day to see how the apologetics of Amos sweep away the apologetics of Amaziah. Men still seek signs. But no signs shall serve them, save such as the signs of the prophet Amos. It is in living wrestling souls that God gives His unconquerable inspiration.

(*c*) Already we have seen in our analysis of the book that chapter v. verses 1–14, are a picture of a keen struggle in argument between the brave prophet and the self-justifying Samaritans. But a keener struggle far records itself amid all that outer fighting. The prophet turns from the audience at every question or objection they propose, and turning to his great Lord, he seems to question Him and wrestle for the true answer he feels God must give. Not this chapter alone but the whole book is a constant controversy. He ranges the whole horizon round to condemn the surrounding peoples in preliminary argument, as it were, that he may justly condemn his own people. He stretches out fearless hands to unveil the bosom secrets and companionships of God, the Divine loves and purposes; the things of high heaven are his arguments, if by any such means he may convince men. He plunges down to

Sheol to forge there his last argument for his last terrific oracle. That place, marked by its very name as the weird mystery that men for ever peer into and question, is ransacked by Amos for the sword that shall cut off all sinners from Israel. Wrestling, restless, the man Amos grasped oracles from God for men, and men have listened with trembling ever since. We do not wonder at this; yet the man's power is a great wonder.

§ 2. *His revelation was breadth and keenness of conscience.* (a) *The tribal conscience;* (b) *the first writing prophet is the prophet of conscience;* (c) *Amos's demand is righteousness;* (d) *the wrongs of his time.*

What revelation came to Amos in such wrestlings? Let us give the answer at once: A wide and keen conscience. And now trace its genesis.

(a) In early tribal days "every man did what was right in his own eyes." That well-known simple historical fact means that men strove to do what was right, but their horizon was not large. They did not take into consideration any man who was not of their own family, and who did not serve their own God. They heard a controlling voice in the soul demanding righteous conduct, or in simple words they could not escape the law, "Do right." That was Divine law to them. But what was right? This was defined by the horizon that marked off the interests of their God; and so long as He was only a tribal God they were bound to care for the tribe's interests only. This is a first fact in the investigation.

But in Amos's day there had come a greater revelation of their God's power and interests; He was Over-Lord, Jehovah of hosts, God of gods. This second historical fact we have discovered already. And now a third fact is that Amos's first and last and constant oracle is a keen demand for a righteousness broad enough to bless all the peoples that Jehovah ruled over.

(*b*) It is remarkable that the first great writing prophet is essentially a prophet of righteousness. His adoption of writing may be partly explained by the troubles which the proud world-empires brought, as we have seen. But still more certainly was it connected genetically with the widened faith in God. For when Jehovah rules the nations far and near then all must hear of Him; and the man of God sees that duty is a far more serious matter than before, a matter to be laid on all men's hearts far and near. Therefore he writes his vision, and makes it plain on tablets for all to read near and far, present and future.

(*c*) This illustrates the essential feature of Amos's oracles. Their characteristic is demand for larger righteousness; and to this task Amos rose through his sense of the overlordship of Israel's God. To the soul of the man of God, finely hearing, devotedly watching the work of his Master, the vision of the wide sway, the hitherto undreamed of sway of Jehovah, becomes at once a vision of vastly enlarged duty for men. With the new interests spring new cares, with the new brotherhood come new needs. Those who once were foreigners have now duties to Jehovah, to each other, to Israel; and Israel has new duties to them all. Simultaneously with multiplied duties comes finer sense of duty. The mature man has finer conscience than the child, for moral exercise brings moral skill. No wonder then that Amos has written his character on Hebrew story as the stern keen preacher of righteousness. He is by no means indeed only a moralist, but in comparison with Hosea the duty of man is to him almost everything, and religion or the sense of man's need and God's mind almost entirely wanting.

(*d*) But let us be more exact. What was righteousness with Amos? There arise two questions: What sort of evil deeds were common then; and how far had Amos risen to condemnation of them? We must be careful, for it is easy to decry moral conditions if they be different from our own. But taking simply Amos himself as a standard for judgment of his own times, let us compare him and his times, and the great difference will move us to say, Here is noble exaltation over against base degradation; here was one singularly alive ethically amid a very want and death of character; here amid men and sin was surely a revelation of good and God. Do the ethics of Amos and his code of morality approve the claim of his cry, "Thus saith God"? What are his ethics? What does he see to abhor round about him?

(α) There is much of brutal cruelty. Torture of prisoners by dragging iron harrows over their bodies is brutal enough, and Amos knows the practice well. There was also horrible torture of women with child by tearing them open, so adding awful mockery of the function of motherhood to the fiendish hurt. It is ghastly. And that was the environment of Amos! Is the individual the product of society? Or was there another element in his environment, unseen but real, purposeful, almighty, creating righteousness?

(β) There was dishonour of manhood. Slave-trade was common, and it was greedy and heedless. Perhaps a tolerable slavery may exist in a patriarchal system of government, where the home-born slave is always honoured and cared for as part of the family and as a son or daughter in a secondary sense. Missionaries tell us we must be careful not to condemn altogether modern Semite slaveholding. But Amos thunders against the capturing of whole villages, and the sparing of no soul among them.

The dealers take and sell all for accursed gain. This class of investment is customary still in our own traffic and society; the wonder is that 2500 years ago Amos was far above such a level. But to his mind there is an added baseness in the slavery he sees: they steal and sell whole villages of their own kinsmen. There are indeed such deeds to-day, and strange it is that to-day social interests can be sacrificed for selfish gain; educational interests, ay, pure religious interests, can be set aside for the sake of selfish gain. But more strange it is that yonder, two thousand years ago, many centuries before Christ, in a society closely like that of our slave-trading African Arabs, a man rose to denounce this selfish gain. He would not endure such mean dishonour of the manhood of the enslaved.

(γ) He revolted against dishonour even of the dead. To rifle graves and burn men's bones, especially a prince's bones, into lime, was an unmanly deed to his mind, but it seems to have been common. And Amos condemns especially such treatment of the body of a prince of Moab. Conscience was larger than once it had been.

(δ) There was still worse dishonour common, he says, for prisoners lying under indictment or out on bail, but not yet proved guilty, were robbed of their bail-pledges and of their means of defence in court-trial. Amos abhorred and condemned all who sway courts of justice to either side for partisan advantage. Here was a demand for justice recognisable surely as, on the one hand, no mere gift of ghosts, and as, on the other hand, a mark of the prophet's like-mindedness with God. Unless God Himself forsakes eternal righteousness, this prophet Amos was a man of God. Surely the Spirit of God and the spirit in Amos were one.

(ε) The Israelite dishonour of man went further. They dishonoured themselves by falsehood in commerce, by untrue certificates of the value of their yardstick, their pound weight, and their coin. This was double dishonour.

(ζ) But they added one black shade more, Amos thought, when they polluted the fountains of human birth. Here fathers, and mothers too, dishonoured their own high prerogative when they flung out the life that was to be to worse than orphanage.

(η) Just at this point Amos's morals and condemnations throw a strong light on the religious nature of his countrymen. When they give rein to their lusts, says he, they ease their conscience by regarding their deeds as religious performances. The cause of such regard is not far to seek, and it is important. The wine-drinker, thirsting for his excitement, counts the uncontrollable impulse in his body as the moving of a god within him; so likewise thinks the most lust-swayed debauchee. Evidently all forces that work uncontrolled by will of men, as lightning or lust, the fructifying rain or the pestilence, alcohol, reproductive power in tree and animal, all these the men of those days counted the work of Elohim. We may say that their thoughts rose at once from the conception of such powers around them to the conception of beings unseen but otherwise somewhat like themselves, though stronger, whom they named "Far-reachers," "Elohim." It is idle to regard all this as the outcome of watching the bodies of the dead, and of wonder where the departed souls were wandering. The notion of God steals over us as we feel all the influences of the home whence we go forth into the world; it is voiced by the busy whisperings of life around us to the eager listening of life within. God is manifest to us first in birth rather than in the looming shadow of the bourne to which we go, and whence no traveller returns to be a familiar guiding friend. Even the vicious excuse for vice in Amos's day shows that.

We see plainly that Amos shares the fancy that there

are other deities besides Jehovah, some of whom receive and relish the honours from the drinker and the lustful. Only he insists that honour done to those deities is dishonour done to Jehovah. When a father and his son go both to one poor girl to please themselves, to her ruin and their offspring's and their own, then they may be giving pleasure to the god called "Male-master," "Baal," but they also put to shame Jehovah's devotion to themselves and to their nation. He is their national God, pledged to care altogether for them; He is their "Qadhosh," their "Holy, Devoted One;" therefore deeds that mean any respect for the Baal, or any pleasure in him, profane Jehovah's devotion, His character, and His name. Thus the Jehovah religion condemned lust, drunkenness, and superstition. Here are valuable facts in the history of this religion.

(θ) As we naturally expect, all these moral characteristics already seen in Amos are accompanied by qualities of still higher and deeper sort. There glistens in every look he gives a kindly remembrance of the suffering poor, there mantles on his cheek at every word a reverence for the pure, there glows at his highest climax such a longing for the simple ideal good, that we may fairly say Amos preached afar yonder in Samaria the Christ that was to come in Galilee. And it was no orphaned or helpless hope for an ideal good that Amos preached, but this Tekoan of 800 years before our Lord was perfectly convinced of the high dignity of personal communion with God, of its reality in himself, and of its possibility for all. That high privilege was to him, and was to be to all, the most momentous ground, spring, and cause of all highest morality. Such was Amos, a contrast to the society about him, an oracle of the God within him. He was emphatically the prophet of righteousness. He was the revealer of the God of righteousness.

§ 3. *His conception of man.*

Who were to be influenced by this Amos-revelation? What did he himself think of them? Or, in other form, let us ask what the soul of man seemed to him to be? The answer will tell us perhaps less about the actual hearers than about the preacher's power of understanding them. This will be itself a picture of the mind of the times, inasmuch as it will tell us how far the more thoughtful men of the times understood the soul's nature. Amos's psychology will certainly give us insight into the contemporary Hebrew mind; and this is essential to a grasp of the Hebrew religion of that day. His psychology will tell us more; it will reveal to us the providential method by which it pleased God to reveal Himself then. We are coming thus to the inner centre of religion in that age, and to the vision of the supernatural moving of God there.

To be perfectly plain from the outset, let us say that here Amos's mind is the white-hot crucible of the analyst, and all his thoughts of the nature of the soul are in the intense flux of readjustment, and of change to a far grander, finer form. For—

(*a*) The common faith of the time, which Amos shares when not driven from it by reflection, is that Jehovah has to do with the Israelite people as a whole only—He does not speak to individuals. "Oh, children of Israel, the whole family which I have brought up out of Egypt. You only have I chosen out of the nations! therefore I will punish you for all your iniquities." "The virgin of Israel is fallen . . ." "Thus saith Jehovah unto the house of Israel, Seek ye Me, and ye shall live." "O Lordly Jehovah, cease, forgive, I beseech Thee. By whom shall Jacob arise, for he is small?" "Behold the eyes of the Lordly Jehovah are upon the sinful kingdom, and I will destroy it from off the face of the earth." This Israel, whom Amos exhorts, is a state, an organised unit; and we may add that it is materially endowed, and continues in life by continuing in enjoyment of cities, fields, corn, and wine, and cattle.

(*b*) But the soul of the prophet is not at rest in this theory. The nation remains Jehovah's, and he himself is Jehovah's; but there are foul and manifold sins done in the nation, against which at least *his* soul revolts, and other souls like his revolt as well. He prays, and knows he is heard. He knows he is himself a servant and friend of God. There are other prudent souls also who condemn and have no part in the evil deeds. They do not shout in the revelry, they sit silent for shame in the courts of justice. They abjure by that silence the shameful excesses about them and the shameful decisions of the magistrates. Their silence is prudent perhaps; but it is compulsory also, for they are forbidden at their peril to speak. The evil-doing men in authority know them very well, and regard them as separate from other men. And Amos too is learning that these are not like the mass of Israel. They are fit companions for Jehovah. It is dawning on him that not all Israel is Jehovah's people. In the paragraph (chap. iii.) where he argues that only those who are agreed with Jehovah can walk with Him, there specially does he speak of Jehovah's servants and confidants as a limited number, and not all Israel. He is leaving one faith and advancing to another.

(*c*) Now rises the question, What is this difference between the two classes that is becoming clear to Amos, and already characterises his exhortations?

The class which he condemns is large and important, including sons and fathers, merchants and magistrates, paramour women and men of the highest rank, artists, rulers, a priest of highest position. These are the sinners in Israel who say, "The evil shall not overtake nor prevent us." But such were present quite as much in the older days when the whole people was counted the true Israel: the title, "People of Jehovah," was previously applied to all Israel, including just such men of evil sorts. It was not the case that some had begun to do wrong where none had done wrong before. Doing wrong was not a new feature that had been added to Israelite nature. What was new? It was not some fact in Israelite character that was new—it was only Amos's knowledge of a fact.

(*d*) Amos had become aware that true Israelite character needed one feature more than had been demanded before. So he moved toward clearer understanding of the individual value of men. How remarkable that it was an advance in the moral estimate of men which led towards truer estimate of human personality. Amos doubtless did not reflect on this psychological fact in himself, but its appearance in a practical earnest life is of highest importance. This fact in the story of men confirms the reasoning of keen philosophers, who tell us that such ought reasonably to be the case. The starting-point of all true philosophy is ethical and practical.

(*e*) The true Israelites, according to Amos's new idea, are those who do good. Does then the difference between these true men and the false depend on some radical difference of nature; or can a false man become a good man? And how? Amos's only answer is "Seek good." "If they will seek good, they shall live; for then Jehovah the life-giver will be with them." The sinful men *can* do good, thinks Amos. At an earlier point he had said that evil cannot be in the land unless Jehovah hath done it; and again he had said that it is Jehovah who gives to man his thought. To Hebrews of a few generations later the apparent conflict of this Divine control with the command "Seek good," caused difficulty. We understand the mysterious conflict of the great facts, but Amos had not reflected so far on the persistence of character. To him the act of conversion was therefore as yet a light matter. It was to his mind entirely in the individual's hand and power to change himself from badness to goodness. This was the natural outcome of the hitherto universal faith that Jehovah had chosen the whole nation; for that choice implied that all Israel was naturally quite likely to do good, or, in other words, it implied that there was certainly no inherent evil nature in Israel, nothing there essentially obnoxious to Jehovah. Very certainly no one had ever hitherto raised the question of the essential personal character of a man, good or bad. But it is a part of the Amos-revelation that in God's Providence the prophet comes close up to the question, and leaves the world henceforth the richer by this glimmering dawn of a sense of the importance of personal character.

(*f*) If Amos is coming but slowly to the grasp of this one particular feature of character, he is nevertheless coming to it from various sides. When he utters his most awful oracle, the climax of all, crying, "All the sinners of my people shall be cut off," we start back in horror at first. Then feeling about for some ground for such a dreadful sentence, we are compelled to think it must have been because the prophet identified thoroughly a wrong with its wrongdoer. He seems to have believed that the cleansing God must cleanse away all sinners if He would cleanse away all sin. A happy day is to come, he believes, when all will be righteous, and the Davidic days, the golden, perfect days, shall have come back again; but to this end all that is bad must be cleansed away. Therefore all sin and all sinners must be destroyed. So we discover again from this side that he is learning the inherent nature of evil character. He is not learning it scholastically, but practically; the form which the faith takes with him is that inherent sinful character begins with the act of sin, while he does not know any inherent sinful character preceding the actual sin. Here we feel at once that he is drawing near to eternal truths; therefore when he says of this dread oracle, "Thus saith Jehovah," we answer, "This is the finger of God," and bowing reverently, we kiss the page.

Instinctively we look now for some dawn of faith concerning atonement. Amid such revelation of judgment we wonder whether there was mercy. And the instinct is correct. For here in fact begins the story of grace. But before we look on that another line of reflection holds us for a moment.

(*g*) Amos identifies the sinner with his sin; he does not rise to identify the good man with absolute good. This would have been Christianity. When in that wonderful and profoundly valuable fifth chapter we see him driven back in his argument that only the seekers of God shall live, and the answers of his audience or of his own traditional faith, "God is in Israel," "God is in our sanctuaries," only call forth his loud and louder, No! No!; then at last he declares his ultimate oracle and faith, "Seek good, and so Jehovah shall be with you, as ye say." But the troubled hearer could at once cry "And where shall good be found?"[1] Now undoubtedly Amos was with God, and God was with him, according to his own firm conviction. If he had bidden the seekers after God to come to himself, to the man of God, they would have found God. They would have found good; they would have found the fountain whence flowed his great demand for righteousness.

---

[1] This is the soul's constant cry through the ages: "Who will show us any good?" "What good thing shall I do?" "What must I do to be saved?" Monasticism, "Imitation of Christ," "Rules of Faith," are all illustrations of the same cry.

But Amos had not risen to that height—that great revelation was not yet come. The need for it was to compel men yet for many a day to "look forward for Another." In other, greater words, the inspiration of God made Amos's commands and his awakening influence an insufficient gospel and an utterance of need of One who should say, "Come unto me all ye that labour and are heavy laden, and I will give you rest."

§ 4. *Amos's view of the ways of revelation.*

Here arises the question, What were then understood by Amos as the ways in which God manifested Himself to men? With this question we begin the study of the prophetic faiths in atonement. There are at least three sorts of answers; and in all of them is again evident that flux of thought, that process of the soul's alchemy, that advance from one way of thinking to another, which singularly and most truly marks men who are in close fellowship with God.

(*a*) First then, to Amos the very soil of Palestine had a certain contact with Jehovah, and to walk upon it was to be with Him. On the other hand, all lands outside lacked this blessed presence and were polluted. To dwell in them was sorrow, to die and to be buried in them was to be accursed.

There is one passage indeed, although there is only the one, which calls one spot in the sacred land peculiarly sacred. "Jehovah roars from Zion, it is from Jerusalem that he utters His voice." And yet there is no denial by any writer of any land or time stronger than Amos's denial of the doctrine that Jehovah is to be found in sanctuaries. Quite true it is that that grand outburst of denial is in the first place a denial that to seek Bethel or Beersheba or

Gilgal is to seek Jehovah. No doubt the local prejudice of Amos and his tribal love for Judah helped him in this condemnation of the Israelite Bethel, the venerable house of God where patriarchs saw their promise-speaking Saviour. But it is doubtful whether there was any tribal prejudice in Judah against Beersheba, that sanctuary in the far south, more venerable still than Bethel, or against the Gilgal, some one of the many Gilgals, *i.e.*, rolled-up stoneheap altars, probably that one which a Samuel's prophesying and judging and priestly offices had made dear. Possibly it was prudence that forbade his mention in Samaria of Zion, the capital of Judah, and the very youngest among all the sanctuaries, although it was already a few centuries old.

But Amos leaves us in no doubt; he goes right forward, and rises far above faiths or fears concerning all or any material sanctuaries. He cries, "Jehovah is where good is; He is not where good is not: seek good, and then Jehovah shall be with you truly, as ye now falsely think He is." Unquestionably Amos rose here to a new and higher conception than he had held just before, moved perhaps into an atmosphere too rare for him long to breathe. But he rose; and in that marvellous soaring we recognise God's inspiration. Revelation consists in—to borrow words from Amos—God's giving to man his thoughts. The gift may be, in the highest instance, an eternal, absolute truth, like Amos's grasp of the fact of God's abode with good; or it may be only a deeper vision of relations, deeper than men have ever had before, to be left behind again by the soul that searches still deeper and beholds more of the ways of God. We learn then that our prophet found manifestations of God in material things, places, soil, but that he was also moving forward far beyond that stage to one more profound and spiritual.

(*b*) Secondly, Amos does not think of any manifestation of God to the wrongdoer as a personal regenerating Saviour. The oracle is simply, "Do right, and you shall live; seek good, and you shall find Jehovah, the Life-Causer; but whosoever does wrong shall be cut off; all the sinners of my people shall die." It has not dawned on Amos that God seeks out the individual wrongdoer to woo him and to regenerate him. And no wonder, for the whole circle of his religious interests moved round the tribal body as the unit and centre. We find then that if the idea of forgiveness was coming in, it was not to be at first a reconciliation for the individual. We shall discover as we watch thinker after thinker that a reaction awoke against Amos's awful oracle of death, but it awoke first as a hope for restoration of the whole people, then of a class among that people, then for individuals, and finally for other nations. This absence of thought for the individual helps us to understand what Amos does say of forgiveness. For he does mention it; he pleads, "O Lord, forgive Jacob;" but it is Jacob the nation, and the land, and the harvest that are in danger of devastation. He is not pleading for personal forgiveness, and yet this very mention of forgiveness illustrates again the struggle in which we have seen the prophet's soul constantly wrestling. "More light, more life," is his cry, and his need; and herein is his intensely real prophecy of an atoning Saviour to come.

(*c*) But there is a finer feature than all these in his conception of God's revelation of Himself to men, and it is one which shows most strikingly that constant self-contradiction, that very living flux and upward advance in his conceptions. He has the firmest faith that Jehovah has spoken to himself, and commissioned him to speak. Here is his precious central spring of estimation of himself. The nation may be the chief or the only being that he thinks to move by his speech; individuals in general may be nothing, but there is one individual of value great enough to enjoy the fellowship of Jehovah. Indeed, he knows well a whole class of men who have made like claim to be direct messengers from God; prophets some of them are, with a message in speech, ascetic Nazarites others are, with a message in symbol. And he has defended these against sacrilegious scoffers. He counts them in some sense a gift of God, a link of relation to Him. That is one side of his changing thought, but there is also the other very different side. These men are a class privileged by birth or by some formal initiation to receive and give messages for God. But his faith in his own possession of a message lacks all those external marks, and rests wholly on conviction that he has talked with Jehovah, and that a certain still small voice within him is God's own voice telling him to prophesy to this people all that he feels he ought to say.

And Amos was standing here on an ultimate fact. We have never since got beyond personal consciousness of— an unflinching categorical imperative, shall we say?—or, more simply, an unavoidable controlling voice; that is, God speaking to us in the facts of ourselves and around ourselves. We never shall get beyond this. To say so is a truism, for to get beyond it would be to get beyond ourselves and to cease to be.

But Amos did not see that every other soul must have some such intense personal value, just as he had himself. Here the full light was still beyond his horizon. There was, however, a faint promise of it in the fine faith he had in his own personal inspiration and power to arouse men to seek more knowledge of their own value. This was after all an unfailing prediction of some Greater Soul to come who would proclaim, "What shall it profit any man if he gain the whole world and lose his own soul?"

§ 5. *His view of the nature of God.*

Now let us gather together in conclusion the features of God which we see in Amos.

(*a*) The fundamental idea of God in this prophet's mind is a thought of an unseen Lord or Authority, and Friend or Helper, peculiar to this nation or this body of small related tribes. Amos does not come to his conception of Jehovah by arguing from a primary conception of an absolute, single, Divine Being to the idea of God revealing Himself in the Jehovah character. The language of the prophet indicates the opposite process. Constantly he speaks of "Jehovah" (יְהֹוָה) as a Being before whom his soul bows with reverence as the inevitable Lord. Occasionally he adds the adjectival word אֱלֹהִים, Gods, and says "Jahweh Elohim," or Jehovah Elohim, *i.e.*, Jehovah of the gods, Divine Jehovah, Jehovah belonging to the "far-reaching ones."

This and the Christian mode of conceiving God in Christ mutually illustrate each other. We find in our Lord Christ Jesus our all, our ideal, our conviction of sin, our forgiveness, the mighty Power that regenerates us—in one word, our atonement. We cry, "Thou, Jesus, art our Lord and our God;" and we build our conception of God from our picture of Jesus. So with Amos: Jehovah, the personal Lord and Friend, whom he felt he knew by the story of the past providences, theophanies, revelations, was all in all to him. From this he was beginning to rise to an absolute conception of the Divine Being.

(*b*) Even more naturally still does Amos think of the nature of his God as like his own human nature. Jehovah loves companionship, talks of His plans with His servants among mankind, chooses a particular people as a family for whom He will be Patron.[1]

---

[1] Theologians have sometimes considered this way of conceiving God as a sort of foreshadowing of the Christ idea. The mode of thought is rather an

(c) Perfectly natural therefore do we find the modes in which Amos and the men about him expect intercourse with God and seek it. They make feasts in His honour, in which they expect Him to take pleasure; and as odours rich and fragrant rise from meats and wines with gratification to the guests, so they think Jehovah will breathe the smell of the feast with favour.

They look to a class of habitually eager speakers as the natural message-bearers that Jehovah will choose, and look on ascetic men as symbols of due devotion to Him. They count the spots of earth where theophanies have been of old as most likely to be still the favoured resting-places of their God on earth.

But Amos feels rising within him a strange scepticism about it all; and probably he only speaks out the fears of a large number. Their God surely cannot, does not mingle in all the assemblies of these sanctuaries, for has not His character come to seem too pure for that?

(d) The widened thoughts of Jehovah's control over lands and men has brought with it far deeper sense of His righteousness. Cruelties and impurities they once thought He overlooked are known now to be abhorred by Him. They are in awful contrast with Jehovah's purpose and character. He will not abide in the abodes of wrong; He will be found only where good is sought.

(e) The good He loves is indeed very specially הַטּוֹב, "that which is pleasant," viz., what is needful for physical life; but it includes certainly also due regard and respect for rank and for sex. It rises higher; it includes respect for Jehovah's preachers, whether members of a traditional class

illustration of the constant, instinctive, true mode of conceiving the Deity. The Christian mode is thus the central declaration of the eternal truth for life, and the normal method for thought. A brief expression of it is, God reveals Himself in man, or man's highest conceptions come through a Son of man.

or whether single specially sent men. These are all valuable and precious to Jehovah. But his own character is the most precious thing of all; offences against other precious things are bad especially because they dishonour his name—that is, His character.

(*f*) Finally, Jehovah has purposes all in perfect keeping with His pure character. He means to purify the earth on a great day to come which is already commonly expected with a well-known designation, "The day of Jehovah." Perhaps we may suppose that even Amos used this phrase, as Jeremiah does 150 years later, with the meaning "The day of Him who is called He establisheth," that is, The day of fulfilment of expectations and ideals, the day of reward and retribution. If so, then we have thus early the germ of our later conception of the Day of Judgment. In any case the title given to the day implies that it was a day when Jehovah should have all things exactly in agreement with His own mind. Then Jehovah would cleanse away all evildoers. Sheol should not conceal them from Him, but should help His judgment. A biting serpent too should be His avenging instrument. Then should the old golden age of David come again, when life, earth, men, and manners should all be good. Such was the nature of the God Jehovah, whom Amos knew and proclaimed as the highest religious conception of the Hebrews of his time in the beginning of the eighth century before our era.

§ 6. *The problems he left unsolved.*

Amos left problems unsolved: he started the thoughts of men along lines of new questioning. It may seem strange to say this of a book and a man apparently so little known; but in the study of some who followed him, and chiefly in

Isaiah, we shall learn something of the direct influence that he exerted. Meanwhile, in preparation for study of Hosea, Isaiah, and others, let us mark what difficulties Amos perhaps unconsciously set up and certainly bequeathed. Let us here observe that the comparatively lengthy treatment of Amos has not been a discussion of him alone, but a recording of the highest position reached by the whole complex of Hebrew religion in Amos's time. Without such full record his followers could not be fairly estimated; but upon the basis now laid down we may build with much briefer handling of each individual stone in the building. What problems then did Amos leave for his successors, or incite them to raise?

(*a*) Assuredly chiefly this, What is good? We have seen him driven ever further in his argument until he falls back on his final gospel, "If ye would find God and live, seek good, for there is His abode." But only the more intensely starts afresh the cry, "What then *is* good? Where shall we find *that?*" Here is the main line along which prophets after Amos for ages to come must search into the deep things of God.

(*b*) The awful oracle, "All who sin shall die," was sure to work a recoil. A tender heart could not feel the dreadful sentence without terror for those it loved and a yearning for some door of hope. Could God do nothing to convert the wayward sinner into a seeker after good? This reaction we shall find rising at once.

(*c*) But can even the righteous live under the severity of Amos's oracle concerning sanctuaries? Must the souls of men have no help from sight and touch? Is Jehovah a God who conceals Himself altogether, save from the purely spiritual? And are men already able to pursue Him along such unseen paths? Are all able, or are even few? Nay, shall ever any souls on earth be satisfied without seeing

Him so as they have seen Him in the sanctuary? Here again reaction was speedily to set in.

(*d*) And Amos has unsettled the unconscious sleep of individual life. No longer can the organised nation, or its representative leaders, be the only responsible actors. Dimly for many a day, and yet surely shall men wonder and reach out from the infancy towards the full conscious strength of personal religion, for the dawn is near. The question must be asked and pondered by all men henceforward, Who are the righteous? What is *my* sin?

(*e*) Amos's expectation for the future holds a doubt locked within its very self. Why had the golden age passed away? Could the evils that had hurried it away be ever overcome to let it return again? Whether men asked these questions consciously or not, their equivalents must have stirred in their breasts. And certainly Amos's prediction ensured an ever more eager scanning of the signs of the times, to discover whether at length the promised glad day should break. Delay, disappointment now could only make peoples and prophets ask with more longing and with a scrutiny more unwilling to go unsatisfied, "Why does Jehovah delay His coming?"

Such then are the first writing Hebrew prophet and his book. Short though the book be, it is richly fruitful to the student; and when we begin in earnest to read its records, profound reverence for the man fills the soul. The oracles written 2000, nearly 3000 years ago, will minister life perhaps more richly still than ever they have done before.

PART II.

THE RELIGION OF HOSEA.

CHAPTER I.

GENERAL CHARACTER OF HIS BOOK; ITS CONNECTING THREADS.

§ 1. *Chronology.*

THE chronology of Hebrew affairs from 900 to 700 B.C. has been ably discussed by Professor W. Robertson Smith in his "Prophets of Israel," pp. 145, &c. Sufficient be it here to urge the student to learn from so admirable a master. We have simply to accept and work upon the results furnished by Professor Smith which immediately affect our own problem and investigation of the steady progress of revelation of God to men, and the insight of men of God into His character.

It seems then most probable still, as it has generally seemed to Old Testament readers, that the work of Hosea was begun in Israel, the northern kingdom, some short time after Amos of Judah had visited Samaria and begun his mission there. Professor Smith has shown that the earlier known events of the eighth century have been usually assigned to dates that are probably too early by ten or even twenty years. In the books of Kings two different sets of dates are given for these events, doubtless due to the rise of the records in the two different kingdoms. But working from the date of a total eclipse across Western Asia in 763 B.C. (*see* Geo. Smith, Ep. Can., p. 200) and the date of the fall of Samaria, which is concurrently fixed by all records, Hebrew and Assyrian, as falling in or very near 720 B.C., we are led to shorten the duration of most of the activities, national, royal, prophetic, and otherwise in the century so far as they precede the fall of Samaria. The relative order remains largely the same.

Hosea's oracles are occupied with the affairs of the state, the king and his court, far more than were the words of Amos. He was evidently a man of high station, and he lived in Israel, the northern kingdom. The state was in much trouble in his time. The background looming through his utterances corresponds well with that story of revolutions which we read in the books of Kings concerning the successors of Jeroboam II. of Israel, the contemporaries of Uzziah, Jotham, Ahaz, and Hezekiah, kings of Judah. It is enough to call attention to these external features, as we now turn to the religious features exhibited in the book of Hosea.

§ 2. *The perplexities of the book, in text, &c.*

The book of Hosea is quite simple at the beginning, but soon leads us into a very labyrinth of perplexities.

(*a*) It begins quite systematically, and so it continues through chapters i. to iii. So far there is regular order and sequence of paragraphs, and clear sequence of thinking and argument. Likewise is there at the close a beautifully-ordered section that speaks of the unseen expected future. At various points in the rest of the book we find short passages with very orderly, decisive treatment of the matters in hand at the moment.

(*b*) With such exceptions, chapters iv. *ff.* seem to be a

collection of material for a book rather than a book itself. The materials are evidently such oracles of intense moment as had been noted down at the times of utterance, no doubt fully suited to their special occasions, but then put together somewhat like an incompletely kept diary. If Hosea had succeeded in arranging them according to some central principle in his own mind, they might then have given us better light on his own grasp of that principle, yet they might have been even less indicative of the progress of his mind in searching into the things of God. As they stand, however, it is difficult to trace any long-continued thread in them, and to this difficulty is added that of a very awkward text. This last peculiarity is connected doubtless with the position of the book in the MS. from which all our copies are taken, as Professor de Lagarde has shown in his treatise on Proverbs. The book stood first no doubt in a roll or volume containing the shorter prophetical books, and therefore suffered damage from finger-marks and rubbing in general, like the first few pages of any book, especially if it be unbound, or if it be in the form of a scroll. But the details of these things are matters for the careful textual interpreter, whose results we have here to receive and use for our own historical purpose.

It is sufficient for us here to sketch the book's general features, and then to give an analysis, which shall show the presence of these features and shall also furnish the basis for further work.

§ 3. *The unchaste society.*

Prominent everywhere amongst these features is Hosea's acquaintance with unchaste society on every side of him and all through the times. Lust and licentiousness are almost the commonest matters of sight and remark. There is either a common belief, or a common tendency to believe, that some deity, perhaps deities, Bă-ālim (בְּעָלִים), master-gods, are moving this passion, and that these deities are to be honoured, worshipped, and secured as friends by unchaste indulgence.

Hosea knows intimately the feelings of an outraged husband. He lives among men who would readily outrage his own wife, and he knows women who would readily forsake a husband like himself. The whole society in which he lives is honeycombed by such disregard toward vital obligations. But at the same time these obligations are held very sacred by some; they are obligations of religious import and sacredness to himself and to such as he. This kind of unfaithfulness was so common that then the preacher and others could speak of it constantly as we cannot speak of it now. This makes our comprehension of the times very difficult; it lessens our knowledge of the religions of the age. For we are apt to suppose Hosea much like ourselves, and to conclude when he speaks often of whoredom that he means idolatry under a strong figure of speech. But figures of speech must have some source in reality. We cannot use to-day these figures as he did; society may be as bad indeed, but it is not so openly. Hosea may be at times using these awful imageries as figures; but the more awful realities were common about him. The open condition of society was unspeakably revolting.

§ 4. *His general idea of Jehovah and Israel.*

Hosea's series of utterances concerning Jehovah's character are even more intensely full of import than those of Amos. The new prophet searches deeper than the old. Observe the details a moment.

(*a*) Hosea has the same unhesitating Semitic faith that

his God causes all things. The creation of men, the working of events, the establishment and destruction of states, are all Jehovah's deeds. The people's path is ordered of Jehovah, and He commands the prophet's steps as they enter into bitterest shame and pain.

(b) The national relationship of Jehovah is of vital moment to Hosea. Israel has always been the very chosen one of Jehovah; and the relation of spouse, not that of a mere friend, but spouse of a man's own bosom, pictures best what the prophet loves to think of the relationship. He gives this as Jehovah's own thought of that relation. There is a further and even finer touch in the portrayal. To many Easterns husbandhood was only masterhood, little more than the relationship of a male animal to his female mates. Many amongst the Hebrews, like many round about them, thought chiefly of fruitful seasons and a good harvest and plenty of food, when they prayed to their gods for favour. The chief task of heaven and God was, in their mind, to fertilise the earth and the herd, and also the race. The gods were the great Bäälim (בְּעָלִים), masterly generating animals; and Israel, says Hosea, had too often counted Jehovah as her Baal, her husband indeed, but husband in that sense, unsatisfying to the deeper soul. "But ye shall no more call me Baali," my master, says he, "but Ishi," my husband, my man, my all that woman soul knows in the great love of a man soul. Here is one of the delicately fine features of Hosea. He is truly human. In Amos we saw the fierce boldness of the mountain shepherd bursting through vain forms until we thought he would touch the inmost centres of philosophic truth, but as we gazed on there never came the calm full-orbed harmony of soul. In Hosea, on the other hand, there is a higher estimate of every human possession and joy, and instinctively we feel he is a greater man. In his generous and loving estimate of all that is about him, whether of nature or custom, he belongs so thoroughly to his time that we count him a genuine man and therefore a real brother for us all. He who thus truly knows all that is in man is the true seer and revealer of God's mind.

(c) Much more than Amos does Hosea speak of all non-Hebrew lands as unclean. Words of dislike, contempt, disgust for Assyria and Egypt are constantly on his lips. And with his love for argument, which we shall presently find to be quite remarkable, he reasons that in Assyrian or in Egyptian slavery all wine and flesh and bread of solemn gatherings shall be as food of mourners and polluted, because it cannot come into the house of Jehovah. Certainly he seems thus at first to be on a lower level than Amos; but this is only seeming, for from his far greater consistency with his position and with his time there comes to us a sense of natural harmony in the whole character of Hosea, finer than finest art, due perhaps to more care, due certainly to higher nature and ability than Amos possessed.

(d) The faith in the David age as the golden age of the past, and as the picture of the happy days to come is even more clearly proclaimed by this prophet than by the last. And while this is at first thought startling in a man of the northern kingdom, yet we recall the story that David himself, while he lived and reigned, held the thorough devotion of all the tribes, and it was from his sons after him that the annoyed ten tribes revolted. All claimed David as their great past king, although not all claimed Rehoboam. And here again it is natural to find Hosea speaking out a national faith with much more of the national enthusiasm than Amos felt. Hosea was a greater man, and this is manifest in his more accurate utterance of the national mind.

(e) The faith in Jehovah's overlordship over all gods

and all peoples seems to be less asserted by Hosea than we saw it in Amos, but it is more thoroughly implied. The golden day is coming again certainly, although Egypt and Assyria are meanwhile to prey on Israel as Jehovah's scourges. The two great oppressor nations are far oftener named and far more terribly described, but only the more surely is their final utter confusion foretold. Israel shall laugh at last at Asshur, who shall not save, for Jehovah is Lord of all hosts, and His words alone rule all the world. Faith that Jehovah is God over all gods has become the current faith among the Hebrews.

§ 5. *His political knowledge.*

Hosea knows more clearly than Amos the actual political movements round the horizon of Israel, and far beyond it.

(*a*) From Amos we heard only generally that trouble murmured round the sky, and danger was looming on the far horizon. Amos's knowledge of the political powers that might soon bring death and decimation on Samaria was only vague, or it was largely concealed. But Hosea knows, and he speaks very fully. He has probably intimate acquaintance with the discussions of the court, and with the dangers well known there threatened by potentates eager for world-empire. Hosea gives us, we may say, the first contemporary record by a statesman of the movements of the great world monarchies. Since the history of these makes up the bulk of the world's most striking history, Hosea's book is an important document.

(*b*) He pictures Assyria and Egypt very clearly, and he draws his picture with no timid hand. The native religious faith, indeed, of the prophet prevents that, and makes him write, as we have seen, with abhorrence and contempt for the very soil of those far lands, as lands not precious to

Jehovah, not blessed by His presence and temple. Moreover, he knows and describes again and again a glorious deliverance in the past from Egypt, that is now once more threatening harm. Amos showed us, but far more does Hosea, that in those days, from 800 B.C. onward, a story of deliverance from Egypt was well known.

The question whether our book of the Exodus was in circulation at the time is evidently another question entirely, and one to be examined elsewhere. What Hosea shows us is, that the story and glory of the Exodus were too great to be absent from the people's thoughts when they sang with one another by their firesides and in their field labour, when the fathers told the children, and the preachers preached to men what work Jehovah had done in the times of old. They heard with their ears, their fathers told them; they believed Jehovah had brought their people out of Egypt, and they trusted and feared not for their own day. It is *that* Hosea uses, that well-known story, to draw from it strong ground for hope now and in coming danger. "Jehovah," cries he, "was our God in the Egypt days; and He who delivered us then is mighty to save now." But he has a still happier inference to draw from that past deliverance, for it was a deliverance wrought at terrible disadvantage, a deliverance of a helpless people who had a dread wilderness to cross ere they could be free, and "for leader," says he, they had "only one of that class so much despised, only a prophet." "By a prophet Jehovah brought Israel out of Egypt, and by a prophet was he preserved."

(c) But Hosea's reproach to his own people, and his confidence in deliverance from the rival potentates, rests not on the past only. He knows something else concerning the secrets of Samaria's court. Assyria and Egypt have been trying an easier weapon than the sword; they are rival wooers for the little people's confidence and obedience.

Foolish Israel has been coquetting with each; she has gone in turn to each for help against the other; and worse, she has sought there for help in her own internal quarrels. She is being snared by both fowlers.

(*d*) Therefore her subjugation shall not be delayed for one day. That is absolutely certain—nay, it is to Hosea the centre of God's plan for the future salvation of the people. Righteousness is the demand of Hosea no less than of Amos; judgment is the prediction of both. The outcome in Amos of the rise to faith in Jehovah's overlordship was faith in Jehovah's demand for far greater righteousness in men than they had risen to before, and faith in His unchangeable purpose to secure such righteousness in all the earth. Not one jot or tittle of this demand does Hosea relax. But while Amos is to get this universal righteousness by the destruction of all evil things and evil men, Hosea believes God is to obtain it by the disciplinary corrective effect of the terrible judgments and sufferings. Hosea rather deepens the emphasis of demand, and he does this by searching beyond Amos into the depths of the righteous reason for all the demand, the righteous result aimed at by all the judgment. He proclaims the righteousness which he counts sure to be produced among the men of Israel by such judgments.

So with no word of discussion whether Jehovah be Lord of all, but resting in unquestioned conviction of that great faith, Hosea, true to his finer power, pours out warning after warning, picture after picture, each new picture ever more awful in its minuter revelation of the coming judgment of Jehovah, Lord of hosts.

§ 6. *His love and esteem for men.*

Yet just the opposite of judgment is Hosea's joy. He was called "Hoshea" (הוֹשֵׁעַ), "He hath brought salvation;" as long afterward the Lord received the same name in Greek form, "Jesus, because He saved His people from their sin."

Let us try to understand this, yet not here from full examination of his theory of salvation, for that must be studied further on; rather listen now to him uttering, one after another, a series of singularly high estimates of the value of men. He who with persuading and pleading brings to men a high and fine estimate of their own value, does by that very service in some sense save them. By such service at least he shows his own great desire to save them; he shows that his delight is in mercy rather than in judgment.

(*a*) Consider, then, how much Hosea argues with men, and appeals to their own minds as sufficient arbiters. His method is full of reasoning, while others so constantly give command only. In their own souls he sees the ultimate power which must bend them, and which alone can bend the will; no external authority avails much here. And he would see that inner authority exalted, truly honoured, strengthened, sweetened, made pure and godlike.

(*b*) We may call him the first theologian, so prominent and characteristic is his argumentative method. It is directly illustrated in his discussion whether this or that symbol can be a god, and in his conclusion that, because a workman made it, therefore it is not a god. The argument is not a bit of rhetorical play, but a train of reasoning that he feels he needs for his own soul's sake. This is evident from his pathetic cry elsewhere that symbols of deity are necessary for men's true life, and the lack of them is a sore calamity. Here then, again, is a sign and a part of his gospel of salvation. He yearns to save, and pleads that men be reasonable, and look for help to sources whence alone help can come.

(c) Even more strikingly illustrative of his theological method, and his dependence on argument, and his high estimate of the soul, is his discussion of a method of salvation. It fills his second chapter, and it pervades the whole of the book. He says, men do wrong because they do not know the right thing to do. Their ignorance comes from the dull and dazed state, physical and mental, which drink and lustful habit produce. Therefore life is to be saved by removal of these causes of death; salvation lies in solitude and restraint. If only the debasing drink and license be far removed, then the man, or woman, or people, sitting alone and silent, will think, will reflect, and will choose the right and do it. "In their affliction they will seek Me early." This gospel of Hosea has failed, as we know, and as the story of the Hebrews specially shows; but this first prophet of it was a soul that loved men, and longed to save them. The very utterance of such a hope shows that he was well called Hosea.

(d) But there is more. The man that so argued could not be content with arguments that seemed in any sense based on his own wish only. He was too much of a Semite for that; it must be a declaration from Jehovah that he makes known, for it is He alone that can afflict or save. The New Testament statement concerning the prophets is very true touching Hosea. They searched what the Divine spirit in them did signify concerning salvation. It was an ethical and psychological quest indeed, into the methods and forces of salvation; but the Hebrew was sure there was a Great Person working in those forces, and it was His methods that Hosea strove to know. That sort of search was peculiarly Hosea's life-study. So again we find him thinking out a great theological argument. He seems to say (chap. xi.), "Can Jehovah save? Can Jehovah fail to execute the dread oracle of Amos, 'All the sinners shall be destroyed'? Can He refuse to cleanse the earth of unclean men?" In a passage of sublime pathos and power, his heart pours itself out in a picture of the great Divine heart that yearns and cannot give up Ephraim to death. Then in one great throe he bursts away beyond the limits thus far dreamed to be the limits of what God could do, crying, "Jehovah is not man; He is not limited as we are; He is not bound by the possibilities that Amos and all us have thought to be His utmost possibilities; He can satisfy His great, great desire to save; He will not come to destroy us." The prophet plunges down deeper than he had ever thought before into the arcana of God's heart. He sees down into depths of agonising love, where Amos's gaze had seen only the crystal purity of the Great Heart and its austere demand, "Seek good." Far nearer to the still distant centre gazes Hosea, and sees some gleam, faint yet glorious, of that grace that was to be utterly revealed on the cross. It is not strange, but most natural, that Hosea, while so beholding, was filled with the sense of perfect oneness with God, and cries out—not concerning God, "He is gracious," but with the very voice of his God, "I am God and not man; I will not return to destroy." Thus does the prophecy of forgiveness and atonement begin, amid the agony of this man's soul, and with his rise to a revelation of God in his own person. The most valuable human joy comes in deepest human pain, and in agony comes the divinest exaltation of man.

(c) Hosea's argumentative and winning method is illustrated again by his constant appeal to the story of the past. Amos had merely alluded to the story; he had not argued much from it. Hosea points to the early nomadic days, long before Egyptian slavery, and bases his pleas on that; and again and again, over and over, he tells of Egypt and the sufferings there, pleading that, since such oppressions have been, they may come again. Now, both Egypt and Assyria are on the watch, ready to overwhelm both the present prosperity and the present wrongdoings in Israel; therefore Israel may well be wise and provide for themselves a strong refuge.

(*f*) Another mark of his esteem for men and desire to exalt them is his introduction of the figure of a covenant between Jehovah and Israel. Professor Guthe's admirable monograph on Jeremiah (*De fœderis notione Jeremiana*, Leipzig, 1877) is at fault in a vital point. In the *Conclusio*, p. 66, my loved fellow-student and faithful friend says, "*Jeremias primus inter prophetas notionem fœderis in usum religionis conclusit aliis deinde secutis.*" But Guthe speaks himself (p. 10), of Hosean *loci* vi. 7; viii. 1, *quibus ad religionem applicatur vox* בְּרִית (*fœdus*). The matter is of much importance for the appreciation of the Deuteronomic Reformation in 622 B.C. under King Josiah. We need not discuss here the use made of the idea of a covenant in that Reformation. We need only note that not indeed in Amos, but very naturally in Hosea we can see the early springs of that popular mode of thought which made the covenant under Josiah possible, and led on to Jeremiah's discussion of covenants, and to his fierce criticism and condemnation of Josiah's national establishment as utterly inadequate without a new covenant written on men's hearts. Hosea does not indeed say a great deal about covenants. But the man who felt into the very secret of God's normal relation to men, so that he called it the love of espousal, could scarcely miss speaking of the slighted troth between such lovers. We expect him to speak of a bond, a tryst, a covenant between the betrothed pair, and so we find he does. Hosea was fitly the forerunner of that profound teaching concerning covenants which Jeremiah expounds, and which Christian theology has so highly exalted.

(*g*) This fine feature and thread of humanity running all through the book stands out also in its judicious valuation of symbols. Judicious it is, for while on the one hand Hosea judges that these are certainly "not God, for the workman made them," and is not misled one step by his readiness to give its due to every human fact and need; yet, on the other hand, he does give that due, and counts symbols valuable. He says it will be a deplorable day for Israel when there shall be no prince or law, no priest nor sacrificial meal, no ephod nor sacerdotal robe that makes the wearer a very oracle of God, no pillars or maççeboth, like Jachin and Boaz before Solomon's temple, no teraphim, and no household shrines with their emblems of Jehovah. Hosea is more evidently filled than Amos was with the faith of the time concerning cleanness or uncleanness, and sacredness or otherwise of external things. Hosea felt the need of holy objects, holy garments, holy places, holy ritual, if life was ever to be "saved." He foretells exile to Egypt and Assyria, and counts it a horrible thing to die there, and be polluted after death by the sleep in a grave that does not belong to Jehovah. Life there will be even worse than death; for no feasts of joy can be eaten where the food of the feast has not been made fit by being slain and fired in Jehovah's own sanctuary. Hosea is here most humanly consistent with his time and with himself, while Amos was in part inconsistent with both.

(*h*) Finally, the most constant evidence of Hosea's thorough humanity is his attack not on sin, but on sins. Amos was vague in his conception of good, and not minutely definite in his picture of the evil deeds of men.

But Hosea's chapters heap awful detail upon detail of wrongdoing, until one almost revolts at the story. We do not revolt nor lay the book away with dislike, for the terrible moral earnestness of the writer holds us and carries us on with him. We must listen to him, as we listen to the terrible denunciations of an aroused conscience. There speaks the man, the true soul, not cataloguing sins for the curious and the prurient, but crying with a great horror upon him, "Look, look, and help. Save men from this awful death." The book is a most human record of ceaseless love for men, and of pain over human wrongs.

Such is a general characterisation, which, of course, must rest for verification on the following analysis, and careful detailed study of the book.

CHAPTER II.

ANALYSIS OF THE BOOK OF HOSEA.

A. Chapters I. to III.—*Symbolical expositions of the sin and salvation of Israel.*

(1) Chap. i. ver. 1 ; the title ; vers. 2–9 : The husband. Hosea's home sorrow, used as a picture of Israel's hurt done to Jehovah. It tells the story of unfaithfulness, and threatens retribution, for which there shall be no relief for Israel, although there may be for Judah. This latter exception reads strangely, and arouses suspicion of its authorship.

(2) Chap. ii. 2–23, with chap. i. 10 to ii. 1. The latter part seems to have been misplaced, as might easily happen with the outside sheet of a MS. The former tale is told again. But the saving love of Jehovah is proclaimed. The method of that grace is to discipline by solitude and privation. Then sober thoughts will work wisdom, devotion, joy, and the old Davidic union of the kingdoms shall be restored.

(3) Chap. iii. The same wrong, and the same mode of righting it, with even more explicit hope of a Davidic restoration.

B. Chapters IV. to XII.—*A collection of brief oracles without clear arrangement.*

(1) Chap. iv. Of corruption and its causes : vers. 1–3, Israel is unfaithful, ignorant, unnatural ; vers. 4–10, the very teachers teach ignorance ; vers. 11–14, how debauchery blinds. Appendix, vers. 15–19, Judah is as bad as Israel.

(2) Chap. v. 1–14. Nemesis: vers. 1–7, its seed sown by the leaders who mislead; vers. 8–14, Assyria, the fancied friend, shall be the desolating enemy.

(3) Chap. v. 15–vi. 7. Jehovah's gracious method and His whole desire: (*a*) v. 15–vi. 3, He will leave Israel to suffer; this will move them to return. (*b*) vi. 4-7, while they are so uncertain, His desire is changeless and simple; not burnt-offerings, not any sacrifice does He seek, but mercy, with true regard for men (חֶסֶד) and knowledge of God, which is thoughtfulness worthy of the children of God.

N.B.—(i.) Hosea requires חֶסֶד, "love," where Amos requires טוֹב, "what is pleasing." (ii.) He considers the "heart" to be the organ of knowledge.

(4) Chap. vi. 8–vii. 16 (end). The degradation of Israel. Unfaithfulness, a human failing, yet unmanly. It is כְּאָדָם, common to men generally, mere men, but not what a true man, a husband (אִישׁ), would show.

Here and there are murders; everywhere is unchastity. The prince riots with his councillors in drunken bestiality. So revolution chases revolution across the throne.[1] Yet when panic rises, the foolish look now to Assyria and now to Egypt for help. When they seem to come back to themselves they do not come to Jehovah, their own God. They know well He is supreme, for they blame Him for the calamity, and so excuse their rebellion. Their anger over calamities does not turn into earnest counselling with Jehovah.

(5) Chap. viii. Stern warning based on formal argument. The Amos-like passage closes with a quotation from that prophet. So his preaching seems to have given direct incitement to Hosea. Because Israel breaks the relation to Jehovah (בְּרִיתִי), and refuses teaching from His oracular

---

[1] In 2 Kings xv. we read of four revolutions within forty years.

representatives (תּוֹרָתִי), "Therefore," says Hosea, "let them look to those other gods," who will certainly not save them from perishing. Because the calf-god that stands in Samaria is made by a workman, therefore it is not a god; it cannot save, and it shall be destroyed. Because Israel has sown the wind, therefore they shall reap the whirlwind. Because Ephraim has multiplied altars on account of his sin, therefore these altars are the evidence of his sin. In other words, Ephraim, being in trouble, has thought his troubles were the angry strokes of many gods whom his deeds have displeased, and therefore he has held sacrificial feasts at many altars in honour of those gods, in the hope to propitiate them. And, therefore, just these sacrifices and altars are the evidence that Israel has sinned, and that he knows it. And yet, when the Jehovah-teachers, the prophets and the priests, tell Ephraim Jehovah's mind, and His desire for mercy or for goodness, Ephraim pays no attention. Such counsels are a strange thing to him; he prefers his sacrificial feasts which Jehovah does not desire, and does not count a justification of wrongdoings. Therefore judgment must come on Ephraim.

(6) Chap. ix. Joyless pollution shall be the reward of polluted ways. Israel shall go into slavery in Egypt and Assyria, where there can be no pure food, for there is no Jehovah-house. On the days for the feasts of Jehovah there can be no feasts at all in those lands of exile: but there shall be death and polluted burial.

This is the reward of unfaithfulness. For the unfaithfulness has grown into disregard of the highest quality in man, the power to prophesy, the power to be filled with the Spirit.

And the nature of the evil is very evident. "The pollutions of to-day," says Hosea, "are the same that polluted the days before David." They who have fallen away from the national unity and exaltation that David brought in have also fallen back to looseness of life, like the abominations that the pre-Davidic judges strove in vain to stamp out.

The root-evil is too plainly seen. Hosea's denunciation of unchastity is no mere figurative denunciation of idolatry. The home has become, by unfaithfulness, the world's worst misery.

(7) Chap. x. A deeper shaded copy of chapters viii. and ix. Lurid light from the Amosian judgments plays fearfully through the scenes. The winsome land and its winsome people are blood-spattered and weed-covered.

But there is a gleam of Hosean grace in one verse (ver. 12). It is indeed almost modelled on Amos's stern law, "Seek God," yet it is so touched with hope of mercy, grace, kindness in men and for men, that it becomes long after a worthy quotation for Jeremiah, when he would preach a way of deliverance to the people of his day.[1]

(8) Chap. xi.–xiii. 13. Opening with the word "Love," Hosea rises away now to his very highest vision of the heart of God and its gracious power. Then follows a story of that grace in the past. The awakening, trembling purpose of love is manifest in the oracle, "At least Egypt shall not have again her old triumph of Jehovah's people." If they go captive it shall be to Assyria. Yet no! How can He give up Israel so? Must He? Perhaps men cannot but mete out dreadful justice, but Jehovah's love is greater, and His authority also. "He is God and not man." He is the one God who is devoted to Israel; He is the Holy One of Israel. He will indeed visit His people, but not to destroy. They shall yet walk after Jehovah. Like migrating birds that return to their own dear land, so the people

---

[1] Hosea must have been well studied, for he is often quoted in the Old Testament. He was well known by Paul and men of his day.

shall come back out of all slaveries, out of all follies, and God shall let them nestle in their own homes.

The story of the past is a tale of evil done by Israel indeed, but a tale of good and only good from God. Many of the patriarchal scenes of which we read in the books of the Pentateuch and Kings are familiar to Hosea, *e.g.*, the story of the birth of the twin patriarchs, the divine vision in Bethel, the Syrian betrothal, the trafficking ways of the Hebrews, the Exodus, the sanctuary in Gilgal. There are characteristic features in these allusions: no deliverer from Egypt or after the Exodus is named, but two of such are described as "prophets." Twice over, especially in xiii. 4, there are words strikingly like a formula of Deuteronomy, but there is no appeal to any authoritative canon, nor any allusion to such.

(9) Chap. xiii. 14 to the end (xiv. 9). The golden days to come.

(*a*) Chaps. xiii. 14–xiv. 1. The opening is a sublime declaration that nought hereafter, not death, not the grave, can resist Jehovah's delivering power. Here first were uttered the great words, used again by a Hebrew in the exalted song of Isaiah xxv., and finally sealed by the Apostle Paul as the grandest chorus of Christianity, the creed and song of resurrection.

The triumph is also over nearer ills; the desert winds may destroy, yet there is deliverance in Jehovah.

(*b*) Chap. xiv. 2–8. Now begins as it were a dialogue between the kind teacher and those who begin to call on Jehovah. The people is pictured as a thirsty soil, which Jehovah will bedew and clothe in all the fair luxuriance of a tropical Eden.

(*c*) Chap. xiv. 9. This final verse may be a gloss by some later true man of God. It was certainly a well-known and well-loved thought, for it is used again and again by later men: by Jeremiah (Jer. ix. 12), and by the writer of Ps. cvii. (ver. 43), and it is echoed by the Apostle James (James iii. 13). It suits Hosea's hand, however; it is confident in men's ability to be wise and good, it is greatly hopeful for that wisdom and goodness which he has said all along shall save them, but it is touched with anxiety and uncertainty. He has no doubt of Jehovah, but he seems to doubt his own Hosean plan of salvation. Will it succeed, or must they look for another? The very question mingled with the faith in Jehovah is a virtual prophecy of deeper depths in God's heart than Hosea had found, and of a greater gospel yet to come.

CHAPTER III.

THE MAN HOSEA.

§ 1. *His home.*

THE features which analysis has given may now be clustered in one portrait of the man as he lived and walked. But be it borne in mind that evidence of the features comes only through closest reading of the book; and from that source only can come also an acquaintance with him which shall fit us to make him known, and let him bless others to-day. First, then, we recall his home.

(*a*) It was in Samaria, the fair centre of the happy, wealthy, northern kingdom, Israel. Round the fortress-like hill, with its crowning city, the vine-clad slopes and hill-sides beyond blushed rich in rivalry with the green and yellow grain-covered plains. It was as when some dark maiden flushes in the contest of beauty over against her golden-haired companion, and all about are moved to admiration and gladness. Amid such beauty Hosea grew.

There were few bare hills here, and few gloomy glens like the many in southern Judah, that sterile home of safety, but of austerity as well. Few foreign invaders would care to plunder Judah; but Israel, called so often Ephraim, which may be interpreted "the hill whose either side is a fertile field,"—Israel's beauty and plenty, Israel for booty was the delight of the invader. From earliest days the adventuring sheiks from abroad plundered her, and like our modern France she was always soon ready again to be plundered. The captivity of the north came a century before the exile of the south, because Ephraim, the home of Hosea, was a rich and comfortable land.

(b) The rich land and people could early grow luxurious in knowledge and thought and utterance, as they did. Schools always spring up first in rich centres: Italy, Greece, Egypt are examples. We find, accordingly, that the number of prophets, thinkers, teachers in the northern kingdom, as the books of Kings describe them, was far greater than the number in Judah. It may be readily asked in reply, do not the most of the records concerning the kings and other leaders of the people seem to have been written in the north and by northern men, and by men fond of the north? Does not the very full account of Elijah, that thorough northerner, seem to be from a northern pen? Very possibly, but this thoroughly confirms the belief that the north produced more of such men, writers, speakers, thinkers, than the south produced. On the other hand, it is just in those more luxurious centres that carelessness first comes. Hosea is an early witness to this constant feature of history. Amid the abundance of comforts and pleasures, men may revel in assurance and mastery to very intoxication, blindness, and folly. Where there is no struggle for life there may come emasculation. So it has been in southern Europe; and so it was evidently in comfortable Israel, as many a Hebrew passage hints. Hosea learned in such schools, and God led him through such dangers.

(c) The low level plains of Jezreel that led to the Philistine coast were the easy highway between Africa on the south and Asia and Europe on the north. They may become so again; and the wise prophet Isaiah, who counselled so long ago concerning that world-highway, may prove to be a prophet for the coming twentieth century, forecasting some iron road to run from Cairo to Damascus, and all lands beyond in east and west. Such highways bring culture, and they are culture, a God-provided culture. But they bring also and certainly large occasions for deterioration. For example, the Hebrew language may be one of the younger sisters of the Semitic sisterhood, but it is the most deteriorated, the worst preserved. It has been rubbed and worn, like a well-used coin, by the ceaseless friction of the many, many strange tongues that passed to and fro, up and down that road for all the world's traffic, the little Hebrew coast of the Levant. As English speech is becoming a traffic speech for all the peoples of the world, and, as used by them, it looks to the philological student like a bagful of worn, defaced coins, without inscription or figures, a puzzle in date and origin, lacking everything save brightness and value, so was Hebrew a language of merchants and passengers, and it lost nearly all its fine detail of form. The language of the far-away interior of Arabia remains to-day almost as full and as gracefully perfect as when it reached its highest development probably thousands of years ago, but the exposed speech of the great west road was actually worn out and disused two thousand years ago.

The people who spoke it deteriorated like their speech; rapidly they rose, rapidly they sank. They learned the favours of the great nations to north and south, and, coquetting with them for more, their luxuriant life became licentious. They learned the possible falseness of those neighbours too, and they fed on shame till they grew like the shameless on the street. Hosea grew up among all this, and pictures it very truly.

(*d*) There had been already a reformer in the north. The course of providential events which brought forth an Amos, prophet of righteousness in Judah, gave earlier birth to a reformer in Israel. But something quelled the reforming spirit. It was in Israel that Elijah had preached, now thundering forth his faith, now hiding it. That faith, now majestic, and again a trembling spark, was the new faith in Jehovah the Over-Lord, God over all the Baalim. With mixed fearlessness and fear he had offered this to the test. He was victorious; the people were rising to a reverence and purpose like his own. But hesitancy followed. His lack of the tremendous self-assertion of an Amos explains perhaps the delay of the rise in the north of great moral teachers like Amos; and the failure seems characteristic of the northern people. They knew even more than Amos knew, but they lacked the severe assertive power. They could question, and by their sharp questioning it was, doubtless, that Amos was driven to grasp at the grand facts of God he found and proclaimed. That was their peculiar share in the seeking after God. Hosea has all this peculiarity in himself, a keen humanity that will ceaselessly speak out its feeling, its needs, its questions, its certainty that there is still uncertainty, its faith that God's heart has yet unsounded depths.

§ 2. *His rank.*

That he was of high rank seems evident from his familiarity with the court and all its ways, even when the facts are anything but noble or honourable. He knows of royal conduct that has been careless and unkingly, and doubtless hidden from all but boon companions or responsible guardians.

His evident culture confirms the opinion. He knows the past well. Probably the events of the Exodus which he mentions were matters of current tradition, talked of by the fireside; and yet there is fulness of detail, and a readiness to draw argument from the story, which suggest much more than the ordinary acquaintance with the past. He seems to have been well versed in statesmanlike knowledge of the history of the state. Amos scarcely gives a hint of such knowledge.

And the present relations of Israel with the great world-empire rivals are well known to Hosea. Amos knows there is danger of foreign trouble, but he scarcely names the rival empires. Not so Hosea, who even knows the simultaneous traffickings that have been foolishly carried on with both Egypt and Assyria. He was surely of high rank.

His whole disposition and fineness of feeling argue also a man of unusual experience and cultivation. It may be added that the preservation of the work and name of this one alone of northern writers in a collection like the canon, so thoroughly influenced by Judah, and furthermore the very frequent, almost unusually frequent, quotation from Hosea by later writers in Judah, mark him as one of the most notable of all Hebrews in every sense.

§ 3. *His personal story.*

This is written in all his sentences. The true man is never a masked character, but bears the lines of God's carving on his brow. His soul's portrait is well drawn on his cheek and in his earnest eye; its voice is never muffled nor ambiguous. What had Hosea done, or what had he suffered?

(*a*) His parents we do not know indeed, but he has made himself in a special sense the child of his people, for he has read and fed on the story of its past and its fathers until we learn them well if we only learn to know him.

(*b*) His name, as we have it, may possibly have been given him by father and mother. It means, "The bringing of salvation," or, "One hath caused salvation;" and perhaps the parents saw in their child an answer to some great cry for help. But it is almost as probable that the nation whom he loved, for whom he lived, in whose very fullest, finest joy he sought all his life, the nation whom he preached to save, and so did save, perhaps it was they who called him Hoshea. At all events, it is they who have told us his name, for in their love for him they saved his words, and handed them on with this name to be saved for ever.

(c) But we know far more. He had a sad, very sad experience. Perhaps his terrible picture of a doomed home is only what he saw with awful sympathy in the house of some friend. He says it was his own experience; he says, in strangest and strongest faith, that it was God, Jehovah, the God he trusted, who led him through the experience. Why do we doubt it? Why do we doubt that good men have gone through worst pain, the pain of astonished and appalled recoil from God's providences? Did not Jesus cry, "My God, why hast *Thou* forsaken me?" There is much to appal us in the providences of God. Why should there not be depths inexplicable or unexplained in His ways? He is God, and not man. Why should not He cause pain, and bitterest pain? For pain is that keen reminder of Him to which every human soul listens with the quick, terrified cry, "O God!"

Hosea knew the awful sorrow only too well, whether he himself had gone through the agony, or had simply stood by a stricken friend, and given him counsel to strengthen and to save him. In it all he had the wonderful faith, "My God does it," which faith is itself altogether a salvation. The sight of such a faith saves others too. No wonder that this man's words were gathered and preserved.

§ 4. *His mind and way of thinking.*

Let us consider a moment his mode of thought; let us become acquainted with his mind.

(*a*) How keenly he reflects. The scenes he sketches are all so finely traced that any explanation of them seems unneeded, all the causes of the events seem quite plain, and all possible ways of hope amid the evils seem clearly disclosed. Finely he can trace the subtle relations of circumstances and events, just as finely and strongly can he grasp and tell the whole story of his people, the past, far and near, the present, its inmost secrets and its outmost contacts.

(*b*) How closely he argues. You shall have reason for all he bids you do, and for all he believes that he himself must do and say. The firm philosophical spirit seems born full-grown in him, for he teaches that knowledge of the nature of sin, and grasp of a satisfactory theory of it, are themselves a cure for the evil. This knowledge comforts him and those whom he persuades. He teaches, and rests in the teaching, that to know good is to be certain to be good. He believes that the soul which sees full reason for a certain course will certainly follow that course. Indeed, his theory is that sin comes only through ignorance. Know, and you will do, says he; see, and you will follow. It is a singular Hosean doctrine that the *reasoner* will always be *righteous*.

(*c*) His reasoning is large-minded. He can argue against a custom because of any falseness that is in it, but he can also bewail its ceasing, for he can discover the valuable features of it.

§ 5. *His heart and feeling.*

Now touch his heart. It is laid bare by its own warm beating. You see it through the garment's folds. You hear its pulsing, its nervous start, the sigh that wells from it in a cry of lament or of hope.

(*a*) He was truly a man, for he could love a woman with all the thirst we know. God made that thirst in earliest Eden, when Adam saw Eve, and felt that his breast was her home, and she must ever abide there. Ever since that day this love has been one of our earliest, surest, richest treasures, blessing all our life, and all life that shall be of us. Hosea was a real man, for he knew this love.

(*b*) He was a father, and had all a father's mysterious solicitude for his children. Home meant the children along with the wife. And when he wept for his lost spouse, he could talk with the children over their common awful loss as a wise man will seek counsel in the sacred circle of his own hearth. Home was a blessed comfort to him, which he understood.

(*c*) He could love the traditions of his people. The stones where the patriarchs worshipped, because they had slept and dreamed beside them of heaven and of God, brought to Hosea like visions of God's presence and care.

He knew his people's story, its past leaders and prophets, because his heart went out to them in affection. His heart sought company with hearts that were its kin.

(*d*) He loved manhood, and could not think God would fling it away. It is his own heart's yearning that speaks out in those wonderful words, "How shall I give thee up! . . . I am God and not man!" Let conventional sense of duty towards wrongdoers be what it will, and let it cry doom against them! Let it seem impossible to pass by the evil deeds! "Yet," he cries, "the heart yearns after them; it struggles to hold them, to stay with them, to bless them." Hosea's heart struggles thus, and in his simple but sublime faith he counts his own heart's moving to be a moving of God. Hosea's great heart received disclosures of God in its own great love for men.

§ 6. *His inner soul.*

Finally, then, let the words "Hosea's soul" gather together into one all these features without and within the man, and make for us a complete picture of the man of God. It is a precious picture. The man companies with God; they walk together. The one is the other's agent; they work together. Hosea's face shows the face of God. Here is one example comprehensible by us all of the pre-existence of the Body of Christ, that Word of God. A child of God Hosea was, and he saw into his Father's heart. So Amos too had seen; but as one star differeth from another, so to the eye of one child is given one measure of insight, a deeper measure of insight is given to the eye of another.

So Hosea saw and has told us of God's far more than human heart, as his wider sweep of vision caught and understood far more of the whole circle of the needs of men. So he looked far beyond visible things, and saw in the land and people fruits of God's own husbandry more precious to God than could be appreciated, save by "whoso is wise." Such was he in mind, in heart, in soul, a noble true man, a man after God's mind, a man of God.

Such a precious picture may we have, so far away and all along the line of Providence, if we but look into the records. Men turn languidly from the Old Testament, and from the New also, and call the volumes of the fathers a waste; they say petulantly, "What have we to do with the Jews?" But he who reads himself into company with those men finds God with them. Then the God who was with them becomes a God with us.

CHAPTER IV.

HOSEA'S RELIGIOUS OPINIONS GENETICALLY CONSIDERED; OR, A HOSEAN SYSTEM OF DOCTRINE.

WHY are we confident that the food of the mouth and appetite shall feed the heart with coursing blood, the muscle with strength, and the brain with quick power to perceive? Why but because one system links all, and linking them makes them no mere mass conjoined, but a body, from any point of which influence radiates directly and duly to every other part of the whole organic system.

The importance of systematic theology is immense, if it duly exhibits the complete relationship between all the facts of religious life. It is vital to powerful preaching, and only its abuse works its temporary neglect. This is true of the systematic statement of our own conceptions of Christianity to-day; it is fully as true of the systematic description of the religious conceptions of any past period or point in history, or of any individual whose influence we would understand and use.

It is certainly an abuse to come to the writings of any individual who lived in days far away from us or even nearer, with a pre-arranged schedule of topics, on each of which we shall demand some deliverance from the old writer. We may not treat any man or any period thus. The abuse becomes vandalism when we insist on an actually positive deliverance in our own favoured sense on each topic as condition of our recognising the writer's fellowship with

God and the Father of our Lord Jesus. Such a Procrustean bed is in essence unchristian; it is utterly ungodly. It may be called religious, but it is so only in a lower sense than heathen religions are.

Our true method of search for the doctrines of a man or a people is first to trace all their utterances to one root, if possible, out of which all have naturally grown. If we be successful, we shall know what root we must plant if we desire the same fruits to grow. Here lies the inevitable connection between a thoughtful study of systematic theology and a sound serviceable homiletic method, or a practical ministry.

If it become evident that not one vital root has begotten all the utterances and all the faiths we are watching, some inconsistency amongst the various utterances and faiths will become clear; and we shall discover thus, as we had not dreamed before, the marks of perpetual need, uncertainty, change, and growth in the life of man or the people. We shall see the strife, the pain, the long subjection to fear. We shall know how to avoid these, knowing their cause, and we shall be quicker to remove causes of similar pain. We shall have finer sense, finer souls, happier days, far truer life. And this shall be ours to give to others also in practical ministration. Such is the value of systematic theology.

It may be that we shall discover, however, away behind the man himself, the one cause which worked both his conflicting currents of faith. The cause may be in the men and things who were long before him, and thus our systematising of the one man's thoughts will help us to feel the solidarity of men. Our own knowledge as to ourselves, and the best plans of life for us, will be seen to depend on knowledge of much else. In fact we shall know our real selves to be much larger than we had thought, and with this expansion will come increased sense of our value. We turn to Hosea and find an illustration. We ask first what is his central characteristic?

§ 1. *The kernel of his thinking.*

The ablest of recent English writers in this historical field has pointed to חֶסֶד (kindness)[1] as the characteristic principle of Hosea's religion. And this is certainly what Hosea counts the true character of Jehovah, and the ideal character in men. But can we say more exactly what it is in Hosea's own character which leads him to this characterisation of God? Let us know, not so much what Hosea preaches as highest religion, but what is his own religion and the root of his own life.

Professor Duhm's admirable *Theologie der Propheten* described Hosea as a man of religion, as distinguished from Amos the man of righteousness, "Das religiöse Moment wiegt einseitig vor" (p. 127). This is true, but it requires closer explanation. To show the need for such explanation let us observe that if we call Hosea the more religious prophet and Amos the more ethical, meaning by religiousness a more special care for the unseen, and by ethical character or righteousness a greater regard for duty, especially toward men and visible things, then we shall have actually reversed the real characters of the two men; for Amos's exhortation to seek good was to the end that they might find God, while Hosea's soul is full of tender yearning love for men, and it is certainly in that love that we find his religiousness and godlikeness.

When Professor Guthe considers the idea of covenant, בְּרִית, as characteristic originally of Jeremiah, he almost robs Hosea of a possession. Hosea is really the first to

---

[1] Professor W. R. Smith, "Prophets," p. 160 ff.

speak of covenants in religion, and, as we have seen, he does so with peculiar fitness. Yet it is something in Hosea's nature deeper than all these characteristics just named which gives rise to his speech of covenants, and gives birth to his kindness, and makes him seem to see the unseen as Amos does not. That nature of his is what we must grasp and keep in mind as his central, fundamental characteristic and the root of the whole system of his thinking.

§ 2. *What he inherited from others.*

Let us pause to recount what he had in common with his predecessors, or had received from them.

(*a*) There filled every Semite, and Hosea too, a sense of Divine omnipresence. All beings, all deeds, all utterances of the soul were the direct work of the Divine Being. God was always everywhere. And to the Hebrew, at least in Hebrew lands, it was Jehovah who did all things and was everywhere.

(*b*) The revelation that seemed to the prophets to fill the David age was that Jehovah was more than Israel's God, more than God. He was Lord of gods; He was The God, the Over-Lord of hosts.

(*c*) In Amos we saw a clear conception added. Amos sees that the Over-Lord Jehovah is the great Righteous One, and accordingly conscience has a far keener voice than it had before, and it points out duty towards foreign men and lands as well as towards the home-born brother.

§ 3. *What was new in him.*

Hosea's new vision into God's heart was Hosea himself. He himself was his addition to the revelations of God that other men of the age had grasped. The kernel of his soul was his thorough *sympathy* with men; and this produced his own kindness, his faith in Jehovah's kindness, and his cry for kindness in Israel. If we seek a definition of his "sympathy," we shall get it from those oracles concerning men which tell us how he estimated them. In technical phrase, we begin the system of his theology by the scheme of his anthropology.

(*a*) He thinks that men naturally do right. Many, or perhaps most, of his fellows are blinded, and cannot see the road they would naturally take. This is the result of intoxication and its stupidity, of lustful excess and its mad carelessness. At one point indeed he seems to hold what may have been a common belief, that mankind generally, and the original father-man, he whose very name, אָדָם ('Adham), marks his close relation to the mother-earth, אֲדָמָה ('Adhamah), is heavy, careless, a covenant-breaker by nature. Yet this utterance, so like that in Job xxxi. 33, marks his faith that Hebrew men, the normal men, of whom and to whom he almost exclusively speaks, are of a higher nature than those other human beings of the general sort. He cannot ignore those others—that would be unlike him—but while he wonders over them, all his working theory and estimate of men refer only to normal men, the Hebrews. Hosea may mean indeed that the Hebrews, alas, are no better than other men but as thoroughly bad when drink or debauchery fills them; but this would only confirm us in the opinion that to him the Hebrew was by nature the perfect normal man.

In any case, very clearly he lays the blame for the sins of the Israelites on that sensuality which blinds and so begets ignorance. Sin, then, is the deed of an ignorant man only. Righteousness will always be, if men have only, first, a clear mind, and secondly, true instruction. How great an advance this is from Amos's failure to suggest any method for changing men from bad to good! We shall have another occasion to refer to this. Meantime we may note that a fruit of Hosea's far deeper sympathy with men is his חָסֶד (chesedh), his kindness toward them, and his eager desire to save them. This truth is not lessened by the insufficiency of his theory; the faulty theory itself becomes his own declaration of faith that the true salvation shall come some day.

(*b*) Hosea's sympathy sees men's natural affinity for knowledge.

(α) First let us remark that the popular psychology of the time regarded the heart as the organ of knowledge. When Hosea says wine takes away the heart, he means that it dulls *the mind*.

(β) Observe, then, that it is knowledge of Jehovah, as the proper God of Israel, that Hosea longs for, deploring its absence. The great need was then, as in Galilee in later days, and now as then, a knowledge of the real way of God. We may call this, in later phrase, the *logos* of God. For as our Lord Jesus is to us our trusted *logos* of God, our idea of our God's way, so to Hosea there was a sort of *logos* of God, an idea of God's way, namely, his conception of Jehovah as the devoted God of Israel, and the Over-Lord over all hosts. The beautiful words in chap. xii. 5 set both ideas in one setting: "In Bethel he will find us, and there he will talk with us: even Jehovah God of hosts." Hosea means that we shall learn all that knowledge which is life from Him who is by name and history our own national God, and who is also by conquest the supreme Lord of all powers. He shall teach us, for his covenant name Jehovah, "Causer to be," and His title Lord of hosts, together ensure it. It was knowledge of this character, and a true estimate of it, and accordant lives, that Hosea longed to secure.

(γ) But he was urging this in place of disorderly religiousness rather than in place of godlessness. Hosea did not charge the people with godlessness. He would replace a loose, thoughtless, debauched, yet strong religiosity by a clear, calm, single devotion. They did care for knowledge of the gods; they were not altogether unlike the Athenians of later days. And Hosea appreciates this characteristic in them. He was a generous man of the times. He and his fellows all felt keenly the sensuous joys of their life, and felt too the mysterious voices that seem to whisper, more to some souls than to others, of the living Cause behind the joys. Semitic souls could hear this speech acutely.

To Hosea's countrymen their luscious plenty, their social luxuriance, their seeming power lent them by the amours of the political rivals, Assyria and Egypt, their self-fascinating coquetry, fanned by eager leaders—all these were gifts of the gods; and they were messages telling the love of the gods for them, wooings to communion with those unseen lovers in boundless feasting on their gifts. So the intoxication of men was wrought by their very seeking after the gods; their delight in knowledge of the gods and their very use of symbols of Divine presence were proving their ruin.

(δ) And Hosea deplores the day of Jehovah's inevitably coming discipline, because it must shut Israel away from all that gives knowledge of the Divine presence. The day is coming when to save Israel Jehovah will take away from them their sacred places, their kings and sacrificial feasts, the pillars that mark the sacred places of Jehovah, the official sacred garments, and all household symbols of Deity. These all speak to the soul concerning God, and the true worshipper desires them worthily. These symbols, and the knowledge of Jehovah which they symbolise and which they bring, are to Hosea the needed and beloved and just means of grace. Men care for them naturally, and Hosea is glad they do. He cares for them himself also.

(є) These things are not evils, but it is the luxurious abundance of them that intoxicates, blinds men, and occasions sin. Hosea's theory is that things of this sort all attract; men are naturally drawn by all they see of the good and the true and beautiful; but order in choice is needed, so that every attraction be suffered to woo only in due measure, and neither intoxication, ignorance, nor sin may result. The soul stands amid a world of lovable things. The question of life is, which of all the soul's lovers is most lovable? How shall we choose Jehovah chiefly, and hold all else in fit place as adornment given from Him, and to be used for His honour again?

Certainly Hosea's is not a complete philosophy, nor a fully written lesson of life; but so high, so beautiful is it that we look away upwards for his teacher. We feel that it must have been some high fellowship that taught him these high thoughts. Only an inspiration from above could give such yearnings as his, and bid his soul speak out such beliefs with such faith. The deep sympathy of Hosea for man and for man's loves was breathed in him from the very Spirit of God.

(c) Hosea's sympathy sees a finer feature still in men's nature. Man needs another's love. Hosea sees this in himself. The prophet, and also every true son of man about him, is susceptible of the fine wooings of some other loving soul, be it of woman that attracts man, or of the Divine Being that holds his riveted attention, or be it the affection of trysted souls like David and Jonathan, whose love surpassed that of women. Hosea knew his own need for more than a mere sight of beauty; he needed tokens of human love more precious than the sanctuary symbols or the beloved national customs. He saw a deeper undercurrent of affections, exquisite even to the simple beholder, but charged with the very vital current itself to the lover and the beloved.

(*d*) A single gleam, shot across the pages of the book, reveals delicately, yet not faintly, Hosea's appreciation of the highest type of man, and the finest possible feature of a soul (*cf.* chap. ix. 7). He tells us, with just a shade of apprehensive trembling, of some who are worthy to be called "men of the Spirit." Such are pervaded by a spiritual quality akin to God; they speak as Divine voices the very utterances of Jehovah. They are God's watchmen, and they stand in His stead before men. They stand in front of God, they appear for Him as the very equivalent of God to human sight. Even the intoxicated people know that such men are to be found, and that they are essential to a nation. So they set up some one, any one, to be their spiritual man and their prophet in times of trouble. Hosea can tell of the past blessing that such men have worked, both by oracles of death and by deeds of deliverance, and he knows in himself the secret working of God that does it all. He speaks from experience; he is himself such a man of the Spirit. His own intensely fine sympathy speaks out in all his description of men who have such a vocation. He believes men can carry such a high endowment. He is conscious of carrying it; and to his perfectly sympathetic soul all men may be as he is. He believes in men. He believes in Jehovah's sympathy with men. Such was God's way with Hosea; such life did God make possible and real in him. Such was the Divine inspiration of Hosea.

(*e*) Finally, Hosea's high instinctive appreciations of man are indeed somewhat disturbed and hard to follow in the book; and the prophet may not even have thought them through in very orderly fashion. Nevertheless they are no passing fancies, but the very essence of the man and of all his oracles. Just as we saw in Amos an overmastering devotion to righteousness, so the characteristic sympathy of Hosea, and his high, fine, gracious estimate of men, are written on every page and passage of his book. He was a man of sympathy.

§ 4. *His doctrine of men.*

For this very reason his doctrine of man implies a strongly marked doctrine of men—that is, of the people as a whole. Indeed, he addresses his prophecy of counsel and of blame and warning to the nation, and not to individuals, with more consistency than Amos had been able to use. While the figures he uses are of individual action and character, and so an estimate of the individual underlies all he says, yet his application of the figures is national. In other words, he is thoroughly a man of his time in all his formal expressions. His fineness of sense only deepened this feature.

(*a*) Thus it is Israel as a people whom he charges with adultery from Jehovah. This consists in their breaking away from the Davidic house, in their coquetting with Assyria and Egypt, and, above all, in the immorality utterly unlike Jehovah's ways, that is practised among leaders of state and of worship, and among the body of the people.

(*b*) The force of this charge lies in the faith that the true relation of Jehovah and the state should be that of a tenderly loving spousal pair. This conception it is that gives deep significance to the description of other peoples and other lands as unloved, undesirable, unclean, and even polluted. The strong expression must be read as coming from a man of that time. If Israel was the beloved and betrothed of Jehovah, and the espoused wife of His heart, then all other peoples were the rejected maidens, unloved, whom His love desired not in comparison. The land of Israel was the bower and home of the bride where the Divine Lover would willingly be for ever, caring for no other spot, but counting all other lands unhappy and unholy.

(c) How natural to Hosea, therefore, was the covenant idea. There is no occasion for fancying a bargain struck and signed with formalities and difficulties, as between seller and buyer, servant and master; none of these things underlie Hosea's conception. But the lovers have met and trysted; without visible touch or nearness they have known each other and loved. Heart has felt heart's embrace, and rested there. Each has taken the other to itself. That is the covenant; it is a lover's troth; it is the flash of love that needs no word to utter it, no speech to make it fact and vow.

But note a finely significant shade in Hosea's words. If the loved people become in any way like mere men in general, and lose the particular, national something that is so loved of Jehovah, and that yearns so toward Him, then the plighted troth shall vanish though it were plighted or engraved on tablets a thousand times. When they are mere men כְּאָדָם (K'Adham), then they break the covenant.

This covenant is only possible between two who are like man and wife, different in each other's eyes from all other women and men. They are the only two in each other's eyes; so Jehovah would be nothing but the Ishi (אִישִׁי), "my own one man," for Israel. We have not synonyms in English as they have in Hebrew to speak out this shade of love's intense devotion. But the Greeks and the Romans had them, and so have the Germans. They all can say of the spouse, *vir meus*, *mein Mann*, &c., where *homo* and

Mensch, &c., would mean only " some man unloved, not my own one." Such is Hosea's thought.

Let us observe that while he pleads with the whole people as one beloved being, his figure and his words have all sprung from his own personal experience and tenderest human fellow-feeling.

(*d*) We may indeed find some confusion in the figures and the facts. And we may say that Hosea's exalted conception of the people as an individual tends to melt away, and he comes to speak of individual men and women as the real units. This is true. Hosea's very words are faiths, and a prophecy of something more yet to come. His faithfulness to feeling makes that certain. And yet that faithfulness reminds us that his conception of the nation as an individual must have also some inherent truth. Certainly the idea of a people of God *is* an eternal truth. Amos had spoken of God's people Israel with customary sternness almost bordering on indifference; but Hosea's finer instinct finds far more reality in all the current phrases touching Israel. He is a seer of humanity and reality, and so he is a preacher of that great true Unit, all mankind. The kingdom of God, the brotherhood in Christ, the temple not made with hands, the solid mankind knit together of true sons of men, is a great necessary truth alongside that of individuality. Hosea's conceptions make us feel how truly all the great facts of life, old and new, were gathered together in Christianity, and how the Hebrew preachers were prophets of the Son of Man.

(*e*) And this doctrine of the true people of God which he sketches implies a story of the love of God to such a people in the past. So Hosea speaks much of that story. Whatsoever documents may have been already in existence and in his hands, and howsoever hard or easy it may be for us to recognise in Hosea's language marks of his possession of them, this is evident, that he was far more interested in such narratives than was Amos. Among thoughtful men of higher rank and greater leisure written notes of the story of the past were evidently coming into use, and therefore were being more and more constructed. Hosea wrote, in 775 B.C., notes of the Exodus and of the Patriarchs' life. Whatever may or may not be proved to have been written earlier, we see that this writer gave and his readers received a brief story and theory of Jehovah's relation to Israel's past history. Such a theory and teaching the Hebrews called a Torah (תּוֹרָה). Here was a Torah of Jehovah. It was a Torah concerning a deliverance from Egypt, and concerning a deliverer, a Mosheh (מֹשֶׁה). The word "Moses" is never used by the prophet, and the deliverer, whatever may have been the personal name Hosea would have given him, is simply called a prophet, and not at all a lawgiver in the modern sense. Our Roman idea of law has awkwardly confused the Hebrew picture of Hebrew Torah, and our English speech has blurred the meaning of the Hebrew word. Hosea wrote a Moses-Torah in the sense that he wrote a theory of the deliverance and deliverer of Israel; and he wrote it in faith in God's agreement with him, God's gift of it to him, God's inspiration of himself as he wrote it. We find then in Hosea an implicit theory of the revelation of God written in the story of the people of God.

(*f*) There is in Hosea the germ of another important conception. Israel is the child of God, Jehovah's son. The beauty and tenderness of the marriage picture should not obscure this other and even more important figure. The faith in the Fatherhood of God is by no means originally a Christian doctrine; it is at least as old as Hosea. The infinite significance of it indeed dawns on us as we stand in the presence of Jesus; but even that will not be understood unless we know what sonship of God meant to a

Hebrew seer like Hosea. The language of his time and of all his people after him makes this plain. When a Hebrew said "son of" he meant "one of the same sort." Son of cattle (בֶּן־בָּקָר) meant an individual ox, sons of Ammon (בְּנֵי עַמּוֹן) meant Ammonites; son of prophets (בֶּן־נְבִיאִים) meant a prophet, and son of death (בֶּן־מָוֶת) meant one destined to die. Thus, to a Hebrew, the cry "Ephraim my son," uttered by Hosea in the name of Jehovah, implied that in the prophet's estimation Ephraim shared, in some deep true sense, the very nature of Jehovah. The mode of thought was indeed an inheritance from far simpler earlier times, when the people were counted as the offspring of their God; and the sacrificial feasts were presented to Him, and eaten with faith that their patron God, who was really their first Father, feasted with them. A very full and fine exposition of this may be read in Professor W. R. Smith's "Religion of the Semites." Hosea's use of the mode of thought, with his thorough sympathetic sharing of all the reality in it, is a vital stage in the advance to the day when Jesus declared Himself both Son of Man and Son of God. There is a word including both ideas, the coinage of a far later day, which has become the symbol of the ever-growing grasp of the eternal verity. God is revealed in men—His children. We are learning to call Jesus the God-man. With singular suggestiveness and force does the Gospel, whose text is "The Word became flesh," conclude its wonderful argument with the personal confession of one who felt Jesus' creative power and cried to Him, "My Lord and my God." Hosea's faith in Jehovah as the Father of Ephraim is but an early stage in the rise of the soul to ability to comprehend and receive the revelation of the " Son of God " in Jesus.

(*g*) One feature further marks Hosea's thoughts concerning society, and it marks them with nobility. He is a monogamist; the age of justifiable polygamy has for him quite passed away. All the more valuable is this feature because the prophet seems to possess it in common with the most or the best of the people; we have here really a note of the process of history—not of an individual, but of the Hebrew people.

It may be that the deplorable picture Hosea gives us is a relic of the old system of polyandry which seems to have prevailed in early days. In any case society is rising far above it, and learning to regard each woman-soul as a precious unit, co-ordinate in value with the individual man-soul. The rise to this view is an advance in grasp of the thoughts of God; and God's leading of men to this height is strictly a process of revelation. It is most significant that this evident revelation of a new high estimate of woman, and of man as husband, and of home, is a revelation in and by that prophet whose distinctively new revelation of God is that He is more than man and yet is altogether devoted to Israel.

§ 5. *His idea of God.*

This is both complex and incomplete. The final picture of Jehovah's control even over death is his normal thought as it is his highest thought, but there are many stages of anxious doubt and wondering whether Jehovah shall be able to overcome all men's resistance to His power. Let us watch the different elements which work together to produce this Hosean theology or doctrine of God.

1. To Hosea Jehovah is a national God—that is, He is co-ordinate to some extent with the Baals and other national or tribal deities. He has been called by Israel "My Baal" (בַּעֲלִי), and Hosea's hope is that this exclusive relationship between Jehovah and Israel shall be exchanged for the other

exclusive relationship, "My husband" (אִישִׁי), "mine" as distinct from any other nation's "husband."

As such a national God, Jehovah guides all the affairs of this people. All their past history, all their institutions, the Exodus, the royal line, the Torah-teachers (Morehs), whether priests or prophets, the coming relations to Assyria, all are the special work of Jehovah. "When Israel was a child, then I loved him and called him. . . . I taught him to go. . . . I am Jehovah *thy* God from the very land of Egypt."

But this national Israelite God is also to Hosea, as to all his people since David's day, the Over-Lord over all national deities. Hosea believes firmly the revelation of the Davidic conquests. Jehovah has mastered Egypt, and fears not Assyria. Even death itself and the powers of Sheol will He plague and conquer.

The fine Hosean touch upon all these faiths is the evident wondering and trembling uncertainty how this Divine power shall be made good. There is indeed no lack of certainty that it shall be made good. But the utterly sympathetic man has a sort of filial sympathy with his God in the quivering strain of heart and nerve and hand amid real work.

2. Hosea shared most thoroughly in the Amosian advance from all these previous attainments to the grander grasp of righteousness. Not Amos alone beheld in vision Jehovah's demand for a justice far wider than Israel had once counted perfect, a justice between man and man wherever the Davidic empire had reached. Not Amos's conscience alone had grown deeply tender while it had grown so large. For the words of Hosea (x. 12), which Jeremiah quoted 150 years later, tell how the later great prophet of personal godliness learnt righteousness at the feet of that twin-prophet of Amosian purity. In evidence scan Hosea's words closely.

(a) His idea of purity stands out all the finer for that very revolt of his soul that so startles us as we read it and blush. He had to speak. He had to rise from the dark sorrow. And more, the pain is pictured by him as a feature of God. Hosea thinks of Jehovah as so sacredly pure, that His purity has a concrete well-defined character. Here is no vague sentimentalism, but a clear demand for a certain treatment of the souls of men and women.

(b) This view of Jehovah's righteousness is accompanied in Hosea by condemnation of the other great wrongs—wrongs against property and bodily life. And at these very points it is the priests who are heavily blamed; because they ought to be what they are not at all, true exponents of Jehovah's mind. They ought to give true Torah, and so stay the evil; but they are actually bloodthirsty and thieves. Jehovah and Hosea are utterly against them.

(c) The righteousness of God which Hosea exalts is like to that of Amos and also different; it is of a higher grade. The very features which mark the two men as akin reveal singularly the higher rank of Hosea. We shall see presently that to him righteousness and knowledge of God are virtually one, and graciousness of character is highest righteousness. But these peculiarly Hosean thoughts stand best in a later setting.

(d) Let us observe as we advance how evident it is that we have here learned something of the general level of religious attainment of all the best men of the people. What is common to both Hosea and Amos is no mere individual characteristic, but may be counted as the general faith of their best men. Certainly the Hebrew people of that day, although not indeed every Hebrew, believed in a God, Jehovah, who cared chiefly for the right. It may be said right is itself a relative thing, varying as the ages move on.

But we know now that Jehovah, whom these men believed in and obeyed, valued each soul of every Hebrew man or woman, with its endowments of body and property, of affections and of reason, as an essential part of the divinely-prized Israel, and He prized all surrounding peoples as secondary indeed, or even subject to them, and yet all indispensable to Israel, and therefore within Jehovah's ruling care.

3. Now we can understand Hosea's own peculiar addition to the conception of God; we can see the vision which was given to himself alone. What had he which was neither the common inheritance from the fathers and the Davidic age, nor yet common to himself and men like Amos? That special feature which we have already traced in him, his strong sympathy of soul, will be our clue here again as we watch his closest gaze on God to learn the new depths he saw there.

(*a*) It is through his sympathy with men, and his own fine humanity truly prizing itself that he counts human graces worthy of Jehovah, and attributes them to Him.

(*a*) So he thinks that Jehovah has the heart of a husband, husband-love, a husband's ways.

(β) He is a Father also. The doctrine of the Fatherhood of God was not new in Galilee. It was at least as old as Hosea, and Jesus showed us the fact of it. He has not merely left us a doctrine: the Son of man *was* and *is* the Son of God. And Hosea felt and prophesied 800 years before that his heart said this must be true, Jehovah must have a Father's heart.

(γ) Hence too He must be a great Leader of the nation; the patriotic zeal that flamed in Hosea must burn in Jehovah.

(δ) Altogether He must be of the same nature as the men of Israel. We saw his faith in the converse of this doctrine. Men are of the same nature as God; that is the declaration of the preciousness of men: but God is of the same nature as men; that is the foundation of all theology, all philosophy, all knowledge, all possible peace of mind, for it means we can learn something of God. It is the eternal truth of the cross, God manifest in the flesh, even unto that death. It is the answer, an answer of faith alone indeed, yet a great full satisfying adequate answer to all the deep craving of the soul. It is the Gospel that Jesus revealed and that Paul declared; it was also the soaring faith of old Hosea. Well was he called " Hosea," " He hath caused salvation." By that profound instinctive sympathy for men which the Divine Creator-finger planted in him, and the hand of Divine Providence nurtured in him, Hosea thought of God, beheld God and declared Jehovah is of us. Not completely defined was his treasure, but he had it; the true light that lighteth every man beamed into his eyes, and from him so far away the bright beam comes flashing through the ages. This has been a glorious world, and is, wherein such visions dwell.

(*b*) It was said above that Hosea's conception of God's righteousness has lineaments which are finer than any in the Amosian conception. The finest moral graces of men which Hosea knew and understood, because he shared them, were richly prized by his sympathetic soul. They were invaluable, they were Divine.

(*a*) Jehovah must love knowledge, and must seek it as the greatest righteousness, because Hosea and men like him did. Jehovah's great demand, cries Hosea, is that men should know Him. This is the prophet's declaration of the vision of God's soul which has been given him. Jehovah, cries he virtually, exalts knowledge as a supreme element in righteousness. To grow ignorant is deep sin, and Jehovah fights against that ignorance, that He may fight it away. Accordingly He exalts the power of reason; God honours the reason of man singularly by constant argument with men. He is scrupulously reasonable Himself in all His deeds and purposes; and He, the great King, is ready to submit all His ways to the judgment of the wise man. In this high faith Hosea is almost unique, for few Hebrew religious thinkers of far later days have traced so profoundly the authorship of God in the human reason. And yet again and again they have quoted Hosea's eulogy of the wise, when their own words perhaps could scarce have framed such faith.

(β) But most fair of all the attributes clothed upon his Jehovah by Hosea is that gracious character, that *chesedh* (חֶסֶד), a thing so full of meanings and of beauty that many words are needed for its translation. Grace, which is favour to the ill-deserving, is implied in it, and the gracious way which sets every present heart at peace, and the gracefulness which delights and makes the hearts smile for gladness; that grace it is that knows no barrier to its loving, its kindness, its royal benediction. That was the sort of righteousness Hosea required from men. He must have known its sweetness, and to know it is to have it within the soul, filling every passage of that labyrinth. He counted it the thing Jehovah required, and so the thing Jehovah knew and loved and possessed. Such a law of righteousness could be given only by such a righteous lawgiver. Amos had exalted Jehovah's severe command, "Do right," "Seek good," until the task seemed mysterious and hard, almost impossible and cruel. Hosea speaks of Jehovah's grace, and all the trouble and fear fly away like a morning mist. The righteous God is gracious; there is no impossibility now.

(c) From the same source in Hosea's soul, his singular regard for all he has in himself, rises his picture of the

Divine anxiety amid His working. The prophet attributes to Jehovah a sense of anxiety or uncertainty as to the way in which His ends shall be accomplished. This is the inevitable accompaniment of the reasoning with men which runs through the whole book. It is, of course, most dramatically exhibited in the scenes of the second chapter. There, as we watch the wayward tempted and tempting ones, and turn to the husband, stricken, yet bent on saving the life he loves, we can see the wistful eye, and, as the brow is knit in close study, we almost hear the anxious questioning: How shall I convert the heart back again to goodness and to me? Tell me what can I do. This way I will try! How could I give the beloved up! Oh no, I shall find a way! Difficulty! Yes, yes, indeed, almost beyond thought, well-nigh past power. But the wise must win; the prudent soul shall know, shall walk on, and at last shall behold the light.

The scene is marvellous, and almost unique. But Hosea's vision of the very living God, quick, striving in intensest agony of mind, was the far-away forerunner of the profoundest philosophy of creation, of Providence, of Triune Father, Son, and Spirit God.

(*d*) This leads at once to the highest element in Hosea's conception, his declaration that Jehovah is not human at all. Strange fact, that the very man who can prize his fellow-men most accurately and most richly can estimate God most grandly. We are often superficial, and speak of God as of a great noble in our race; His name sounds like a great family name of our known kin. But let our vision grow keen by gazing into the dark for help when no man's help is seen, and then the truest human reason knows best that its God is more than itself. He who cries in darkness for help, convinced that his voice will reach a kindred ear, is most certain that his helper shall be one more powerful than himself.

Let us trace the reasoning of the prophet's soul in that classic passage (xi. 8–12) that records his profoundest gaze into the very heart of God and God's peculiar word to Hosea himself.

(a) Invasion is coming, he cries; and the terrible judgment-oracle of Amos is as righteous as it seems inevitable. "He shall not return to Egypt, but the Assyrian shall be his king"—king of that Israel, child, son, that "I loved and called out of Egypt!"

(β) Yet how is it possible! Hosea's love, his manly love, his patriot love, his husband love, all mount and beat in agony against such undoing. No! they cry, he cries; and in his faith, that springs highest in the hour of need, he declares his own yearning to be God's yearning too. God's yearning, the fountain, is the same, only it is far greater than this stream of Hosea's. More truly we must say, according to our own faith, God yearned in love, and yearned to tell His love; but He had no voice save the voice of man, which He had created, by which to speak the language that man's ear could hear, and therefore He breathed, He brought forth the faith of Hosea, and thus Hosea's words.

(γ) In Hosea's speech is Jehovah's speech:

"I am Israel's Devoted One.
My home is in Israel's midst.
When that home fails, then my heart fails.
Truly do I come likewise from afar;
For I rule all, even the Assyrians who march from afar.
But I am Israel's Devoted One:
I come not to destroy Israel."

(δ) Now turns the manly soul of the prophet to give answer and reason to the questioning of men, and of an Amos, and of himself, How can Jehovah thus pass by wrong? We know our own heart's declaration, "All that sin shall die;" and we have declared this in the name of Jehovah, saying for Him, "All the sinners of my people shall die by the sword." We know not how He can come hither without destruction in His hand.

"He is God, and not man,"

answers Hosea, the man and seer, who sees beyond man. But how can due retribution be left undone?

"He is God, and not man,"

answers Hosea. Men know not, but God knows. But how can He dwell with evil?

"He is God, and not man,"

comes the answer. The Devoted One, who must dwell in the midst of Israel, can create again what man has undone. But can Jehovah cleanse away evil from men and make them good again?

He is God, and not man.

He will come, but not to destroy. He will be as the dew unto Israel.

> Take with you words and turn to Jehovah.
> Say unto Him,
> Take away all iniquity.

Thus a gospel of reconciliation is dawning. The preacher of salvation begins to proclaim:—

> "I, Jehovah, am thy God, even from Egypt:
> There is no Saviour beside Me."

What is now prophesied with trembling shall yet be preached by a great host of voices.

(c) Is it finely characteristic that the whole book closes with the appeal to the wise (the חֲכָמִים), and to their prudence? Is the verse not Hosea's, but a note on the last flyleaf from some thoughtful reader? If so, that reader was the truest pupil of Hosea. He spoke the very heart of Hosea; the prophet spoke through him in this verse. It sums up all the trembling hope, all the boundless faith in God, all the certainty that righteousness is right, all the kindly, manly estimate of man. We too may close thus: Whoso is wise, even he shall understand Hosea; he shall understand and love God.

CHAPTER V.

THE ADVANCE MADE AND TO BE MADE.

§ 1. *The material pathway for this.*

It is well to gather here in short outline the results thus far in order that, holding them in mind as points of attachment, we may quickly build again in our imagination the living religious society of the time. But what time? one naturally asks.

Let us first, then, recall the chronological data on which we have been working, and are to work for some time. For closer investigation of dates the reader may consult Professor W. R. Smith's Appendices to his Lectures on the "Prophets of Israel."

The David-era culminates with Elijah about 850 B.C. Then evidently the faith that Jehovah was Lord of hosts, God over all gods, had become the fixed Hebrew belief. During the next hundred years came about those developments which have given to us written prophecy. The earliest preserved works of prophetic men, Amos and Hosea, were uttered between 800 and 750 B.C. We shall see that the lad Isaiah had his first vision (chap. vi.) say in the year 750, when he was probably some fifteen years old.

This first half of the eighth century B.C. was the era of stern consciousness of duty. Certainly the demand for righteousness made by a few is itself proof that many lives were far below that demand; yet even these must have understood very clearly the words and the standard of the preachers. It was the age of conscience, and it was also the age of comparative comfort. The very long reigns of Uzziah of Jerusalem and Jeroboam II. of Samaria partly produced and partly were produced by this time of ease.

But darkness was creeping on. About 750 B.C. Assyria's last great assertion of world empire and her last terrible conflict with Egypt began together. Beginning about 750, this grew fiercer as the century grew. In the second half of the eighth century she was to be the terror and the destruction of Palestine and its Hebrew peoples. That belt of land, the eastern coast of the Mediterranean, semi-tropical yet well-watered, and fairly level, was the great road between three continents, and especially the highway from the valley and plains of the Euphrates to the valley and delta of the Nile. The march of the caravan in peace, or of the army in war, was seen every day. Here, from Amos's day onward for a hundred and fifty years, the advance or retreat of Assyrian or Egyptian hosts was almost ceaseless. If those greater armies rested a while in their homes, then other bands and masses of marauders coursed to and fro. These were at times the near Syrians from the white mountains and rich valleys of Lebanon and beyond, or they were later on the hordes of wild Scythians from the far-off lands we now call Russia and Tartary.

The dread warnings of Amos meant that he heard the thunder-mutterings along the horizon. In his high mountain-home in south Judea all was comparatively safe; the foreigner's tread would scarcely ever leave the easy coast-plain and the road through Philistine towns to plunder Judah. But in Samaria, the rich market-town in the very centre of the great highway, and above all at the court, both he and Hosea saw the certain danger of the city and its lands. Traders, travellers, and courtiers from the far north were bringing in the first rumours of Assyrian purpose and march.

Hosea tells far more fully than Amos of the nearing war-flood. His picture of intestine quarrellings, overturnings, recklessness, revolution, scarcely needs the story of 2 Kings xv. to give it definite line and shade. Simultaneously with the death of the two strong chiefs Jeroboam II. and Uzziah, Assyria and Egypt began their invasions, or at least their rival grim coquettings. Had the strength of the two Hebrew princes prevented earlier attack, or was it their prudence only? Perhaps they had understood, as Jeremiah understood long after, how to adapt themselves to the advances of the overwhelming powers, and to study the comfortable safety of their subjects rather than a greedy love of mastery for themselves. But these princes died, and at once, terror rolled in from far, and the fever of disorder broke out within.

Now we see the setting of the burden of these prophets. While brightness still beamed on every side they demanded righteousness worthy of their blessings, and pointed the demand with earnest warning that possible evil was not far away. But the evil began to lower darkly; and now still maintaining their high demand, and their estimate of men's responsibility, the prophets stretch out the hand and cry for unseen help. It was sorely needed in those fifty years that followed Amos's preaching. Let us then gather here in summary what truths Hosea proclaimed as comfort in this day of darkness, and then we shall ask what greater problems still he left and compelled his followers to face.

§ 2. *The advance made by Hosea.*

Here then is the peculiar height that Hosea reached, or here, rather, are the special depths he sounded in the great heart of God.

(*a*) He has grasped some hope for the sinner. The story of faith in atonement has begun.

(b) That hope speaks out in a definite theory of the way of salvation. This is no mere vague hope, but the man of faith tells us he can conceive a great possible plan for atonement, and he tells us what it is.

(c) The plan springs from a new, greater and diviner conception of God's character. It is no new God that has been made by men, but the great Spirit has touched men with new power to see, has revealed Himself as never before. They behold, and cry, He is God, not man. He is Israel's Devoted One. When He comes it is not to destroy the evildoers. He can show favour to the fallen.

(d) And this new superhuman view of God springs amidst and from a far profounder, richer view of the value of man. Included here must be the richer view of history which we find, and the fine, unostentatious, yet dignified self-estimate of the prophet. The knowledge of the value of men comes because the speaker has learned his own value.

(e) Here must be singled out a special feature of this high estimate of man. Knowledge is exalted, and ever presses to the front as the secret of goodness. Hosea's special claim is that it is knowledge of *God* which saves; none the less emphatically is it *knowledge*. It may be possible for us to grow much wiser than those old writers, but there is an eternal truth in this Hosean doctrine. That recognition of facts and truths in God's ways and deeds, which in a word we call knowledge of God, is essential to life; we may well say it is life. They who would give life must give knowledge, and they must have it themselves abundantly.

(f) Let us set out by itself another new trait in the humanity of Hosea which sheds beauty on every side from its own beautiful nature. He exalts marriage far, far higher than it has been before. Not with words of plea or praise, but with tenderest respect he lifts the love of man and woman into almost loftiest sacredness. Israel seems to him the beloved wife of Jehovah.

(g) To close, we observe Hosea's advance far beyond Amos's position towards worthy valuation of formal religious observances. Only symbols they all are, and not God, for they are the work of men's hands; yet such priests as they have, and princes too, are God's voice. Such sacrifices as they may have, more or fewer, for he says little of them, are, or ought to be, blessed occasions of family fellowship with the Husband, Father, Jehovah. As for their symbolical pillars of stone, their ephods, whether of precious metal or of woven stuff, their teraphim, each is to Hosea a possible shechinah, the abode of God, where the soul may find the very gate of heaven.

§ 3. *The advance still needed.*

Hosea leaves problems still unsolved. Certainly no man can declare all the revelations of God that other souls need, else those souls would not know the revealing grace of God towards themselves. They would have no personality in their life. The new questioning which rises within each soul is simply the outcome and the proof of the new individual personality. The great way of God is indeed always the same; He will always answer the questionings of the sons of men. But no son of man can enter into the joy of the sons of God save by crying to God himself for the answer to his own individual life's needs and questionings.

Hosea's failure to solve all problems was itself a true solution of life's problem; it was a law and a prophecy. "Ask still, and revelation shall still come." What questions do his words start, and yet leave unsolved?

(*a*) His theory of regeneration must fail. Affliction does not make men good. In pain men cry out, indeed, for help from the unseen; but often they curse bitterly the afflicting hand. Men do not kiss the rod; it is rather the saviour, the defender, him who wards off the stroke, that they learn to love.

And ignorance is not the cause of all sin. Rather to him that knoweth to do good, and doeth it not, to him it is sin. A plan of regeneration must indeed set every motive, all knowledge and light, before a habitual wrongdoer, but then, besides, it must win him to do what he knows to be most reasonable, most happy and best. From Hosea's plan men turn away, and long for a new creation, a power to be "born again."

(*b*) Hosea's lines of advance from the faiths of Amos bring eager hopes rather than clear possessions. His large human and sympathetic love bids faith rest in the love of God; but henceforward concrete *methods* must be definitely proclaimed, tried, and moulded into ever new fitness to the lives that use them. Henceforward there must be reflection on the profound faith of such as Hosea. Philosophy has begun, for Hosea himself has reasoned and argued; and men must now listen for the revelations of God in the hidden reflection of their own mind on the *way* of the Grace of Jehovah.

(*c*) For, to speak more particularly, Hosea has breathed out his own and all men's need of some visible manifestation of God, but that very need will demand the time and the place and the form which alone are holy. Because men need a sanctuary, therefore ere long a sanctuary-law shall be exalted, and for a time obeyed. Sacrifices will not seem sacred unless they become separated from the family meal and the common places of resort. More still shall men need. They cry now to God for forgiveness, and sit with priestly teachers round the feast of propitiation for sin; but the penitent soul in its hour of subdued reflection craves special and minute direction lest it sin again. The sympathetic prophecy of Hosea is not enough. Law must appear; ritual must be used in the ages to come.

PART III.

THE RELIGION OF ISAIAH.

CHAPTER I.

A SKETCH OF THE WHOLE COURSE OF THE DEVELOPMENT OF HIS THOUGHT, AS MANIFESTED IN HIS RELATION TO ZION.

§ 1. *Perspective in history.*

ATTENTION has been often turned of late to the meaning and beauty of the book of Isaiah. A gifted, but alas! now vanished hand has written gracefully of the beauty hidden in our common English version of the prophet's oracles, and has bidden us share the delight he found in the wondrous visions. But that beauty in Isaiah's book grows fairer far if we will look on those visions in their true perspective.

For there is a perspective in life, and one event ranks there after another, with thought following in the train of thought. At one point perhaps a new conception is nearing the dawn, and behind the translucent darkness there is swelling the rich wealth of brightness that in a moment shall burst in joyous vision on us, now as never before, and never perhaps again. Or perchance yonder a giant form of faith is withdrawing, mellowing into a dream of the past, fair still, but speechful only as it quietly points to its great followers, prophesying a greater future. Therefore let there stand here before the book of Isaiah a portrait of the man we would describe as frontispiece. And let it be a portrait of a living man, not in stone, but in action, not a motionless soul, but a man actually receiving revelation from his God.

In the full study of Isaiah all the rich detail of his thought must be enshrined; here it is enough to trace one bright beam along its quivering path. Let us begin acquaintance with him by watching his ever-deepening grasp of his plainest faith and his wondrous work as he imprints that faith upon the very traditions of the people. Let us look at Isaiah's personal development in his thought concerning Zion.

§ 2. *The faiths before Isaiah concerning Zion.*

Recall for a moment what we have learned of men's faith Zionwards before Isaiah's day.

(*a*) What the young prophet could inherit from the pre-Davidic days was the faith in a great Deliverer, God, and in His hovering presence at many a sacred spot in Canaan where patriarchs had met Him. This was the faith on the one hand; on the other was the consciousness of feebleness in the people throughout all its loosely knit families and tribes. They could only cry to their God for deliverance from themselves, and strive to weld a stronger union more worthy of Jehovah. The bond was welded by David's hand, and held well for a while. So Isaiah looked back to the great man who was after Jehovah's heart, for he had made the tribes all one Hebrew nation, and he had taught them too that their Jehovah, the God of Israel, was also the God of all hosts. This faith, which King David founded by his sword and sceptre, the prophet Elijah sealed finally by his oracles and command. Jehovah, God of Israel, was henceforth to be Jehovah alone, the only true God.

(*b*) Amos had risen to a far higher faith. The Lord of hosts was Lawgiver and Judge of hosts. The Deliverer was all-righteous, and demanded all righteousness. "Seek good and ye shall live," he cries, "for so Jehovah, God of hosts, shall be with you, as ye say." It seems almost the climax of truth, it sounds like a wonderful anticipation of the Teacher who sat by Sychar's well and proclaimed, "God is a Spirit." But there was an awful phase of Amos's faith utterly unlike the gospel of Sychar's Saviour, for he healed the woman's sin-sick soul, but Amos knew of no forgiveness. Amos's gospel had no room for mercy in it. It cried only, "Seek good, and ye shall live," for "All the sinners of my people shall die by the sword."

(c) Hosea's deeper insight saw man's need of forgiveness, and also God's need to forgive. He too demanded perfect righteousness, but he searched for a way to better life and joy for the unrighteous. He felt the wrong of sin, and cried again God's judgments against wrongdoers; but he felt in behalf of man, and in behalf of God too, that God must be gracious, and must know some way of grace beyond men's knowledge. He knew, moreover, men's need of visible, tangible tokens; and while Amos, the lone mountaineer, had scorned sanctuaries, Hosea, the man among men, knew the blessing that hovered round altars, shrines, symbols of God's face.

(d) Isaiah's coming doctrine was to bind together all these faiths. He was to centralise the faith in a material revelation of the gracious love of Jehovah in the sanctuary of Zion. That rock and temple were to be to him, and so to the Hebrews, and thence to the world, a symbol of the devoted love of God. But ere the prophet saw that, he was to try the stern Amosian faith in Divine righteousness, and to declare the Amosian oracle of judgment. Forgiveness was not to be at first his remedy for awful sin.

(e) Let us look back on the story of the Zion sanctuary hitherto.

(a) Students are aware that only some three and a half centuries before Isaiah's day Jerusalem was not a Hebrew town, but alien from both Judah's land to the south of it, and Israel's land that began immediately on the north. While David was ruling in Hebron, the future seat of his long dynasty was the stronghold of his bitter enemies, the Jebusites. But David besieged and reduced their fortress; and then he made his military skill and his statesmanlike tact notable for ever by his choice of that spot of neutral ground as the seat of his government over the united north and south, Israel and Judah.

(β) In David's day, and for generations before, it was Shiloh, some fifteen miles north in Israel, that seems to have been counted the chief among the many sanctuaries, where David and Samuel, the patriarchs, the judges, the kings and the people worshipped. Shiloh became neglected and dishonoured, as many records tell us, but its abandonment does not seem to have been held due to a substitution of Zion instead of Shiloh, as if Zion had been discovered in David's day to be the divinely ordered spot. Shiloh was abandoned, not at all for Zion's sake, but because of wrongdoings in Shiloh itself. Jeremiah, long after Isaiah's day, says so, and warns Zion that its present distinction, due to no more inherent grounds than Shiloh's, may easily be forfeited for similar reasons. No Zion had ever been, if Shiloh had not sinned; Zion might become nothing, exactly as did Shiloh. It took many a century, and a long exile, to change into a Divine oracle the cry which Jeremiah had scorned, "The temple of Jehovah, the temple of Jehovah are these." Indeed, the honour paid to Beersheba and Bethel by the patriarchs, and to Mizpah, Gilgal, Shiloh, and many another altar by the prophets and all men of the Davidic days, lead us to think that Zion was not a favourite sanctuary before Isaiah's prophecies. The slight regard for Zion that Amos, Hosea, Elijah had, confirms this.

(γ) David built an altar to Jehovah in his new capital, but the sanctuary where it stood was of the simplest nomadic order. Where he met his God, there, like Jacob, he set up his altar, and there he spread a tent for the abode of Jehovah, and for the ark, the symbol of His oracle.

Solomon built a magnificent temple upon that spot, where his father had prayed; he lavished on it his own great skill and the immense wealth his greater father had won and bequeathed. But Solomon seems to have dazzled the sight of his austere people with the glory of this sanctuary, gorgeous like the glittering shrines and ornate symbols of Tyre and her luxurious sisters. Moreover, Solomon's temple was to be a pantheon. The whole family of the gods must lodge here, thought the exalted king, for his heritage of power over all peoples, from Egypt to Euphrates, must be symbolised by his assemblage of all their heavenly lords in this central palace. Jehovah was doubtless counted the Lord of the hosts here marshalled; but His simple worshippers must wander through a distracting maze to find their own loved God, if haply then they still prefer Him before all that glorious company. How strange that after all this such high blessing came in Zion. It came slowly, and it came through Isaiah.

(δ) Watch how slowly it came. There is an under-current of connection, not obscurely expressed, between that Solomonic luxuriance of religious eclecticism and the speedy revolt of the northern Israel from the house of David. Thereafter Ephraim never worshipped with Judah, nor bowed to her sceptre; and for the unhappy division of the kingdom in twain Solomon's religious unwisdom seems to have been sadly to blame. The rent in the royal power was a heavy blow to Judah and to David's throne, but it was a heavier blow to the prospects of Zion. Zion had become the occasion of the estrangement, the rock of offence to kings and people. To predict that she should become the centre of all light, of all love, of all nations, seemed impossible.

(ε) For many generations even Judah herself did not consent

to worship in Zion alone. Certainly there seem to have been few shrines in the poor bare south as compared with fertile Ephraim's many sacred spots, yet Isaiah, in his early days, had not learned to honour her altogether, as his taunt in his opening text of chapter ii. tells. And quite a hundred years after Isaiah had preached his great faith in Zion there were many country altars to be broken down by Josiah. Jeremiah himself, of that date, was one of the priests of Anathoth; hence perhaps his condemnation of Zion; hence perhaps also Ezekiel's surprising condemnation of Jeremiah along with the people whom that saint was toiling to bless. Of course by that day, 600 B.C., the inhabitants of the royal city, and Ezekiel among them, had learned to honour their temple and her priests, the Zadokites, as the best and only true institutions.

We have to trace how, in Isaiah's own day, and by his faith and word, that great change began to dawn. To Isaiah, not at first, but after long years and toil, came a vision of Jehovah's gracious healing love pouring forth from Zion for an unclean people in the hour of deepest spiritual despair. We have seen, then, the story of Zion before Isaiah, and before his own awakening to his Zion-faith.

§ 3. *His own experience in Zion.*

We turn to the story of Isaiah's own experience.

1. He was born probably between 770 and 760 B.C. That was a time of manifold importance in the world's story, for just then, far to the west, two great peoples were awaking into consciousness, as the dating of the Olympiads and the founding of Rome tell, and far to the east the old nations of the Tigris and Euphrates were all astir in deed and word, seeking world-empire, and recalling and recording their older and their younger story on the slabs we find and read to-day. Yet perhaps the greatest, and far the subtlest, of all the factors for later life was the wondering about God

that filled the Jew boy Isaiah in Jerusalem. We can fancy his boyhood among the courts and lanes of the rocky capital. As he played he watched the new fortresses a-building under the Prince Uzziah, well named thus "Fortress of Jehovah." The lad would scarcely dream that this loved Zion had ever been aught but the sacred centre of the whole world's strength. Did he play in the gorges beneath those towering walls? Did he step beside his father Amoz, "the firm-treading man," along those echoing aisles and toward those smoking altars that had stood now three hundred years? Did he not gaze in wonder at the splendour Solomon reared, and the follies of his unwise successors had scarcely marred? Surely to the young poet-soul that sanctuary might seem the very abode of the God of Ages—the glorious throne on earth of Jehovah's heavenly glory.

Doubtless the lad heard often in those wide courts the rapt utterances of strangely-clad seers from southern ravine and rock, or from more northern fruitful vale. Perhaps he strayed after these men of God as through dark lane they threaded out to market-square "Rehoboths," to cry aloud there of sin and for the right. Doubtless he would hasten home, and in some housetop corner he would brood upon their words, then ponder over the written sayings of the older prophets, storing in his memory their burdened cries and wondrous faiths. So probably did he learn that text, full of high hope, which he was to write one day over his own first lament for his country. The words of the past seer prophesied that light should flow out of Zion: the lad must have caught up that hope eagerly; he was to learn from the present seers to doubt it. He was himself publicly to deny it, and then most wondrously to assert it. His faith and word touching Zion should be the light to save and bless all Hebrews and all men. He was to compel into the one focus of his soul all heaven's beams that shone down through the past, and all that burst daily through the darkness of the present. He was to move all souls around him that seemed so dead. He was to illumine all the past, and to send on through all coming ages a light to lighten men by revealing the very face of God Himself.

2. In those early years the lad had a strange experience. The great chieftain Uzziah lay a-dying. It may be that his leprosy-bitten form lay already cold in the rocky tombs, and his spirit had returned to God from its busy, weary toil. Was it this failing of the strength of men that sent the sensitive Isaiah away to the sanctuary, to sit silent there, shaken to the soul by this strange thing, a king's death? Such a dread day the boy had never known before; scarcely even his father remembered the like, for it had not been in Judah for well-nigh half a hundred years. The trembling soul drew instinctively toward God for help. But he was to tremble yet more awfully amid his search for God's comfort. Bowed and covered he sat, buried in his thought. Then God shook the earth. The foundations of the great temple quaked, the boy's heart quivered, bright flashes flew across the darkened halls. A light that was not of earth filled the boy's soul: he saw God. He saw and lived. While he lay stricken to the earth with awe God talked with him. God came to him; God gave him clean lips to talk with God. There was other converse also; the heavenly ministrants spake together with veiled voice of the holy devotion of Jehovah to His own. God thought on the lad. Was not Isaiah the representative there of Jehovah's own beloved, and did not all the movements of that vision seem like a wooing of Isaiah by Jehovah and for Jehovah by His angels? How singular the suppressed eagerness of God to win this boy's help. Jehovah is burdened with a care, and cannot speak out His will to men. He needs a human voice to reach human souls, and therefore suppliant He seeks His angels' counsel whom to send. The angels cannot go, but the young man rises at the thought. This desire of God is a command to him. He

rises filled with the sense of a Divine commission, and with its strength.

3. What was this commission?

(*a*) The question becomes complicated at once when we reflect on the well-known but peculiar position of the vision in the course of the book. Why does it not stand at the beginning? Had Isaiah begun to prophesy long years before he had the vision and its call? Had he already declared all the stern judgments of the earlier chapters, when this theophany came as a revelation to close and even to reprove that early tone, and to introduce an entirely new and truly godlike utterance? Or was the vision indeed the occasion of the lad's first dedication of himself to prophetic work? Were his first call and ordaining here, as commonly supposed? Why then, in this case, does it not stand first among the chapters? Perhaps he received the vision twice? Or he may have obeyed it at first with partial grasp of its great meaning, and then recalled it again amid his troubled work, remembering then the grace of the Hand that first ordained him, and feeling that thus far he had prophesied only of judgment, and now must prophesy of grace also? Was this the reason why he set the story of the vision there, as the preface to his new and gracious declaration?

(*b*) Known dates do not help us much here. If Uzziah's death fell, not about 760 B.C., as has been supposed, but as late as 750 B.C., as juster calculations say, and if Isaiah died about 700 B.C., when his prophecies cease, then to read chapter vi. as the story of the initial vision is to count the prophet a lad of say fifteen to twenty years in 750 B.C., and a man of sixty-five to seventy at his final words and death. This seems a reasonable theory, and it agrees with the tenor of the story of the vision, for this would seem an unnatural picture unless the boy were comparatively young, untried, and tender. But why then does not the chapter open the book?

Perhaps the vision came after the the first period of prophesying. In this case the year 750, when Uzziah died, must have found him already a man of strength and skill, a man surely of some twenty-five to thirty years. At his death he would thus be seventy-five to eighty years of age. The theory is possible, and would agree with the calm strength of the last words of the great soul. But it does not fit well the tenor of the call and of the response, for it would be strange to see the man of chapters ii. to v. put on the simple untried attitude of chapter vi.

(*c*) In either case, however, this chapter vi. may stand where it does as introduction to a new period of work, whose tone and aim is remarkably different from that of the early chapters.

Take the former theory. Our wonder over the vision grows intense as we think that perhaps Isaiah himself wrote down or told the tale long years after he had seen the vision and obeyed the call.

Did the man, in his searching after God, in his diligent inquiry what the Spirit in him signified, look back across the vista of years once full of hopes, then full of toils, and finally growing clouded in failure? Did he wonder, as he recalled the vision, whether in his first young eagerness he had taken in all the deep meaning of the revelation? Did the old vision become a new vision in the light of the experience God had given, that divinest "theophany of experience" that comes to every man? He would feel justified indeed in all the work he had done, for the impulse to it was all given in that first sacred hour; but he would feel now that far more was given him than he could then comprehend. He would see now, in the vision's meaning, truths far higher, far diviner, truths too big for any soul to know till it had tried life, but truths which he must now lift up before men and proclaim to the last ever more and more fully. If this was the order of events, it was very natural; we can understand it thoroughly.

If, on the other hand, the vision did not come to him until after his first period of prophesying, then two things are evident. He must first of all have had some sort of initial call sufficient to send him out on that first mission of judgment, and then at its close this vision (*cf.* chap. vi.) revealed to him the profounder truth of Jehovah's grace toward the unclean, and sent him out to a very new and different task from the first. The second theory then resolves itself into a somewhat less natural case of the first.

There is of course the further theory possible, that not Isaiah but compilers arranged the order of the chapters. This would only signify that the compilers saw long ago an order and progress in Isaiah's utterances; and seeing the vision's deeper truths, the kernel of the later work, they put its story in chapter vi. as the introduction to that later work. We may leave untouched a remaining theory, that the position of passages is due to haphazard collection. To discuss it would be fruitless toil; better assume any of the others.

(*d*) Falling back then on the first theory, let us enumerate the *momenta* of the vision, and then we can proceed to watch in the progress of the book and the man the successive rise of each faith into controlling pre-eminence.

(*a*) Clearly the Amosian doctrine of stern judgment, and only a remnant spared, is prominent. Mr. Matthew Arnold said truly that Isaiah proclaimed the faith, "A remnant only shall return." The prophet carved his faith upon an enduring monument when he gave the name Shear-Jashub ("It is only a remnant that remaineth") to his son. Isaiah firmly believed this doctrine in his early days. But Isaiah was not the first to believe it. Doubtless he learned it from Amos, who proclaimed it before Isaiah. Isaiah received many inheritances from the past, and this was one. So when the vision came, and struck out into vivid form the faiths which God's providence had been sowing thus in the young soul, then this dread note sounded deep and strong in the chord. The stern Amosian tone was certain to prevail for a while in the words of this second Judaean prophet of the century. He was sure to follow his own compatriot's teaching; and a young man who cares for God is always most ready to insist sternly on absolute righteousness with no compromise, no escape for the evildoer. This is the great prerogative of young men, so Isaiah speeds away out to proclaim terrible judgment; of this stubborn people only a few shall escape deserved death. The oak-tree of the nation shall be stripped of all its leaves by the winter blasts, although within indeed its life shall hide safely.

(β) The certainty of this safety is the second *moment* of the vision. The prominent character of Jehovah revealed to the young man was His holiness (קָדֹשׁ). This holiness meant devotion, the devotion of Jehovah to His own peculiar chosen people. Here we find again a note sounding across from the past, a heritage of Isaiah from the ministry of Hosea. Amos had known it, but Hosea had loved and declared it. Is it strange that to the lad this fair thought of God seems to be the chief meditation of the heavenly ministrants? Although it was an Israelite, Hosea of the north, a foreigner, who had taught the doctrine, its beauty had won the instinctive love of Isaiah's heart, and even enshrined the faith in a sacred place in his imagination.

But consider the meaning of the faith. We read the seraph's cry, "Holy, holy, holy!" What was this holiness in the Hebrew sense?

(i.) There is certainly something of the idea of "separation" in the word Q-D-Sh; but what sort of separation, separation "from" something or separation "to" something?

(ii.) The consequences of the theophany tell us of its nature. For observe that the vision of the "holy" Jehovah aroused in Isaiah first a sense of sin, then a sense of forgiveness, and finally a sense of vocation and power. Such results would never have been produced by an attitude of separation and removal of God away from the man; only a kind gracious approach to him could work this. Not a cold, crystalline, icy purity, but the warm tender embrace of love can thus win. It is the holiness of devotion, not the holiness of distance, we see here; it is the holiness of *separation unto* men and to their benefit that humbles and heals and holds men's hearts.

(iii.) If we trace the Hebrew idea of holiness through the history of ceremonial practice, we find it constantly equivalent to the idea of appropriation. The "holy things" described in Deuteronomy xii. 26 are various kinds of food which may not be eaten at home or in any chance place, but in the central sanctuary only. They are however the property and the food of the worshipper, and are not separated from him; and they symbolise his relation to his God. They say "This man, his food, his all, are devoted to Jehovah." The holy things are the things appropriated to the symbolical acts of honour towards God. Such, then, was the meaning of the word to those Hebrews who adopted Deuteronomy as their political constitution in Josiah's reign in *circa* 620 B.C.

About the same date Jeremiah preached, "Make holy a war upon Jerusalem," *i.e.*, Appropriate a war to her, do it thoroughly, in all solemn earnest. Devotion is the idea the word conveys.

After the Exile the people who used the various directions of Leviticus as their rules of worship had constantly in mind the fundamental law, "Men must be holy, because their God is holy." The meaning is evidently, "Your God is devoted to you, caring for you chiefly among all the peoples, therefore surely ought ye to care for Him chiefly, devoting your souls to deeds in His honour. Bear ye His ensigns, for He has chosen you for His special care." The essential feature in this old ceremonial holiness was the mutual devotion of Lord and follower. Of course the followers of one chieftain are *separate* from any other chieftain's flag and feast, but the *devotion*, and not the separation, is the essential matter. Men who are essentially *separated* men are essentially friends of nobody. It is not separatist-holiness, but something of the old Hebrew holiness we need to-day.

Most clearly was it such holiness of devotion that Jesus exhibited and required. We read in the vision of His last prayer that arose so wondrously in His followers' hearts, "Sanctify them in Thy truth; and for their sakes I sanctify Myself." On the eve of crucifixion He did not flee from death, but devoted Himself even unto it, thus devoting Himself to men. His holiness was no separation from sinful men, but a coming down to them, even unto the taking all their form and woe upon Himself with perfect willingness. He was holy in His clasping souls to His heart, though the souls had sinned and the love meant death.

(iv.) Philological discussion need not be extensive, for the matter is simple, if but simply handled. The meaning of the stem Q-D-Sh can be best illustrated by its actual use in its various derivations. Of these observe—

First. Qâdhosh. Jehovah is called Israel's Qâdhosh. The form is infinitive, the *nomen actionis;* and it is distinctly active, certainly not passive, and not even stative. Therefore Jehovah was to the Hebrew one great act of separation connected with Israel. He is not passive, separated by Israel, He is essentially active. He is not a Being actively hedging Himself away, else why should this action respect Israel alone? Why should He separate Himself from Israel alone, and not from other men as well? Duhm has pointed out that while He is Qâdhosh towards Israel He is "Exalted" towards all the earth. The best translation of the words Qâdhosh Yisrael is "appropriating self to Israel," or the "devoted one of Israel." Jehovah is that Deity who devotes Himself to Israel. Professor Robertson Smith reminds us that other Semitic nations use the expression, each applying it to its own peculiar deity.

Secondly. The word "Qaddishin" is used by the Babylonian queen in the Aramaic of Daniel v. 11 to describe the gods. The Babylonian is pictured as counting all the gods so related to men as Jehovah was related to Israel, namely, caring for them with all devotion.

Thirdly. The word "Qadhesh," a stative form, was used to describe those devotees of various sorts who frequented sanctuaries, sacrificing by their own act their body, honour, life to the honour of the deity.

Finally. The remaining term "Qŭdhsh" is a strict passive, and means something separated, devoted by the worshipper to the honour of the deity. This word, used as an attributive, appears in the expression "a hill of a devoted nature," or "hill of holiness," *i.e.*, holy hill.

Now, arranging all these expressions in derivative order, we begin with the stem, following with the monosyllabic, dissyllabic, duplicated (frequentative), and extended forms:—

Q-Dh-Sh = Appropriate, or devote.

Qudsh, or Qodhesh = A thing appropriated or devoted.

Qadhosh = An act of appropriation or devotion; or, used as an adjective concerning a person = One who devotes all to some one else, and is all in all to him.

Qadhesh = A devotee.

Qaddish = (Aramaic) One ever appropriating or devoting himself, a national deity, a *numen proprium*.

Qaddesh = He appropriated, devoted, sanctified.

Hithqaddesh = He volunteered for war, &c.

(v.) Finally, the suggestion of Duhm that the idea of holiness is an æsthetic one is correct, but should not lead to the mistake that "to be holy" means "to be separate from something." Of course the devotee is likely to wear some badge of distinction, some monastic robe, some æsthetic garb, and hence the generalisation that holiness is simply the æsthetic form which marks the devotees of a deity. But the generalisation fails just at the crucial point. Jehovah is the chief Holy Person, and His holiness is more than an æsthetic garb, it is His devoted love, His guarding, healing, and even forgiving grace.

Such then is the second *moment* in the vision. As we recall the faith of Hosea, we feel that there was a providential impression of this faith in God's grace passing over many hearts in those years. Isaiah may have learnt from Hosea, perhaps he did; perhaps he was moved by Hosea more than his patriotic aversion from an Ephraimite was willing to allow. In any case, Hosea and Isaiah were both moved, and to the same thought, by the Spirit of God that giveth to man his thought.

(γ) We find the third *moment* of the vision in the fact of its occurrence in the sanctuary in Zion. We recall the stern cry of Amos, "Seek not sanctuaries, but seek Jehovah;" and we know how natural it was that the lad Isaiah should bend toward his countryman, Amos, as the most favoured teacher. Yet the far more sensitive soul of Hosea had uttered the far deeper truth. Man needs visible tokens of God. A man needs sanctuary. And when Isaiah looked back upon his early vision for more light on his troubled path, he remembered God "so as he had seen Him in the sanctuary;" he remembered the altar that had seemed indeed the Father's table whence the angels had fed the child with the fire, the cleansing, the Spirit, and the words of God. Amos condemning all known sanctuaries, and Isaiah scorning Zion in his earlier oracles, stood both of them, indeed, on the level of their time where some sanctuary was sure to be the very gate of heaven, if one could only find the true one. And in Zion Isaiah did find it, for he saw God there. His faith in Zion, springing up after many days, grows into the glorious form wherein he enshrines his faith in the love of God. Immanuel is to him Jehovah in Zion.

The course of development of this phase of his thought, will now become evident if we run rapidly along the line of his utterances touching Zion.

§ 4. *Zion in the early discourses.*

(Chaps. ii.–v. 24; ix. 8–21; v. 25–end. *Circa* 740–735 B.C.)

1. These passages seem to date from about 740 B.C., when Uzziah's glory had passed away, and when Jotham's regency and reign had altered the state little for either better or worse. Ahaz was beginning to rule while yet a boy, and under harem control. He was gifted indeed, but seems to have been graceless; he was thoughtful and studious, but lacking the grasp which his name (Ahaz = grasp) seemed to claim for him; he was religious even to superstition, but without strong faith; he was fond of beauty, but the prey of effeminacy. David's son was no saviour of David's people.

It may be that Isaiah had been altogether silent in the long years between his vision in 750 and these discourses in 740. Perhaps the Hosean influence was breathing on him then, like a fragrant breeze soothing him to patience, although the strong, stern soul of the young man leaned hard toward the sterner doctrines of Amos. It is worthy of note that in these years was, no doubt, born to him that son whom he called Shear Jashubh ("It is a remnant that shall return"). He bade, as it were, his child carry in his name such an echo of the Tekoan prophet's voice that the father calling to the son might ever be repeating the great preacher's righteous sentence.

2. But he who so sternly forbore to speak could at length forbear no longer. The times were rotten. Not the little lad Shear Jashubh's name alone suffices for a sign; out from the father's soul, full to breaking with God's indignation, must break forth His judgment. Now shall there burst

over Jerusalem the most terrible oracle of judgment that the literature of the world contains. Scorn is the theme and fulness of all the prophecies in this section.

3. They open with the quotation of a well-known hope for Zion, the utterance of an earlier prophetic voice (ii. 2-5). But when Isaiah has quoted, he turns from the hope for light from Zion to lighten all peoples, and pictures the sad reality, all superstition, all folly, all bad. He may have once shared the fair hope, but now, if Amos has condemned older sanctuaries, Isaiah will utterly condemn this newer and dearer one; he scorns the hollow claim that Jehovah is manifest here. The torrent of awful eloquence rolls on, condemning wealth, luxury, state, religion, men, women, all that is fair with all that is strong, for all is perverted. From the fierce verdict his thought turns back again to the sanctuary; and there, for a moment, the bitter scorn, as if exhausted, rests in a hope which is itself bitterness. When men are dead, then God can create life. "When once Jehovah shall have blown a burning and righteous wind across the sanctuary hill, to burn away the badness of her best—even her daughters—then at the last there may float over every home of the small remnant in Zion the smoky, flaming sign of reverential feasting. Then every home shall be a pure sanctuary of Jehovah, and every hearth His altar."

The seer turns to song. He would gladly woo to God as he sings of Zion, that richest of vineyard hills. But in vain. All lavish care in hope of delicious fruit there has only been rewarded with bunches of bitter things. Therefore the love-song fades away, and the dirge of woe! woe! woe! begins. At the last there is heard in the oracle only a low moan like the moaning of the cold sea. The prophecy is all dark; the prophet's own soul is in darkness, for the prophet of judgment must himself sit down in the gloom he brings. Isaiah's prophesying has not brought life, but death; his own soul seems in utter despair.

4. Observe one feature of the language of this section. Isaiah seems determined to push aside all suggestion of the holiness or devotion of God and men. Only twice in all these discourses does he use the words, "The Holy One of Israel," and only twice more does he use the word "holy." Like Amos, he avoids the thought. In chap. iv. 3 it is when he has uttered the sentence of death on all who sin, and has pictured Zion's desolate gates, that he allows a hope, an uncertain hope indeed, that then all who are left alive by the scourge of Jerusalem may be called holy, and be filled with devotion to their God. In chap. v. 16 is spoken the dread faith that when proud men are all laid low, then Jehovah's holiness, His devotion, shall be manifested in the unwavering firmness of His awful judgments. In verse 19 of the same chapter the prophet records the blasphemous sneer of the debauchee over God's name, "The Holy One." "Let this devoted God use more speed in His devoted work," they cry, not knowing that the long-suffering of God is their life. Then, with indignation and words that wax white-hot, Isaiah calls down quick destruction on "such as have despised the Holy One of Israel." These four utterances of the word tell how Isaiah here counts Jehovah's love a jewel far too precious to come near evil men. He thinks of this God as devoted indeed, but devoted only to the good. But the hottest fire burns low at length, and Isaiah's preaching of justice ends in failure and gloom. Yet the dawn was near, for man's extremity is God's opportunity.

§ 5. *The hour of change.*

The darkness that can be felt in Isaiah's closing sentences in chap. v. is only the shadow of the darker reality recorded in the picture of affairs and men in chap. vii. Prof. de Lagarde shows (Semitica I. 12) that chaps. vii. to ix. are only a cento formed of lines from many separate oracles uttered, some in the very gloomiest days, and some again as the joyous songs of firmest faith and expectation, and even actual possession of blessing. The cento is arranged as a pæan of joy indeed, and yet one can easily read in it the story of the dark hours before the dawn.

(1) It was about the year 735 B.C. that the weak, harem-guided king Ahaz was threatened by two strong allied tribes. Syria and Samaria exulted in the temporary absence of the Assyrian over-lord, Tiglath-Pileser, and his armies, and they leagued to harry little Judah, and, if possible, to depose its chief, Ahaz. The people of Jerusalem trembled like the leaves of the forest in the wind. Their city was indeed always comparatively safe from the great invaders, the Assyrians or the Egyptians, or the Scythians in later days, for it lay among the hills away from the great road along the coast; and besides, it was of little worth compared, for example, with Samaria and Damascus, both luxuriantly rich, and both right upon the great road besides. But safety from giants was not safety from dwarfs; and the two small allies knew no bigger quarry than little Judah nestling among the rocks. We may as well note by the way that the great story of revelation is not at all a story of mighty kings and countries, but of little folk; for these indeed, "and base things of the world, and things which are despised, hath God chosen, yea, and things which are not, to bring to nought things which are."

(2) It was in such a troubled juncture of affairs that there came to Isaiah one of the most priceless conceptions the world has known. He was ever tender to his fellows when trouble fell upon them. The man who thundered threatenings against Zion's wrongdoing in sunny days sprang to the defence against a foreign foe; for the same strength was strong against every enemy, whether from within or without. Therefore, on a day when Ahaz examined his defences, Isaiah went out to meet him with counsel and with cheer. It was

a heavy task to inspire this heartless prince; it was all the heavier that the prophet came leading by the hand his boy Shear-Jashubh, the silent foretoken of God's coming judgment. Yet this Amos-like symbol was unlikely to win the careless Ahaz; it was a far more significant omen that it was a whispering of the Spirit within him that moved Isaiah to take the lad. God was near to help; yes, even the God of judgment was bringing help.

(3) Isaiah's first words were the stern old Amosian command repeated, "Seek Jehovah, and thou shalt live." Believe that thou *shalt* be delivered. Isaiah's faith was absolute that this deliverance would come. He believed that Jehovah was simply determined to save, and that at all costs He would. Whatever sign of this a man might look for would certainly take place.

Ahaz refused to ask any sign. Isaiah was indignant, and in the fulness of his sense of his Divine mission, and of the Divine presence within himself, he poured forth his indignation as the very anger of God. Rev. G. A. Smith points out with force (Isaiah, 114) that Isaiah was here discovering and exposing an unpatriotic guilty secret of the king's, viz., his plan to hire great Assyria to destroy the little allied enemies by giving his own independence and his country's freedom to Assyria as price. This was the political or material meaning, as we may say, of the acts of the king and of the prophet. We must look what their religious meaning was.

(4) Isaiah first tried to persuade Ahaz by the promise that he should see *any* physical phenomenon, whatsoever he should choose. We may naturally ask, was this a worthy method of persuasion to godliness, to goodness, to trust in God? It is certainly true that the influence of Christ through these nineteen centuries has gradually done away this method. It is not employed. We do not bid men ask signs. We are decidedly not concerned to teach men the immense power of the great Spirit who controls them. They

believe in that, and tremble. We rather seek to teach them the character of that Spirit, that he is the Father of Jesus. So we seek to woo them to trust Him, to love Him, to be good.

Of course, to produce a change in character we must work on the will. We must hold up—a motive for the soul's choice? Yes, but more. We must present such a motive that the very choice of it will be goodness itself. To make a soul good you hold up the best, that is, God. The vision of Him, the choice of Him, the love of Him is good; it is conversion, salvation, goodness, life. The rejection of Him is inexplicable; it is sin.

This is certainly true. But how is a soul to see God so as to choose Him. We must see a revelation of Him. The sense of His presence must come to us along the channel of —of what?—simply said, of ourselves. And that to some men, in some ages, may be "signs." Suppose that the highest apprehension of God must come by way of thought, even that must be *our* thought, linked wondrously all round with all the other characteristics of the human soul, its affections and all its sensations. So to-day. So nineteen centuries ago. One remarkable fact in the Word's becoming flesh is this, that we can get at Jesus only through media of a very material nature. So then in Isaiah's day the command to ask for a sign was the speech wherein an utter confidence in the love of Jehovah reached out to woo the soul of Ahaz to like trust.

We may go further. The prophet made it possible, says some one, for Ahaz to ask some impossible sign, and so turn Isaiah, and even all religious faith, to ridicule. Be it remarked, however, that men of faith are, after all, not very often turned to ridicule in this world. God does take care of them. But in this case one may suggest that Isaiah should rather have proposed, "Ask any sign which a man truly at one with God would ask." This form may seem better, but Isaiah's instinct was more correct. He was himself at one with God; he would not have asked any foolish sign. And he loved Ahaz, and was eager to make the king happy; in pure, honest goodness he expected the man to be good too. He was pure in heart, and he saw God; and he was not deceived. If this seem all too unreal, and such a man too simple for a prophet who ought, think some, to be astute, let us remember that Isaiah had himself received a vision, a sign that was to him as transcendently great as any sign Ahaz could possibly ask. He had learned that Jehovah dwelt in Zion to be gracious there even to the unclean, and even to cleanse them and trust them with His work. The faith coined into the golden word Immanuel was born in the temple-vision. Isaiah saw there God gracious in Zion.

(5) And Ahaz said, "I am not going to ask, and I am not to keep treating Jehovah as a waverer." The language might have come from a saint. It is well that in thinking through the history of the religion of the people, we are not compelled to give verdict on Ahaz: guilty or not guilty. We are concerned with the story of religion in the nation, and may be uncertain here and there concerning individual sins. But Isaiah's verdict in this story was emphatically, "Guilty," and the main point of his indictment of the king was not carelessness, for Ahaz was anxiously careful, but it was refusal to let Jehovah act in the way He purposed to act, namely, to "give a sign." This was what Isaiah called wearisome to God. The prophet was all overwhelmed and filled with his new sense of the grace of God that reveals itself in signs, in a sign, in Zion. It was this sense that the king refused; so he refused what to the prophet was the very word of God. To Isaiah's faith, Jehovah was with him, his speech was Jehovah's word; the thoughts of Isaiah were the revelations of Jehovah, God of Israel.

We have here, then, a religious fact in Isaiah's experience which might and did become a turning-point in the history of the people. But we have more. The king's opposition shows that such faith in Zion's special protection by Jehovah was a new thing. This will be confirmed by other indications as we proceed. The faith in Zion as the exclusive choice of Jehovah, His sanctuary, His pledge of His gracious saving love for Israel, began with Isaiah. A hope there had been before, and Isaiah tells us of it; but now came the satisfying revelation. He grasped the idea, and made it all in all for himself, until the nation too accepted it as their central faith.

(6) The sign which Isaiah finally gave to Ahaz, "A virgin shall conceive and bear a son, and call his name Immanuel, and ere he be grown a lad this Judah shall be all safe, although thou, Ahaz, be discomfited"—this is in essential meaning the same as the sign Isaiah had had in the temple vision. It is certainly also framed in that setting which Isaiah loved so well, the name and life and value of a child as a gift from God. But its meaning was, Jehovah is a God who comes to the wrongdoers in Zion to forgive them. Abide in Zion and be true to it, for there God gives life. Elsewhere is death.

§ 6. *The growth of the new faith.*

A striking side-light confirming the opinion that the Zion faith was new appears in chap. xvii., the passage next in chronological order after chaps. vii. to ix. There we find Isaiah declaring the austere Amosian faith: "In that day men shall trust no altars, nor any other symbols;" but he adds to that negation the kernel of the new faith: But all shall look to Him whose name and nature are "the Maker." For the God of all power is the Devoted One of Israel, Israel's saving God.

Now watch the rapid growth of the faith. Ten years sped away, and in 727 B.C. Ahaz lay dead. Then Isaiah wrote a significant oracle, which we find in chap. xiv. 28 and xxviii. 16. The Philistines, always troublesome, thought to rob Judah when her prince had fallen and his son Hezekiah was but a boy. Mourning and danger hung round the city. Perhaps the boy-king sent to the prophet, who became his close friend, to seek some counsel or some cheer. Then the brave prophet took up his parable, and sang back this message—

> Rejoice not, all Philistia,
> Though the striker's rod hath broken,
> For out of the Nahash root there riseth ever a David seed.
> (Fear not) For Jehovah is founding Zion.
> And there may rest quietly all the loved meek ones.

Our English versions write here, "Jehovah hath founded Zion," but the text is uncertain. The correct meaning we get from chap. xxviii. 16, where the same oracle is repeated five years later and in unquestioned form. Some may say, How could Isaiah write, "Jehovah is founding Zion"? He must have said, "Jehovah has founded Zion." But since Isaiah certainly wrote in 722, "Jehovah is founding Zion," then he could say it more easily in 727, and we may decide that the doubtful words of xiv. 28, which allow this meaning, very certainly did carry it when Isaiah spoke.

A word on the later passage in chap. xxviii. to point out the force of the oracle. Samaria had broken away from the Assyrian vassalage and paid no more tribute. Salman-Assur and Sargon were hastening from the east and closing in their circles round the doomed city. None the less within whirled the mad carouse of the vintage feast. The wine waggons rolled in from the fat vales and sunny slopes about the fair hill-top city, and reckless riot drowned every anxious voice. The senses of people and priests, prophets and princes, were dazed. Isaiah was witnessing like rioting in Jerusalem. He implored his countrymen to learn wisdom from Samaria's madness, for her danger from Assyria might easily become their own. Yet over their cups the very seers flung filthy sneers at their chief, while the priests of Zion staggered to their sacrificial prayer. "We are safe." they cry, "for are not here in our bacchanal march and dance the grim ghouls and gods of night and dark, of Sheol and death itself." The demons were alive, for they were masked men. They shout, "Ha! ha! these devils would deceive Jehovah Himself. Under falsehood have we hidden. If the Assyrian scourge came, he would never find us." We may not stay now to picture the scene of filthy mockery that follows, and is quite obscured in our English version. Enough to tell here how Isaiah thunders the awful and well-known talisman of Fate, "a decree and a doom" that always makes the stoutest quail before the prophet of Jehovah, whom they count the God of Fate. But now when a hearing is gained by fear the great-hearted prophet pours out his oracle of salvation. The great faith speaks. Jehovah is founding Zion, and he who believes shall not make haste.

To Isaiah these years were the foundation days of the sanctuary in Zion. He was steadily entering into this joyful faith, and surely the day when a man plants his foot on a foundation faith is the day when God founds that faith for that man. He was setting it too in brightest, winsome beauty before his countrymen for their grasp and their joy, and the centuries ever since have proved that this belief is a foundation stone of Hebraism.

§ 7. *The changed faith at the fall of Samaria.*

Prof. Guthe (*Zukunftsbild des Jesaias*, appx.) has shown reason for assigning the "oration against Assyria," contained in chaps. x. and xi. to 710 B.C., ten years later than the date which had become currently adopted. In any case Isaiah fears that Sargon will swoop down from the north to desolate Judah and destroy Jerusalem. Now, as always, Isaiah's courage rises with danger. His faith in Zion's safety bursts out in sublime utterance. Has Assyria "shaken the spear against God's beloved Zion? The people that dwell there are safe, who stay themselves firmly on Jehovah, Israel's devoted God." The fearfully looked for danger, and the proudly looked for triumph are sung in high rhapsody in the close of chap. x. "The hosts of devastation may speed on, until on yonder heights of Anathoth the thousand spears stand thick like the forests on Lebanon; but there shall the Great Forester, Jehovah, hew every stem to earth. All shall fall." Here are Isaiah's voice and power in climax.

The raptured seer marches on into that grand vision of Incarnation which has been a weary world's dream and psalm, chaps. xi. xii.; and here the faith we are tracing stands out like a mountain-top:—

> When the spears are all hewed down,
> When Jehovah's forest's growing,
> Where God's living wind is blowing,
> Hurt and death shall be unknown
> In Zion.

The vision of the coming golden age starts questions for study later on. Our present quest is satisfied in that declaration of perfect safety for the holy hill of Zion; and even if chap. xii. should ever be clearly traced to another later hand than Isaiah's, it adds an echo of his controlling gospel in its chorus, "Cry out and shout, thou inhabitant of Zion, for great is the Holy One of Israel in the midst of thee."

§ 8. *Thence to the end.*

We know comparatively little of Isaiah's work during most of the years of Hezekiah's reign from 727 to 700 B.C. Only a few words have come from the years 727 and 721, perhaps from 710, and then more fully from 705 to 700. But if we can rely upon the suggestions of the story in the book of Chronicles, 2 Chron. xxix. *ff*., then Isaiah's eloquence concerning Zion bore early fruit, and the reformation under Josiah in 622, with its exaltation of Zion, was the second and not the first royal effort to establish Isaiah's faith as the state doctrine. And even if, on the other hand, we cannot rely on the chronicler, but must consider that he read into Hezekiah's days the ways of centuries later, still it is remarkable that he felt how appropriate such a royal establishment of Zion would have been in the days of Isaiah.

But amid the terrors of Sennacherib's invasions, 705–700 B.C., the prophet's voice rang out clear and full of cheer. In chaps. xxix., xxx., xxxi., xxxiii., you read his brave, strong alarum, and every utterance is keyed on the old note of faith, "Zion is safe." The Zion sanctuary cannot be hurt, cries Isaiah; the place chosen of Jehovah for His gracious abode on earth is Judah's pledge and place of safety.

(1) In chap. xxix. he sings of Ariel, God's altar-hearth. Her halls, where Judah's families meet for sacred feasting, are in distress; but distress more bitter shall come on those who fight against Mount Zion. For, after all, it is Jehovah's hand that visits her with distress, and His hand will bring relief. The kernel of the faith lies in the words, "The poor among men shall rejoice in the Holy One of Israel," ver. 19; Jacob's face shall not wax pale, but he shall sanctify Jehovah's name, *i.e.*, he shall count Jehovah's character full of devotion. He shall sanctify the Holy One of Israel, *i.e.*, he shall know Jehovah's devotion and live in the faith of it.

In chap. xxx. those who flee from Zion to a fancied safety in Egypt are told their folly. The saving love of Jehovah is the ever-recurring theme of the wooing song. One passage especially (ver. 18) is of striking beauty in its contrast with the terrible judgment of earlier days. The young prophet of judgment cried, ii. 17, v. 16—

> Hide thee, hide in the dust, for terror of Jehovah,
> He will exalt Himself by thine abasement.

But now the prophet of grace whispers—

> He longs to bless, He patient waits to save,
> Until at last, impatient grown, He will arise—
> Yet not to slay,—to woo and win.
> He will exalt Himself by thy salvation.

(2) Among all the utterances of these invasion years perhaps the most beautiful are in chap. xxxi. 4–5; few indeed even of Isaiah's sayings have so exquisite a grace. With majestic strength of figure as of faith he writes—

> Like as a lion sallies out against a shepherd-band,
> Knowing no fear,
> So shall Jehovah come, Creator of all hosts,
> To fight, to save Mount Zion from Assyria.

But now, as if his figure and his tone might seem too fierce to soothe the timid folk he loves, he writes on—

> Like parent birds that flutter to and fro over their nest with cries and courage strange,
> When enemies are near,
> So doth Omnipotent Jehovah hover o'er Jerusalem
> Defending and delivering.
> Let Asshur mark the smoky cloud o'er Zion's altar fire!
> That is Jehovah's ensign;
> His home is there, and Judah's
> Zion is safe. Asshur shall fear and fail.

(3) The siege grew close and hot, as we read in chap. xxxvii. Isaiah's confidence breaks out in a song of glee—

> O Prince of Asshur, hear—
> The virgin Zion, daughter of Jehovah,
> God's fair beloved one, despiseth thee.
> Stay now the battle-noise, and listen to her merry taunt;
> She shakes her head in laughter at thee.

Such was the first strong impulse to fearlessness. But the danger grew, and Isaiah seems to have found that the city must be taken. His brave soul counts quickly over all the resources of the hour, and like a general, he marks out at once the new line of outlook and of action. Only, in it all there remains the one unchanging faith—Zion shall not fail. He issues his oracle—his and God's—for to him his thought and God's are one. He cries, "Even out of the bruised city shall a remnant be saved; and they that escape shall be a seed to fill the land again with fruit, with life, with men of Zion. The zeal of Jehovah, Lord of hosts, will do this," for our pledged Lord would be no God at all had He no people, or were His promise and His power vain. He will do this.

But this is the voice *de profundis;* the seer shall rise to greater things. The siege waxes hotter; so does Isaiah's excited spirit rise. Then he cries, Thus hath said Jehovah—

I will defend this city and deliver it;
For mine own sake, and for my servant David's sake.

The lightness of laughter is not there, nor is it on the fearless seaman's brow in the fiercest storm; but there is the short strong word, while breath is held and death is defeated. We read in independent records, written far away on Tigris and in Greece, that the order of Providence did coincide even with the material expectation of Isaiah. Sennacherib lifted his siege and left Zion safe. But this material event was a light thing compared with the highest of Isaiah's hopes for Zion. That is manifest in the final passage we have to touch.

(4) The final poem was probably chap. xxxiii., written, one can easily see, after the Assyrians and danger had gone. The faith in Zion is its chief theme.

Now hath Jehovah gotten Himself exalted, for He inhabiteth a lofty place. Again and again (ever) hath He filled Zion with justice and stability.

. . . . . .

Sinful people have indeed been trembling in Zion. They fear they'll die and burn in Hinnom; they fear war, hunger slavery.

> But only let thy soul gaze on Zion,
> 'Tis the place of our tryst with Jehovah.
> Look, and with bodily eye behold Jerusalem!
> There is a pasture free from fears,
> There is a shepherd's tent that's never struck;
> Her stakes are never drawn,
> Her cords are never broken.
> For do ye doubt Jehovah's there?
> Is not He our Judge, our Guide, our King?
> But His mind is to save us.
> O! let none who dwell in Zion say, I am sick.
> From the people who abide there iniquity is taken away.

Here are Isaiah's highest words. This is man's holiest hope and God's holiest purpose, forgiveness. It was this greatest need of men that the prophet felt, and God was with the soul that felt it; it was this high gift of God his soul grasped, and God breathed the faith that grasped it. And the revelation to the senses, whereby alone a son of man in Isaiah's day could think this faith and speak it to his fellows, was Zion. In that sanctuary the soul of Isaiah saw a vision of the present healing Jehovah, and the longing heart trusted God. Hosea's hunger for some atonement whereby God should not return to destroy the sinful city was answered. God had told men another sentence from the eternal tale of love; men had gained a new depth of vision into the infinite heart of God.

Such is the story of Isaiah, his life-quest, and his finding, as we see them along one principal line of his being.

CHAPTER II.

ANALYSIS OF THE ORACLES OF ISAIAH IN JERUSALEM, IN CHRONOLOGICAL ARRANGEMENT.

INTEREST is deepening fast and wide in those parts of the Bible which we are discussing. Works on individual parts and treatises on various phases of them are multiplying. Sermons are signs of the people's thinking, and therefore we may be sure the people are thinking of Isaiah. But the sermon hearer and reader are often anxious over the question of the order of the oracles of our prophet, and are ready to lose heart over this best preacher more than over less valuable books.

Prof. Driver's "Introduction to the Old Testament," pp. 194–217, provides large information and excellent counsel in explanation of the prophet's labyrinth, and that treatise is in every way of great value.

The following analysis could not repeat all the reasons for its arrangement; they would be few and feeble reasons if they could be so easily rehearsed. But the lines of study can be suggested.

The reasons depend largely on the contents of the chapters themselves. The good-natured proposal to submit the various questions of Hebrew literature to persons who are masters of the English versions only, revised or authorised, &c., is a good proposal, because it will induce some men to master the English versions. These men will at once discover the insufficiency of those versions. Of course a man who can read Goethe's Faust in English translations only has but a slight knowledge of the story of German literature, its unfolding, its bloom, its richest words. The faithful student of good translations only can know little of he splendour and the keen word and wit and pathos and majesty of the Greek dramatists and philosophers, or of Herodotus and Homer. Such readers crop at the fringe of the pasture; the soul that looks out from the old speech is veiled, and those readers discover it. So with Hebrew literature. The Hebrew reader alone knows its meaning. We have an English Isaiah indeed, who is even held infallible, but he is not the Hebrew Isaiah.

There are external sources of light on the dates of Isaiah's utterances. In his own day great libraries were being written in Assyria, Babylonia, and Egypt, also on enduring tablets, and we are reading those very tablets to-day. They were written quite independently of the Hebrews, many many hundreds of miles away from them, by men who had indeed Palestine within their range of vision, but knew it for one very small land amongst a host of like little lands sometimes tributary to their own great states. They could err, certainly, but they were not likely to be always wrong, even when their statements conflict with Hebrew opinion. Let us gather in brief the general information gained from these tablets which is necessary for our task, and arrange a general outline of chronology ere we proceed to the analysis of our prophet.

§ 1. *The Assyrian canon.*

1. The little book on the Assyrian canon, written by the late George Smith (The Eponym Canon), gives a valuable brief account of the Assyrian libraries, their methods and records. A still more valuable guide in the matter is Prof. Schrader's "Old Testament and the Cuneiform Inscriptions," translated by Prof. Whitehouse.

The languages of the Euphrates valley need not be described here, nor yet the somewhat hieroglyphic style of writing with letters made up of systems of marks shaped like arrow-heads. These cuneiform marks might be made by pressing a square chisel into the clay tablet before baking, or by driving it into a stone slab, according as the country furnished slabs, in the upper valley-lands of Assyria, or the clay, as in the lower alluvial plains of Babylon.

More remarkable is the wide range of records covered by these old libraries. In Isaiah's day writers were busy at works on religion, law, language, history, or chronicles, astronomy, arts, commerce, and the like. And they were busy further in reproducing older libraries written from time to time in many previous centuries. Here we reach the point of finest interest. The Assyrians had a regular system of dating all their documents and the events they described. Just as Romans had their era A.U.C., and as we have our Christian era, and mark the date of an event by saying that it happened in such and such a year B.C., *i.e.*, before Christ, or in such a year of our Lord A.D., *i.e.*, in the year number so and so after the birth of our Lord, similarly did they, making a little era of each emperor's reign.

A closer analogy is the Olympiad system of the Greeks, but the closest furnished by is the method of dating our Acts of Parliament. We say Act 38 Victoria, and we mean the volume of Acts passed in the 38th year of Her Majesty's reign, *i.e.*, in the year 1874 A.D. The Assyrians named the years, not by numbers, but after certain officers of state in regular order, and they dated their chronicles of events by saying such and such a thing happened in the year of officer so and so under emperor so and so. Still we should be helpless but for two fortunate facts. One is that there have been found in the libraries careful tables of the names of the years, and not one table, but several, all agreeing. These form calendars of reference for us when we wish to read a dated document. But it is more important that the Assyrians recorded eclipses in their chronicles, and dated the year, officer, and king in whose days these eclipses occurred. We know when all these eclipses happened according to our reckoning, and can thus readily read all the Assyrian dates in our own style. The astronomical care of the Assyrians warrants us in putting much confidence in all their calculated records. Political pride or religious prejudice may have led them to exaggerate their gods' honours and their own, but they are not likely to trifle with dates.

These are not the only records. Some come from Egyptian sources, notably the so-called Ptolemaic Canon (κανὼν βασιλέων), a chronological work of the Alexandrian philosopher Ptolemy, A.D. 139–161.

§ 2. *Chronological outline.*

Let us note the main events of certain noted years.

B.C. 2500.—Thus early was there regular government in Elam, the south-eastern part of the Assyro-Babylonian region to the north-west of the Persian Gulf. The peoples and their speech were probably of the Turanian or central Asiatic sort. This was the so-called Accadian element in the later Assyro-Babylonian language. The Assyrian emperors called themselves princes of Accad and Sumir. The two words seem to have been the designations of the early Turanian inhabitants, "Accad," of the hill-folk, and "Sumir," of the river-folk, and the title was kept, as we keep the old word "British."

In the course of the next thousand years there was probably an invasion of men and manners, of sovereignty and of speech, from the Semitic lands of the south-west, especially Arabia. These were the Casdim (Hebrew name) or Chaldeans (Assyrian and Greek name). This made the later Assyro-Babylonian nations a virtual part of the family which contained the Hebrews and their brother Canaanites. The centre of this new half-Semitic people was in the southern alluvial plains of the united Euphrates and Tigris. This was the old and at first independent Babylon.

B.C. 1500.—A colony of early Babylon moved away up the rocky Tigris valley (*cf.* Gen. x. 11), and by this date became independent of the mother Babylon, and in the ninth century B.C. ruled over her. A famous king was Salman-Assur I. about 1300 B.C. Doubtless the new mountain region was securer than the old plain from all attack, and furnished besides sturdier warriors and thinkers to frame the future world monarchy. These are the beginnings. It is not necessary for us to trace the various fortunes onwards to Isaiah's time. These can be read in various works. The fact of immediate interest for us is the chronological spirit of those peoples, and the aid they give us in arranging the order of events in their day. We may sum up the matter in the words of Mr. George Smith, "Assyrian Eponym Canon," p. 19: "It is evident from the Assyrian inscriptions that there was a regular chronological computation in Babylonia reaching up at least to the beginning of the twenty-third century B.C., and in Assyria to at least the nineteenth century B.C. . . . If the Assyrians knew the dates of events more than 2000 years B.C., we may safely trust them with reference to the comparatively modern period of the Hebrew kings."

We pass to years and events which concern the Hebrew people and the prophets directly.

B.C. 850.—Salman-Assur II. of Assyria made an expedition to Hamath and defeated Benhadad of Damascus and his allies, including an Ahab. Elijah's work was going on.

B.C. 845.—Jehu overthrew the Omri dynasty of Israel.

B.C. 842.—Salman-Assur made another expedition to Lebanon, defeated Hazael of Damascus, and took "tribute from *Jehu, son of Omri,* silver, gold, bowls of gold, cups of gold, bottles of gold, vessels of gold, maces, royal utensils, rods of wood" (Schrader, C. I. & O. T., i, 199).

B.C. 790.—About this date Jeroboam II. of Israel must have begun to rule, and shortly after him, say 780, Uzziah of Judah. Each ruled some forty years or more.

About B.C. 780 Salman-Assur III. was warring against Tyre, Sidon, Omri, Edom, and Philistia, overwhelming with terror all lands towards the great sea of the setting sun, and carrying off their treasures. Here is the evident occasion of the warnings of all the prophets from Amos to Isaiah.

B.C. 763.—The Assyrian Canon records two events in this year, named after Esdu-sarabe, governor of Gozan in the reign of Assur-daan III. One event was a revolt in the city of Assur. The second record, of first importance to us, is that "in the month Sivan the sun was eclipsed." To be more exact, let us say that the Canon records an important eclipse visible in Assyria in a year which must have fallen about the date 763 B.C., as we know from the general sequence of events. But our astronomers tell us that an important eclipse happened on the 15th of June 763, and affected most severely an area reaching from Sicily to Mount Ararat. We conclude that this Canon-year, Esdu-sarabe, with its events, was the year 763 B.C., and we reckon backwards and forwards from this as a known point in Assyrian chronology.

B.C. 745.—There was a revolution in Assyria. The old reigning dynasty was deposed, and another begun by Tiglath-Pil-Assur.[1]

About B.C. 743-740 Tiglath-Pil-Assur II. taxed Rezin, king of Syria, very heavily.

B.C. 750 onwards.—Israel was ruled by Menahem, Pekahiah, Pekah, one after the other, down to 730.

About B.C. 738 Tiglath-Pil-Assur helped Azariah (Uzziah) of Judah, and enslaved whole bands of the enemies of Judah,

---

[1] Note the possible relations of the first two parts of his name. *Cf.* Tiglath with Di-ig-lat and Hidiglat of the Inscriptions, and Hiddiqel (Gen. i. 14), Assyrian names of the river Tigris. Pil seems perhaps equivalent to the name Phul given to this very king in 2 Kings xv. 19.

taking heavy tribute also from them, and among others from Rezin of Syria and Menahem of Samaria. At this date Judah's trouble was calling Isaiah from his stern oracles of judgment to the new gracious gospel of safety and forgiveness for Zion.

About 734–722 the same Assyrian warrior-king was punishing sorely Syria, the Philistines, Arabia, Ammon, Moab, Edom, Israel also with its kings, Pekah and Hoshea, and Judah with its king, Jeho-Ahaz.

B.C. 730–722.—Hoshea was made ruler of Israel by the Assyrians, but soon led his people in revolt. They kept their freedom until the siege of 722–720, which ended in Samaria's destruction and the final captivity of the northern ten tribes.

B.C. 727.—Ahaz died. Hezekiah, a young child, began his reign, which lasted till about 699. Professor Guthe (*Zukunftsbild des Jesaia*, p. 37) holds that Ahaz died in 714, and was then followed by Hezekiah, But cf. W. R. Smith's "Prophets," p. 416.

B.C. 727–722.—Salman-Assur IV. was emperor of Assyria, and perhaps was a less terrible warrior than his father, the founder of his dynasty, for there must have been some such cause for Israel's revolt. He died while Samaria was still in siege, and his fierce follower Sargon destroyed the city.

B.C. 721.—Samaria fell. The northern kingdom was for ever destroyed, its people largely exiled to far-off Assyrian lands, its sanctuaries were broken down, as the book of Judges (chap. xviii. 30) tells us. No wonder that Isaiah's faith grew stronger in Zion the unharmed, the safe. He must have written chap. xxviii. shortly before 721.

B.C. 721–705.—Sargon was Assyrian emperor. He claims that Samaria fell by his hand, although his predecessor had begun the siege. Many suppose that chaps. x. 5–xi. end or xii. end were written just after this destruction, when every one in Jerusalem might well fear that the terrible Sargon would march to the south and ruin Jerusalem next. But the cities named as fallen in chap. x. 9 had not fallen until the year 717 at the earliest. (Arpad fell 740; Damascus, 734; Samaria, 722 or 721; Hamath, 720; Carchemish, 717 B.C.)

B.C. 720.—Sargon defeated Seveh (So), king of Egypt, at the battle of Raphia.

B.C. 715.—He transported foreigners to Samaria, also took tribute from Egypt.

B.C. 711.—Sargon punished Ashdod for rebellion (Isa. xx.), and the records say that the neighbouring princes, doubtless Judah, Moab, and Edom, were then in league with Ashdod. Possibly chaps. x. xi. were written by the prophet then amid fear of an invasion. It is difficult to be quite certain when Isaiah's faith in Zion's safety came to its greatest strength and strongest utterance as recorded in this oracle.

B.C. 710.—He defeated Merodach-Baladan, king of Babylon. From this year Sargon is counted king of Babylon in Egyptian records as well as Assyrian. Merodach escaped with his life, to turn up again after Sargon's death, plotting insurrection against his successor, Sennacherib. Merodach's visit to Hezekiah (Isa. xxxix.), and Isaiah's condemnation of it, are no doubt to be explained by these conflicts.

B.C. 706 or 705.—Sargon was murdered.

B.C. 701.—Sennacherib, the new Assyrian emperor, marched against Judah and Egypt. The note in Isaiah xxxvi. places this in the fourteenth year of Hezekiah. If this be correct, then Hezekiah did begin to reign in 714 B.C. as Gutho holds (see above). The date of Hezekiah's recorded sickness (chap. xxxviii.) is very uncertain, but perhaps we may fix it by counting back fifteen years (xxxviii. 5) from his death, *circa* 695, *i.e.* to the year 709. If we do so, then it may be that Merodach-Baladan paid Hezekiah his visit just after this illness, and soon after his own dethronement by Sargon in Babylon. If so, the pretext was convenient, but the purpose was doubtless to plot revenge against Sargon. Hence Isaiah's keen-eyed and quick disapproval of it.

B.C. 695, or a little later, Hezekiah's death. Isaiah disappears without a comment at the same time. Such a man's death scarcely needs a record. He lived on in his work as few other men do.

B.C. 681.—Sennacherib is killed, and is followed by Assurhaddon, one of her most brilliant rulers (Duncker, Anc. Hist. ii. 283).

B.C. 680.—Manasseh, king of Judah, Hezekiah's successor, is punished by Assyria, and apparently exiled.

B.C. 671.—Manasseh is restored. Meanwhile the Assyrians' hands are full, through conflict with a rising power, Tirhakah, king of Ethiopia (*cf.* Isa. xxxvii. 9).

Later on Amon rules Judah from 642, and Josiah from 640, while Assyria has one more truly great ruler (668-626), Assur-bani-pal, son of Assur-haddon, who is succeeded by his son, the last monarch, the effeminate Assur-idil-ili. Under him Assyria is overthrown by the Babylonians, and the great Assyrian empire ceases for ever, 606 B.C. One lingers fascinated over Duncker's story of those brilliant days from 700-626, vol. ii. 283 and 290, and then feels almost grief over the tale of ruin, ii. 334. From highest might under grandfather and father, the son brought the great nation to its fall and utter extinction.

§ 3. *The analysis proper in outline.*

Following the clue given in our previous study of "Isaiah and Zion" we shall find our way across the maze of great oracles, and see withal how vistas open along other main lines of thought.

1. We may set certain mottoes over Isaiah's work.

(*a*) First, over the whole of his utterances may stand—

יהוה קְדוֹשׁ יִשְׂרָאֵל

"Jehovah is the Devoted One of Israel."

True, Amos had almost spoken it, and Hosea had flung all his hopes upon it in his hour of agony; but Isaiah first wrestled with it, and even against it, then seized it as a discover seizes on a great truth. He saw God; he saw this great fact in God's character, and he declared it with all his power. But this change in the course of his work divides his life into two great periods, as we have seen, and hence we have two other mottoes.

(*b*) Over the first period and its oracles we may write the words—

שְׁאָר יָשׁוּב

"Only a remnant shall return."

The sentence is what a grammarian calls circumstantial. In the ordinary declarative sentence the Hebrew sets his verb first, as the most important matter; but when he leaves this order and sets a noun in the front, as in the present case, then we know he is calling attention to that noun as the most important thing. He means to say, "It is a *remnant* that shall return, and not the whole people," or as above written, "Only a remnant shall return." Mr. Matthew Arnold called this very truly one of Isaiah's great sayings. So it is, but it was inherited by Isaiah from Amos. The defect of Mr. Arnold's beautiful book is its disregard of this descent of faiths, which marks the ceaseless unfolding of truth and life from God on the one hand, and tells on the other of the solidarity of mankind, the unbroken unity of all true men transcending the single and transitory individual.

(c) For the whole of the rest of Isaiah's work after the first gloomy "remnant" oracles the motto is—

$$\text{עִמָּנוּ אֵל}$$

"With us is God."

God—whose very name, El, means that He reacheth out afar to us, whether in beams of light or streams of rain, or gifts of any far-off, hoped-for blessing—God is with us. God—whose very name tells how we lift up our hands to Him, as we reach and plead, or again, proclaim our solemn oaths, yearning towards the place where His glory dwelleth—God is with us.

God—not "the Gods," not that mysterious sum of powers that work on us from every side, appearing so infinite, and yet all one and working together because all ruled by one Lord of all those hosts; not "Elohim," the Gods, but the single one ruling God, El—He is with us.

With us He is in heart, love, and gracious purpose, in the home He loves best and the spot of earth He chooses—in Zion, and in all its true souls, its kings, its prophets, in their children, in the inhabitants of Zion—He is with us.

With us He is, and who can be against us? for no others have Him with them: God is with us.

Such are Isaiah's three great watchwords.

2. The following is a brief outline of the oracles for ready reference as we proceed to their explanation and to a justification of their order:—

Introductory.—Chap. vi. tells of the prophet's original call (B.C. 740); but its deeper lesson, grasped in B.C. 735, causes it to be placed as prelude to the later oracles of grace.

Chap. i. was probably written about 725 B.C.; but its expression of faith in both judgment and grace led the collector to set it as prelude to the whole book.

The first great division is:—

(I.) The Oracles of Judgment:—
Amos-like in character;
Characterised by the motto,
שְׁאָר יָשׁוּב, "Only a remnant shall return."

Oracles uttered probably from 740–735 B.C. These are chaps. ii.–v., and ix. 8–x. 4. They fall into two sections, thus:—

(A.) Chaps. ii.–iv.—Oracles in plain prose form, which can be again subdivided into—

(1) Chap. ii. 1.—A title.
(2) Chap. ii. 2–5.—A text taken from an elder prophet, extolling Judah's possible future.
(3) Chap. ii. 6–8 declares the actual present licentious state.
(4) Chap. ii. 9–iii. 7.—Awful but sublime sentence pronounced.
(5) Chap. iii. 8–15.—The religious kernel of mischief is laid bare, with exhortation to conversion.
(6) Chap. iii. 16–iv. 1.—Woman, who should be best and fairest, is foolishly bad, and shall suffer terribly.
(7) Chap. iv. 2–6.—Only superhuman power can save a remnant, can purify woman, and can make each fireside an altar.

(B.) Chaps. v. 1–25; ix. 8–x. 4; v. 26–30.—Parable and dirge in regular stanzas. The detailed divisions are—

(1) Chap. v. 1–7.—The parable-song of the "vineyard."
(2) Chap. v. 8–24.—A dirge of six woes.
(3) Chap. v. 25; ix. 8–x. 4; v. 26–30.—The chant of the outstretched hand, and anger not turned away.

We turn to the second great division of the book.

II. The Oracles of Grace—
   Hosea-like in character;
   Characterised by the motto,
   עִמָּנוּ אֵל, *Immanu-El*, "With us is God."

These include all the remaining prophecies from 733 B.C. onward. We may distinguish first those proclaimed in the remaining years of the reign of Ahaz, 733–727 B.C., and then those uttered under King Hezekiah in the years 735–700 B.C.

(A.) The new gracious oracles in the days of Ahaz:—

(1) Chap. vi.—The story of Isaiah's original vision of Jehovah, which he had experienced in the temple in the year 740, is now recalled, and written in 733.

(2) Chap. vii., viii., ix. 1–7.—A cento woven of parts of various utterances spoken amid the events that led the prophet up to the new understanding of God's heart. The bits of utterance are set like mosaic in a framework of story, which tells when and how the oracles were given.

(3) Chap. xvii. 1–11.—A final word of wrath against Syria.

(B.) The Oracles of Grace, as they flow on in the days of Hezekiah, from 727–700 B.C.

We must recall here that possibly Hezekiah did not begin to reign until the year 714, as Professor Guthe suggests. If this suggestion be correct, some of the following passages must have been uttered under Ahaz, while those which refer to Ahaz's death as past must be set down later than we mark them here.

We may in any case distinguish first those marked by much anxiety for Zion, although full of faith, and then those of a later date, with a thoroughly triumphant tone.

(I.) First, in the anxious days; and here stand—

(1) Those before Samaria fell.

   (*a*) Perhaps chap. i., a sermon of pain and hope.

(b) Chap. xiv. 28-32.—The dirge over Ahaz' bier; date *circa* 727 B.C. But see discussion later on.

(c) Chaps. xv. and xvi.—Story of Moab's devastation.

(d) Chap. xxviii.—The greatest of all these oracles, just preceding Samaria's ruin. All her brightness is to be swept away. Jerusalem ought to learn wisdom from Samaria's fall, but many will not. Yet Jehovah is founding in Zion a sure refuge. He is the great wise Lord, Guide, Keeper.

(2) When Samaria had just fallen, Isaiah was, like others, in fear lest Jerusalem should be the next prey of the Assyrians. Probably it was in these days that he uttered chaps. x. 5–xi. A few other passages are related to the same circumstances.

(a) Chaps. x. 5–xi.—The fierce challenge to Assyria, and the high faith in golden days and regeneration close at hand.

(b) Possibly also chap. xxii., at least vers. 1-14, belong here. It is likely an utterance of dread of invasion by the conqueror Sargon.

(c) Chap. xxi. may also be set here with its three short oracles, one touching Babylon, a second concerning Edom, and the third speaking of Arabia.

(II.) We turn to the more confident utterances.

(A.) When no danger is near.

(1) Chap. xx.—Symbolic.

(2) Chaps. xxix.-xxxii.

(a) Chap. xxix.—A siege lifted.

(b) Chap. xxx.—Unearths the plot with the Egyptians; then pours out some of the tenderest beauty the book contains (ver. 18 *ff.*).

(c) Chap. xxxi.—Grows more indignant at the foolish trust in Egyptians, who are men, not God (*cf.* Hosea viii. 6); then moves the fearful by the love of God, more tender than love of men, or mother, or brooding bird.

  (*d*) Chap. xxxii.—A joyful song of the peace and goodness Isaiah believes are coming for state, for homes, for field, and for all souls.

(3) Chap. xxiii.—A wail for Tyre.

(B.) Here follow, as the second subdivision, oracles declared amid the siege of Zion.

(1) Chap. xxxiii.—Isaiah rises to the highest height of faith in forgiveness, as he understood it; and such faith does he fearlessly proclaim, although the "everlasting burnings" of the awful enemy blaze all round the city.

(2) Chap. xxxvii. 6, 7, 22-35.—A cry for help and a cry of trembling confidence in Jehovah amid Sennacherib's worst attack. It may be a picture of what Isaiah said, painted by a devoted follower.

(C.) In a third subdivision fall three utterances that in the view of some presuppose the withdrawal of Assyria from Palestine.

(1) Chap. xxi. 1-10.—Prediction that Babylon shall fall before Assyria. Possibly it refers to an earlier siege of Babylon, in Merodach-Baladan's days, and we have given it a place once already above. More likely Isaiah foretold how it would fall when Sennacherib had returned from Palestine to the Euphrates lands.

(2) Chap. xviii.—A song of the fall of Assyria the Great; the great conqueror, shouts Isaiah, shall at last be conquered. Probably the date is 705-700, after Sennacherib's return home. Here falls also chap. xvii. 12-14.

(3) Chap. xix.—Perhaps Isaiah's last oracle. A prophecy that Egypt shall be humbled, and at last shall learn to worship Jehovah, the God of the Israelites. The close has a still larger hope: Assyria too shall be Jehovah's follower, the third with Egypt and Israel. Such faith in salvation

could Isaiah grasp. The date of the words may be even later than 700 B.C. There is no record then that Isaiah died. His words simply worked on; he lives in them.

§ 4. *Description by paraphrase of the substance of Isaiah's preaching, following the analysis given.*

Introductory to the oracles of judgment it is to be noted here:—

1. The text of chap. ii. vers. 2–5 occurs also in Micah iv. 1–4, in a form evidently more original than Isaiah's form of it. It belongs probably to some earlier preacher than Isaiah, and in any case to an earlier date than here.

2. The date of the whole section, as outlined on a previous page, falls most likely in the earlier years of Ahaz, for the luxury, licence, child-rule, harem-rule, and godlessness that Isaiah condemns marked those days more than any others.

3. The verses, chap. ix. 8–x. 4, agree so exactly in poetical form, and in contents, and date allusions, with the whole of chap. v., and especially with vers. 25–30, that Ewald's and Cheyne's replacement of them beside the latter commends itself at once.

I.—PARAPHRASE OF THE ORACLES OF JUDGMENT.

A.—1 and 2.[1]

Have we believed in Judah's lordship over men ?
Have we hoped to lead all men in Jehovah's ways ?
Did we dream of Zion as Great Arbiter,
Whose realm no angry strife shall e'er disturb ?

Alas for the reality !

3.

This Zion learns from all the low-born,
She bargains with all strangers
That she may gain, gain, and have, and have !
Her soul needs a god, so she buys for it—a nothing !

---

[1] The letters and numbers refer to the brief outline given above, p. 191 *ff.*

4 and 5.

Down on your knees, small and great,
Fly to the hills and to the holes!
    The earthquake comes!
Proud looks shall fall, and Jehovah alone
    Shall be exalted in that day.

His day comes, it dawns o'er all your pride,
O'er all your wealth, your strength,
Your empire, and your forces,
Your far-fetched glory and your beauty.
Proud looks shall fall, Jehovah alone
    Shall be exalted in that day.

Ha! look to those rock-caves and graves.
Look! the bats fly out as the little gods are flung in,
Fly! from His terrible shaking,
The whole earth is quaking.

His day is now, and is not yet to come:
All dignity has fled, and here fools rule.
Brother flies from suffering brother, no help is near.
Who makes God weep has already fallen.

6. Chap. iii. 8–iv. 1.

Only too plainly do they their deeds, and earn their hire.
Women and boys give law here.
He who should right us is he who wrongs.
Oh, let Jehovah come as judge!
We know Jehovah's oracle, wherewith He rules the world.
'Tis this, "Why hurt the poor?"
Jehovah loveth beauty; He created it.
But woman's vanity is not woman's beauty.
Nay, it is her shame, and shall be.
Does she think to do kings' work?
Then kings and men shall die all round her,
Till there be none to cover her shame.

7. Chap. iv. 2–6.

In that day of man's death
God alone shall give life.
Our God maketh many a waste to blossom
Where no hand tills and no rain falls.
When the careless all die, then only shall the devoted live.
Storm, wind, and lightning shall sweep out all disgusting traces of the past.
Then over each pure home the hearth-fire's smoke shall rise, the cloudy token of the family feast, Jehovah's best-loved sacrifice.
Then each home shall be a true sanctuary, refuge from all ill.
This is woman's true beauty.

B.—1. Chap. v. 1–7.

Come, music, aid me, that I hold this easily wearied audience.
Let us sing of love and gardens, of the tawny grape, and of the blushing wine.
Told is the tale.
There lies a hopeless and forsaken vineyard,
Once full of promise because 'twas full of toil.
I toiled, I hoped; I've mourned, I've spurned.
'Twas no poor earth-field, 'twas the life of Judah that I cherished.
Judah's love was the wine I vainly longed to drink.
What more was there to do! Naught, naught!
What is there now to do? Make it all naught.
Why cumbereth it the ground? cut down that vine.
        Ah, Israel!
Who, cruel, frustrated the kindly hand of justice.
        Ah, Judah!
I cried ' Be righteous." I hear a cry! 'tis piteous.

The Dirge.—2. Chap. v. 8–24.

Woe to him who would own alone;
When all the land is his own, he shall dwell alone.
Woe to him who devours: Sheol shall devour him.
Woe to the godless, the deceiver, the conceited, to the lover of strong drink, and to the false man.
For the mocked Jehovah is still devoted to righteousness.

THE OUTSTRETCHED ARM.—3. Chap. v. 25–30, and ix. 8–x. 4.

The earthquake shook;
But His anger burned, and His arm was not turned away.
God has sent the Syrian and Philistine war;
But His anger burns on, and His arm is not turned away.

None sees His hand; and they die, die on.
And His anger burns!

'Twas their burning passion that burned them;
Brother devoured brother.
His arm is not yet turned.

Oh, selfish fools! who but God could bless you?
But his anger burns on!

Hark! the roar of the terrible, the hoof of the swift.
Dark grows heaven and earth; there's moaning like the sea.
Hark! thro' the mist and darkness; 'tis the moan of men.
Woe, oh Judah! Woe's me!

Notes in conclusion.

1. The steady progress of thought in these oracles is remarkable. Many Hebrews lack it, and they give trouble to Western readers. Isaiah carries us on like a mountain torrent.

2. The grandeur of conception and the brilliance of imagery that carries it give these chapters splendid power.

3. There is a fineness of diction all through them which can be appreciated only by the Hebrew reader. The characteristic word play of the Semites is present here in its best style.

II.—PARAPHRASE OF THE ORACLES OF GRACE.

(A.) *Under Ahaz.*

1. Chap. vi.—The story of the call is brought to mind amid the darkness just felt, and yet more fully to be pictured. Light breaks in from the new vision of God's heart.

"Jehovah came to me," writes Isaiah, "when I was unclean, in unclean Zion. He made Zion his home, and He touched my lips. I am His, Zion is His, Judah has received from His love the secret of life."

2. Chap. vii. 1–ix. 7.

(*a*) vii. 1–12.—Of Ahaz's trial and failure. Isaiah's first child, Shear-Jashubh, bears before the king in his strange name at once the token of the prophet's faith in Jehovah's commission to himself and also the omen of warning to the king. Ahaz doubts the oracle.

(*b*) vii. 13–16.—The prediction, nevertheless, of God's kind deliverance of the untrustful prince. A second child shall be, by the name he bears, a token of this kindness, even of Jehovah's ever-present help.

(*c*) Chap. vii. 17–25.—A strange interlacing of warning for the David-dynasty, prediction of Assyrian invasion, and assurance of coming comfort for the tillers of the soil.

(*d*) Chap. viii. 1–8.—A third child shall come, and bear in his name a warning of the dread invasion.

(*e*) Chap. viii. 9–20.—The prophet and all his children are the best token of the devotion of Jehovah to Israel, and of His purpose to save. They are the true token, because they carry the living speech of His love.

(*f*) Chap. viii. 21–ix. 7.—The darkest days and souls shall be lighted up by that devoted love. For He will send a fourth child, a David-heir this time, who shall counsel and work and rule righteously, and so establish the kingdom safely for ever.

3. Chap. xvii. 1–11.—Final oracle of wrath against Syria, which has been the tormentor of Judah by its alliance with northern Israel to vex the southern kingdom. The passage fits so well the same occasion as the oracles just described, and fits it alone so exactly, that it is probably of the same date, 733–727 B.C.

> O Damascus, fair city and old, hear the oracle of the All-Creator.
> A ruin for ever shalt thou be; thou and Samaria shall be sheep-pastures.
> A reaped field, a shaken olive, that once was full.
> O Samaria, thou despisest Zion's altar: despise all altars and seek God alone.
> Hear old Amos's oracle.
> Away with thy tree-worship and thy sun-worship.
> Thy anemones of Adonis, and thy vines of Bacchus.
> They shall away . . . and leave thee a ruin-heap.

Isaiah did not foresee the singular power of endurance Damascus was to have.

(B.) *The oracles of grace under Hezekiah* (727–700).

(I.) In the anxious days.

1. Before Samaria's fall.

(*a*) Chap. i.—A discourse of reproach mingled with tenderness. Interwoven in it are both the great characteristics of Isaiah, his early sternness and his later love. It may well have come from the days of transition in the prophet's mind. The desolations described are exactly what we might expect in the end of Ahaz's reign, when the Syro-Samarian alliance had been tormenting Judah, and when the armies of Tiglath-pilassur and Salman-assur, between 740 and 720, had foraged and ravaged in all directions.

> Listen, O earth and all ye heavens, and wonder.
> God poured on this people all His wealth of love,
> And they have only provoked Him to anger.
> O nation, ye are now stricken, invaded, ruined;
> Why not turn to your Great Lover?
> Festivities of sacrifice, formal holydays are of no use:
> Among such a people they only disgust God.
> Be clean, be good, be kind, be reasonable,
> Else Amos's word shall prove true, ye shall die by the sword.
> Hosea's picture of your harlotry and blood, among your very highest, is too true.

Jehovah is wroth; He will burn, He will purify.
There must be righteousness; will only justice bring it?
Turn, else blight shall fall on you, as it can fall even on the trees
    sacred to the gods.

(*b*) Chap. xiv. 28-32.—The dirge over Ahaz's bier. This must have been written in 727 B.C., unless Guthe be right; if so, this chapter and chap. xx., written in 711. are closely related.

The dirge becomes a song of defiance against the Philistines. Ahaz is dead, but the David house dies not. That Nahash-serpent blood and genius which first led the Hebrew people out from childhood into nationality, maturity, shall lead men still. Death comes indeed, and folly comes even worse than death, but life and wisdom rule still. The proof shall be when Assyria ravages the Philistines' coast and their trembling messengers seek help in Jerusalem. Then let all men know our faith that Jehovah is founding Zion as His sacred city of refuge, and His troubled people shall rest safely there.

(*c*) Chaps. xv. and xvi.—A lament for Moab. The passage with its vivid imagery must have been a favourite. Jeremiah quotes it again and again in his oracle on Moab (Jer. xlviii.). It may be, as Duhm thinks, the work of that early Jonah, a generation before Isaiah, who sang of Jehovah's help for the peoples of Canaan wrought by the hand of Jeroboam II. Yet, in any case, Isaiah seems to have re-issued the oracle with his own touches added. Whoever be the writer, he can use play of sounds very skilfully, lighting up as with a bright glint the things he would have you couple or contrast by using for them words of close-related sound.

xv. 1. For Moab in the night falls blight, eternal night.
2-5. Weep, pray; ye terror-stricken, fly.
    6, 9. The springs are dry and desolate.
        The streams shall run blood, for the lions shall crouch
            there.

xvi. 1–5. Who shall save Moab? Send to Zion! She shall tell.
Cry unto Zion for counsel and for care,
For her king and her throne are perfect,
Firm, kind, righteous, just.

6–12. Oh, Moab is proud of her prowess, and haughty of heart.
But woe to her, wailing and weeping and want
Dread Asshur shall bring.
To-day my heart sighs, to-morrow hers too.
She shall come then to Zion, so weary, so late.

13–14. Has to-morrow come harmless? Three years be the term.
Thus sayeth Jehovah.

The characteristic Isaian faith in Jehovah's care for Judah is clearly uttered here. That care is to be seen in symbol in His gifts of safety to Zion and wise strength to David's heir. And that care can shelter other Canaanite tribes from destruction.

(*d*) Chap. xxviii.—Here follows one of the most striking of all Isaiah's discourses. Its imagery and its poetic energy are very fine; the faith is the same as ever, and the sublime utterance of it has made it a household word for the religious for ever.

הַמַּאֲמִין לֹא יָחִישׁ, in old-fashioned phrase—

"He that believeth shall not make haste,"

but in exacter reading—

"That God who plants thee firm
Can never make thee slip."

The date of the utterance is evidently just before the fall of Samaria. It is vintage-time, and the feast of wine-gathering has become a mad carouse in the fair fortress-city. The vine-crowned are wine-drowned, and the coming Assyrians are altogether forgotten. An awful storm of death is near. But it is to Judah that the prophet cries. She too is in the like carouse, and worse, as Isaiah warns her leaders, and even her prophets babble mockery back. The calm reply is first of warning; justice is certain: yet in that justice is wrapped up Jehovah's devotion; He is preparing in Zion a place of safety for all the poor in spirit, and all the trustful, and

>'Tis the man of steady confidence
>Who never slips his hold!

The closing verses are a beautiful argument for the love of Jehovah, shown in His gift of wisdom to the tillers of the soil.

> 1–6. O vaunted crown of Ephraim's debauchees,
> Thou withering sprig of his adorning braveries,
> Wealthy and well-defenced, yet wine-smitten!
> Lo, one of strong grip comes like a hail-burst,
> A horrid ravager, a wide-engulfing wave.
> His host shall level thee.
> Thy gaiety shall he crunch like early fig;
> Then shall Jehovah be the only vaunted crown,
> The Creator of all hosts, the only adornment.
>
> 7–13. But these too, men of Judah, wine-wild wallow.
> Inspired, aye drunk, their prophets:
> They swallow—aye are swallowed.
> They guide, aye blind with drink, they guide.
> They wander off.
> Maundering they wander off from the very cups they seek.
> Seers they!—ay, staggering seers;
> See them tottering to the place of prayer.
> Ugh! their table's spread with . . . vomit
> Filthy! They lie in it.
> Hark, they babble now!
> They have heard my disgusted cry. What have they made of it?
> Alas! only the words "filthy" and "spewing" have they caught,
> And these they roll with relish on their tongues.
> "Ho! ho! And what's he babbling of?

To infants, weanlings, surely he is rattling off
His çau, çau, qaw, qaw, law, law, caw, caw,
Line upon line, time upon time, the stammerer!"
So hear them hoot and mock the voice that spake,
"Come unto Zion, weary ones, and here ye shall have
   rest."
But no! They care not!
Thus do men often turn from friends for spite,
Call their love gall, and perverse choose the worse!
These tipsy mummers shout, "We're safe;
We've death upon our side. Look at his mask.
See the masked devils, Death, Sheol.
As for Assyria, why, they've passed us by. We're safe!
Ha! ha! We cheated them! Ha! ha!"
Oh, listen to the God who loves you, men of Judah;
He's building now a refuge for us.
Every stone He hath tried, each corner's dear to Him.
Oh, hear, and love and live.
That God who plants this Zion firm
Will never bid it fall.
But lies shall fall.
The awful torrent, the engulfing wave, shall sweep away
Thy refuge built on sand. Day after day,
Again, again, again the storm shall rage. Mock thou
   not now.
Ah, drunkard, thy bed is always short for thee,
Thy covering is too narrow for thy shame.
See, Jehovah riseth, rouseth His dread hosts,
Let His dread watchword, well-known, sober thee—

כָּלָה וְנֶחֱרָצָה "Let the decree be done.

Sobered now art thou, tiller of Judah's land!
God's care is known to thee, made known on every
   hand.
Ploughing and levelling, scattering and gathering,
All in due order, who hath taught thee this?
God taught thy fathers, God was thy teacher,
Wondrous wise, wondrous kind; God is thy wondrous
   Friend.
Trust Him, not lies nor the wine gods.

2. Discourses after Samaria had fallen, all still in an anxious strain, but with rising confidence.

(*a*) Chap. x. 5–xi.—The date of this magnificent piece of work is disputed. The older theory was that Isaiah wrote it about 701 B.C., when the Assyrian emperor Sennacherib was marching across Canaan to strike his mortal foe Egypt, and on the way was ravaging many of the little states that had thrown off the Assyrian sovereignty and leagued with Egypt. Judah was one of those leaguers. The story we shall learn more clearly by-and-by; here it is enough to know that Isaiah was no doubt then in great anxiety lest Sennacherib's march from the north should strike Jerusalem. It was once commonly thought that chaps. x. 5–xii. were Isaiah's shout of defiance, and hope rising to sublime rapture in expectation of glories to come instead of any hurt to Zion. This theory is still that of Prof. Driver, *Introd. O. T.*, p. 200. There are, however, many students of the passage, including Prof. Cheyne, who agree that not Sennacherib speaks here, who did not overthrow Samaria and the other states over which Isaiah makes the victor glory, but that Sargon must be meant, who did destroy these, and that, moreover, long before Sennacherib's day. The horrors of the captivity of the northern kingdom must have been all fresh in Isaiah's mind when he wrote of it so vividly as he does, as we shall hear presently.

Further, Professor Guthe does well to point out that the foremost faith in the writer's soul here is not that which filled Isaiah in the latest days, near 700 B.C., but rather does he pour out the hopes he had in earlier years, not indeed in the days of his oracles of judgment, 740–725 B.C., but in the earlier oracles of grace. For Guthe shows that among the oracles of grace themselves there is a progress. At first, says he, the hopes gathered not round Zion alone, but round the heirs of David in Zion. He had great faith in persons when he began to preach his gospel of hope. We know this; we know how he preached of babes as message-bearers, of himself and the children God had given him as signs, of the David-heir as God's own image. This was indeed the highest form of his faith. As years went on he had less confidence in individuals, was "more practical," as some say, but in reality less grandly ideal, less enthusiastic, and certainly less Divine. We shall read this clearly in the oracles which belong undoubtedly to the latest years. He came down from faith in the power of a Spirit to put his faith more in Zion, in a place, in stone and lime, in material things. It was possible for even Isaiah to pass the meridian of his clearest vision of God.

Now it is the highest height of his hopes we hear proclaimed in chap. xi. He does indeed sing of Zion's safety, but his swelling heart yearns out towards another human heart, great, gifted, good, as God's grandest revelation of His ceaseless love. Guthe seems right, and chaps. x. and xi. doubtless belong to the earlier date.

But Guthe holds also that the date, 720 B.C., immediately after Samaria's fall, is too early, because the other states declared to be overthrown were not all overthrown until 717 B.C. He thinks chap. xi., with its strong faith in the Person who should work all safety and joy for the people, may be of earlier date than chap. x.

But the close relation of both chapters to chap. xxviii. is significant, and may not be passed lightly by. The terrible proverb of chap. x. 23 and the allusions of verses 22 and 26 recall at once the same awful proverb-oracle uttered in chap. xxviii. 22, and the imagery of verses 15, 18. Isaiah seems to have hurled forth both these great cries in the same hot hour of danger. Their stamp is the same.

 5-19. Woe! woe to thee, Asshur, mine angry scourge,
   I, Jehovah, wield thee. Thou art not God.
   A cruel-hearted soldier thou, but I'm commander.
   I hear thy boast. Thou fool!
   " I've kings for captains, states for slaves;

As I have done I'll do.
Samaria, Syria, many more I've felled;
I'll fell Jerusalem.
As I have done to Samaria's God,
So will I do to Zion's."
Big boaster, how thou'lt burst.
"I'm wise," sayest thou, "and mighty; I am lord.
I'll gather towns like eggs; no hen shall cackle me
 away."
I heard a swinging axe scolding its swinger,
A saw ordering its sawyer, as it rose and fell;
A sceptre held a king, a rod ruled a soul.
But look, these rods and sceptres, thistles, thorns,
Are all aflame,
Blown to a blaze by the blast of God.
How Jehovah's devotion devoureth.
He burneth forests of sceptres, till one or two
 standing
Totter to sinking like sick men.

20-23. Then let the stricken lean on the striker no more.
O fallen Israel! once countless as sand by the sea,
A remnant shall yet return. My boy She'ar Jashubh
 cries to thee, She'ar Jacob.
The far-reaching God is reaching out arms of love
To thee. "Let the decree be done," saith God.
But His decrees are all devotion to His own.

24-34. Asshur shall fall. God gave, and God shall take away.
O Zion! thou art safe.
Ay, let him march on, till he's close upon us,
A day's march off, or nay, an hour's,
Till all the villagers about us flee in terror.
Lift now thine arm o'er us, O Asshur!
Plant thy spears, a forest of them, 'gainst us.
Rise now, Jehovah, hew that forest down.

xi. 1-5. Now David's time hath come; his plants shall sprout,
In his tree-tops shall rustle the winds of God,
Wise winds that give kings strength,
Bowing their reverent crowns before Jehovah's throne.
Then shall the poor, the meek, stand firm mid honest
 judges.
A good king's breath is life, his girdle truth.

6-9. Come soon, O happy day! Change all creation.
   Make the fierce lion kind, the pretty snake an infant's harmless toy;
   Change them within; breathe in new laws for all,
   Till every clod knows God.
10-16. Wave David's banner high, till all men see.
   And now come Israel's exiled remnants, gather home again.
   From Afric, Asia, Tigris, Nile, fly on wind's wings.
   Come, Ephraim and Judah, one in the past golden day,
   Now one for evermore in the glad golden day to be.
   Dry up the seas that sunder brothers.
   Sea and earth shall know Jehovah,
   And build His glad people's pathway home.

Here we may not include chap. xii. in our description of what is undoubtedly Isaiah's, for many careful students doubt whether he wrote it. It is a most beautiful psalm, full of the very voice of God whispered through a wondrously gifted soul. Whoever wrote it, it was not unfitly placed here to swell the glad psalm.

But its close relation to the song of Miriam in Exodus xv., and its distinct linguistic alliance with Deuteronomy xxxii. and xxxiii., perhaps also with Psalm xc., taken with its unlikeness to Isaiah's style, place it among those controverted works which cannot be truly estimated until our history's guiding lines are learned from the documents which are uncontroverted.

(*b*) Chap. xxii.—There is a siege. Those who understand the danger are on the housetops watching anxiously the besiegers, and the reservoirs are carefully filled. But, like the Samarian bacchanalians above, the people below in hall and street are in loud carnival!

This is madness, blindness in visible danger. But Isaiah exhorts the careful men too; they have looked to walls and water-tanks, but they do not look on God and God's heart, God's devotion to them and His purpose.

Appended is a warning to a "familiar" of the court, a man with an Aramaic name, Shebna, and so a foreigner from Syria, who had got himself into high place and magnificence and power, and was even coveting a tawdry immortality in Jerusalem, building himself a grand tomb there. Isaiah is annoyed; he thunders anathema, and predicts that Shebna shall fall, and be superseded by one Eliakim. The later chapters, xxxvi. 22, &c., seem to record the fulfilment of the threat.

Isaiah's thoroughly human character appears finely here. The intense concern with "persons," which characterises his earlier work, is seen in this personal attack. He rises naturally also to sing of his highest theme, faith in the house of David. Very naturally too did such an oracle, with its personal features, catch the attention of men long after, and furnish language for the writer in the Apocalypse (Rev. iii. 7, 8). The oracle was doubtless spoken in Hezekiah's earlier days.

(*c*) Chap. xxi.—We need not delay over the three oracles here, save to say: (*a*) the first (verses 1–10) warns Babylon of one among its many attacks by Assyria, and its only theological interest for us here is its splendid assertion of the omniscience of Jehovah, Israel's God, who is Lord of all hosts.

(β) Verses 11–12.—The second pictures Edom asking counsel from Jehovah's prophet. Here again is an exalted faith in God's presence with the soul.

(γ) Verses 13–16.—The third predicts Arabia against suffering, starvation, blood, decimation at Assyria's hands. And again Isaiah speaks his profound faith in God's guidance of his thoughts. What the prophet feels and speaks he knows Jehovah thinks and purposes.

All these are of uncertain date, but we may easily conceive them uttered when Sargon was conquering and devastating on every hand, 720–710 B.C.

(II.) Secondly, more confident utterances. And here again we have three subdivisions :—

(A.) Utterances of the perfect assurance in the prophet's soul, and as yet no danger actually near. Most of these oracles seem to imply that Hezekiah has revolted from the Assyrian suzerainty, and many of the people fear that there may be a new invasion to avenge the revolt. The dates are not certain to a year. The whole may have preceded 711 B.C., when Sargon did invade Palestine again and took Ashdod, as we shall see. Or they may have just preceded Sennacherib's fresh invasion and his siege of Jerusalem, about 706 B.C. In any case, we enumerate—

(1) Chap. xx.—A dated oracle. It was uttered in the year of the siege of Ashdod by the armies of Sargon under the command of a "tartan," *i.e.*, a general. Ashdod was twice thus besieged, in the year 711 and in the year 709 B.C. Some men of Judah in their terror thought Egyptian help should be invoked, but Isaiah pours out supreme contempt for all aid from the African states Cush and Miçraim. He uses no euphemisms, but himself performs a rather strong symbolic act, and then plainly interprets it, declaring that men shall remember with blushing for three years to come the shame of the vaunted African helpers.

(2) Chaps. xxix.-xxxii.—We open now one of the most important sections of the book. Canon Driver's description of it is excellent, one of the finest parts of his little book (Driver's *Isaiah*, chap. vi. pp. 55–56, cf. *Introd. O. T.*, p. 212).

Sargon the great emperor has died, after fifteen years of battle and blood from the day in 720 B.C. when Salman-Assur IV. bequeathed him the siege of Samaria. Samaria fell quickly; and then Isaiah expected a siege of Zion. But there was Hamath away in the north to beleaguer, and when very soon, in 720 too, there was war with Egypt, the warpath lay along the level coast of the Philistines to the field of

Raphia, and not across hilly Zion. Later on, about 711, the great king punished Philistia again by a siege of Ashdod, as we have seen; but this time again Judah suffered little, although she had been plotting with Philistia against the common overlord Sargon. Then in far-off Babylon a prince, Merodach-Baladan, had tried, and failed, to make his country free. He had wooed Hezekiah with courtesies in time of his illness, seeking support from Judah; and Isaiah had feared mischief might result from this. Nevertheless the prophet's faith in Judah's safety had all along proved true till now, when, in 703, Sargon died. Sennacherib, who next took the throne, was a more bitter foe than Sargon. If Sargon was a Napoleon, Sennacherib was an Alva.

Those little kingdoms on the south-eastern coast of the Levant had not considered what Sennacherib might be and do, when at the news of Sargon's death they plotted eagerly for freedom. In Babylon too Merodach revolted again; and now all the states in Palestine threw off the yoke, Judah among the rest, all counting on Egypt as their champion if Assyria should turn again upon them.

Isaiah approved of the independence, but not of any alliance with Egypt to defend it.

The four chapters from xxix. to xxxii. are a set of three prophetic proclamations for these times, 705 B.C. and later, each sounding the same keynote and theme in its initial chords, "Ho! ho!! Woe! woe!!" each with skilful rhetoric interweaving denunciation of Egyptian hopes with cheer for the anxious through trust in the devoted Jehovah. In each the tone swells, and the torrent swells more and more cheerful, jubilant, fierce, till the third is a chant of victory over the Assyrian; and then follows as a final coda an exquisite picture of ideal days to come.

(a) Chap. xxix.—A SIEGE LAID AND LIFTED.

(i.) Verses 1-6.—*Jehovah surely causes trouble.*

O altar, altar, round thee David camped, and round thee
    sacred dances whirl.
Round thee shall wailers wail,
For round thee, all around, shall awful Asshur camp.
Down, down, face to the ground, in haste,
The awful sandstorm's on the horizon!
The whirlwind, quaking earth, the dazzling flash!
Men? Asshur? No, not they; 'tis God does this—
The Lord of all hosts, Jehovah, Zion's own God.

(ii.) Verses 7-12.—*Are God's ways a riddle?*

Oh, who shall read the riddle of God?
Shall the hosts that are swept against Zion to-day,
And to-morrow are swept away, away as the sandstorm!
Have they dreamed the purpose of God?
O ye blinded, ye drunken with dread, can ye tell?
Ho, scholar! ho, yeoman! can neither explain?
Can none of you read God's oracle, written in storm?

(iii.) Verses 13-16.—*To deceivers God's ways are a riddle.*

Why are God's ways so dark? Let Him tell:
My ways are known to the men who walk with me
In heart as in words, in love as in rites.
Does God know naught of your secret Egyptian plot?
Can God not see? 'Tis you, fools, are blind.

(iv.) Verses 17-24.—*O trust Him! He will save.*

We need no Egyptian help; our devoted Jehovah will
    speedily help.
Even blind eyes shall see and laugh
When earth herself is free, and full of the riches of God.
For the tyrant Asshur shall pass away;
That vain deceiver, Egypt, shall pass away too;
Likewise all perverters of justice at home.

> O Jacob! beloved of Jehovah, trust in His love!
> Gaze on His work for thee;
> So learn His love for thee.
> Trust that He ruleth all;
> Trusting, thou'lt never fall.
> Then troubled souls shall know and rest;
> Then murmuring hearts shall see God's way is best.

Note how distinctly religious the writer is. He handles politics, it is true, but not as his primary interest. He preaches a method and place for deliverance, but not with a priestly interest, not as a traditional institution. The form he preaches is a new one, and almost an innovation. But Isaiah's pressing points are, "It is our Jehovah that is so powerful," "How wonderful His ways," "How close He walks with men." "How utterly He loves." Isaiah is all absorbed in his gaze on God. God, God he sees, and must declare.

(b) Chap. XXX.—THE FOOLISH USELESSNESS OF THE EGYPT-PLOT DISCLOSED.

(i.) Verses 1-7.—*The plot is well known, and Egypt's worthlessness also.*

> Ho! ho! an oracle, an oracle of God is in our household word,
> "As restless as a child."
> Ay, restless are ye that should counsel well,
> That should sway men, save them!
> Your plans will fail; there's nothing manly, godlike in them.
> Who knows not that your emissaries have been seen
> In Tanis, Dafne, sneaking in shadow of some sphinx.
> Hear plain speech: Egypt is worthless;
> She never helps her allies, save to contempt.
> I'll sing you a song of the hot land,
> Land of the lion's lair;
> Hot biting vipers glide there,
> They'll be your camel and ass

To carry your treasures away—yes, away!
Go there, and be robbed, and bitten, and burned.
Go and get pain; seek help in vain
In proud, idle Egypt.

(ii.) Verses 8–11.—"*You have silenced true guides.*"

Alas for the day that has heard!
Alas for the record, written this day for our children to read
    and to weep!
This people cry, "Tell us no more of Jehovah's devotion."
They say the seer's dream of God is all a dream!
"Let the preacher stop! To Egypt we must go, our only
    hope."

(iii.) Verses 12–17.—*This Egyptian hope will be your ruin.*

But think what that scorned devotion of God to you means.
He moves me to cry to you,
He who trusts mockery will surely be mocked.
As a wall that towers too high falls with a crash,
So falls he who trusts in pride.
What said Jehovah's seer?
"Trust Him. You're safest here.
Cheer all the timid. 'Twill bring yourself cheer."
What then do ye cry?
"Nay, saddle quick; we must fly."
Then saddle horses, camels. Fly!
Fools run in thousands at that cry
From one Assyrian. They'll die! They'll die!

(iv.) Verses 18–26.—"*Yet Jehovah will save.*"

Like one lone tree left of a forest by the storm,
Zion shall stand—nay, not alone;
Jehovah, God with us, waits too.
Waits to be gracious; rises not to shake
The earth, as once we feared, but to breathe grace, love,
    life on us.
Oh, blest are they who put their trust in Him!
In Zion God wipes all tears away. O gracious God!

He may cause siege for reasons known to Him.
We will be His men, brave to fight or wait
His oracle, His whisper, "This is the way, walk in it here."
Oh, bitterly do we lament our leaving Thee, Jehovah,
To worship other deities. Oh! they disgust us now.
For Thou wilt give us rain and grain for beast and man.
Thou art the great Rain-Giver. Thou wilt circle the dry mountain-tops
With water channels. The days shall be too short
To gather all the harvest, but the days themselves
Shall lengthen, and the night be bright as day.
Siege, breach, Jehovah heals it all.

(v.) Verses 17–33.—*Jehovah will overthrow Assyria.*

Lo! Asshur is coming from afar for war.
Lo! Jehovah comes farther; His wrath's fiercer far.
Asshur's war-drum shook nations; God's breath shakes them all.
Ho! a song! a great feast! God thunders His call.
Flash, lightnings! roar, storm-clouds! rain, hail, fall!
Dash Asshur to death!
Now feast, O fire, in Tophet!
'Twere food for Moloch! Faugh, the stink!
Now, flying besiegers, think
Of Jehovah's storm-breath!

(c) Chap. xxxi.—THE EXULTING SONG.

(i.) Verse 1.

Ho, fools! Woe, fools!
Ye trust Egyptian horses, because ye see them.
Ye trust not Jehovah's care, because ye have forgotten it.

(ii.) Verse 2.

Ye are fools: but God is wise.
He ne'er forgets.
When evil helpers ruin foolish men, then God will rise
Never-failing.

(iii.) Verse 3.

Egypt is human, he's not God;
His horses flesh, not spirit!
Oh, trust in God.

(iv.) Verses 4, 5.

The still voice of Jehovah whispers in my soul; hark:
"Like lion o'er his prey, roaring
When shepherds, a band of them, run and shout to frighten
  him.
But he flies not; no, but roars again—
So is Jehovah crouching, guarding Zion."
Again the gentle Spirit whispers; listen:
"Like fluttering parent birds, over their nest
When danger comes, so I, Jehovah, hover,
Shielding and saving Zion."

(v.) Verses 6–9.

Turn, turn back to God:
Fling away little gods, all;
For 'tis Asshur shall fall by the sword of no man, but of God.
Stricken, faint, sick;
Were he a rock, he'd fear and fall.
Thus sayeth Jehovah,
Who shineth in Zion.

(d) Chap. xxxii.—THE GOOD TIME COMING.

(i.) Verses 1–7.

When kings are firm, and princes just,
When each man shields his neighbour,
Then seers shall see, and all men hear
God near them 'mid their labour.
When churls are known, and churls called,
No high-placed thief called honest;
When loud-voiced fools are not held wise,

Nor clever sneerers bravest.
Then quiet safety shall fill all Jehovah's land;
We shall know the power and presence of Jehovah's hand.

(ii.) Verses 8-14.

O women, veiled yet powerful, beware!
Ye trust in men, and that is womanly;
But men are not almighty,
And least of all, when at your bidding they're unmanly.
Within a year ye'll beat your breasts
Like gleaners in a famine.
Men shall fail, the wild-ass roam,
And you —— ?

(iii.) Verses 15-20.

Jehovah works when our work's done.
Then deserts blossom; vines wax like the cedars;
Where no man dwelt, rise tents, justice, joy
In richest pasture.
Then woman, thou'lt be happier in that humbler nomad home,
Like mothers of old, than in these crowded courts
All wealth and wrong.
O! most blessed are the quiet tillers of the soil.

(3) Chap. xxiii.—A wail over Tyre, with a warning for Egypt. She seems about to fall before the Assyrians. Sargon's inscriptions tell us he did gain mastery in some form over the island city. Isaiah's cry in ver. 13, "Behold the land of Chaldea; this people is no more," means surely that when he wrote the words Sargon had already crushed the Chaldean or Babylonian revolt under Merodach-Baladan. We know he crushed that in 710 B.C. Putting these things together, we can see how Isaiah may well have proclaimed this oracle of chap. xxiii. just after his oracles of chaps. xxix.–xxxii. described above. In these latter he condemned all trust in Egypt. Now he adds, "See how Sargon has beaten Tyre, the help and sister of Egypt! How now will

the heart of Egypt, always weak, be cowed and paralysed with fright! Seek no help there; seek your own Jehovah. He can and will help, and He does help; for are not Sargon's sieges of Tyre, and Ashdod, and elsewhere, while Jerusalem is left comparatively untouched, all fulfilments of our faith? "He is truly founding in Zion a sure refuge!" Here is again evidence that Isaiah is indeed a politician; but his politics are all simply expressions of his religious faiths, on which all his opinions are based. And his utterances touching foreign politics or peoples are uttered for the sake of that folk who are to Isaiah an essential part of the life, the purpose, the joy of Jehovah. Here is the sum of chap. xxiii. :—

THE DOOM OF TYRE.

(i.) Verses 1–7.

O Cyprus! O isles of sea! O straits far over the sea!
Blush for the pitiful fall
Of the merchant-mistress of all!
But thou Egypt, Tyre's harvest-field, blush most of all!
Nay, pale! Shriek! Fall in this fall.

(ii.) Verses 8–12.

Who could do this?
Who devised, who spake, who struck?
Jehovah, the Lord of all hosts, our Lover.

(iii.) Verse 13.

Think ye 'twas Asshur? Think ye that Asshur slew Babel?

(iv.) Verses 14–18.

Our God decreed the past;
Hear Him decree the age to come:
O Tyre, mistress, harlot!
Go, thou shalt hide thee a whole age to come;

Then a harlot, all selfish, thou wilt be again.
But thy gains God will bid thee disgorge
Thou shalt bring them to Zion, to us, to Jehovah.
Jehovah ruled all, and He will rule.

(B.) The second subdivision of these more confident utterances is the oracles declared amid actual siege, chap. xxxiii. and part of chap. xxxvii.

(1) Chap. xxxiii.—Quite true it is that Isaiah descended from the ideal faith in men, in persons filled with Jehovah's words, or covered with His Spirit. He came down to a more material faith in a place as chosen by Jehovah to be the one place of safety in the world. It was, of course, a practical faith; but it is a disappointment. Yet here is a remarkable fact; in the midst of actual danger Isaiah's inspiration rose again repeatedly to a high spiritual level. In the midst of the siege he proclaims the highest spiritual deliverance he ever conceives, and the most purely moral endowment for soul and character that we have thus far seen. It is forgiveness he preaches now—forgiveness for those who live in Zion, it is true, yet forgiveness for trembling sinners.

(i.) Verse 1.

O cruel, false Asshur, God hinder thee!

(ii.) Verses 2–6.—*The prayer.*

Jehovah, save, O save!
Thou giv'st the striking arm strength;
O, therefore, Thou canst save.
Greater than men, than Asshur, Thou!
For dost Thou not brood o'er all!
O God, Jehovah, Zion's Friend,
We're strong, wise, safe—in Thee.

(iii.) Verses 7–9.—*The distress.*

The soldiers weep,
The towns are fallen,

The roads grow green,
The footfall is hushed,
The earth is faint and weeps.
Lebanon, Sharon, Bashan, and Carmel,
Fling off their leaves in grief;
Zion's alone now!

(iv.) Verses 10–24.—*The deliverance.*

(α) Verses 10–13.

Jehovah's shout! "I come!
Asshur, conceiver of folly,
Burn in the heat of thy mad conceit.
Blaze like a beacon, till the world see!"

(β) Verses 14–16.

Sinners in Zion see, and cry in fright,
"Oh, woe! Oh woe! The awful fire
The enemy kindles to destroy us.
We are undone! Who can escape?
Perhaps the righteous—they perhaps!
Oh, we have sinned, we've sinned.
Oh yes, we wronged our neighbour;
Blood-guilt is on our souls!
No rocky fastness for us now!
The awful God has that for righteous souls.
'Only for such,' cried Amos long ago;
Now we must die."

(γ) Verses 17–19.

Nay, look; see near thee God's beloved,
Thy king; thee too He saves.
'Tis Asshur that's on fire;
Jehovah burneth up his host.

(δ) Verses 20, 21.

Look upon Zion, sinner; look around thee
On this trysted meeting-place of God and men;
Can he break tryst?
Jehovah never strikes His tent.

(1) Verses 22, 23a.

Hear, sinner, let Jehovah be thy trust.
His judgment's full of favour to the fallen.
Look unto Him and live. Let Him hold thee.

(2) Verses 23b, 24.

Take, sinner, take Jehovah's gifts;
Thou art in Zion. Here all's well.
Here shall all faintness cease;
Here all are forgiven.

(2) Chap. xxxvii. 6, 7, 22–35.—Some phrases in these oracles suggest the style of a follower rather than the master's hand; and the setting of the words in a narrative which occurs also in 2 Kings xviii. *ff*., strengthens this suggestion. If this should be a correct surmise, we should have in the whole passage an excellent record of the impression Isaiah had made on men by his proclamations of his great faith. The writer, whether Isaiah or another, depicts the prophet's soul as full to the last of enthusiastic faith in his great Zion-doctrine.

The words are a fierce challenge, a sort of weird laughter flung at the terrible besieging host. For a brief hour there whispers fear. Then leaps out again the shout of perfect fearlessness for Zion.

He who set the words in narrative was full of wonder at the great seer's power of faith and deed, and at his power to work like faith and deeds in the king and men of Judah.

It must be observed, however, as one reads the close of chap. xxxvii., that the story's end is very abrupt. What was the "angel" by which God slew so many of the Assyrians? Was it a pestilence? Or was it some successful stroke by the Egyptian forces?

This latter clue is distinctly implied in the narrative. And it is also made probable by Sennacherib's very inscription, telling of what was evidently in his own eyes a failure and severe disappointment. The record is given in Schrader, C. I. & O. T., pp. 277 *ff*. The Egyptians preserved a record of the matter, and gloried over it to Herodotus (ii. 141) long after, quite possibly with some exaggeration of their valour and success.

The important facts for us are, in brief: 1st. Zion was partially, but only partially, delivered from the Assyrian attack. 2nd. Egypt seemed to have proved an important helper in the deliverance. 3rd. Isaiah's ministry appears suddenly to cease; and of his later story we hear nothing.

When we link together this silent disappearance with the double non-fulfilment of the strict letter of the promises, perfect safety for Zion, and perfect uselessness of Egypt to help, we have probably to conclude that Isaiah's final experience was the opposite of what happened later to Jeremiah. The latter prophet rose immensely in popular favour as a predictor. Isaiah surely lost repute, and his last days were hid under a cloud of disfavour. His greater glory was to be the glory of the rising again of his influence in a spiritual and ideal resurrection.

(C.) The discussion of any oracles supposed to be later than those above will now seem strange; but such discussion may be hypothetical; and by allowing the hypothesis the view above set forth will be found to be confirmed.

(1.) Chap. xxi. 1–10 is a warning that Babylon is in danger. It used to be considered as the work of some hand in the Babylonian exile of 590–540 B.C., a shout of satisfaction over the coming of Cyrus to liberate the Jewish slaves by the overthrow of Babylon. But it is quite as likely to be Isaiah's warning to his own countrymen not to trust in help against Assyria from Merodach-Baladan or other Babylonian patriots and insurgents. Viewed thus, it agrees with the probable disrepute into which Isaiah had come. It illustrates the willingness of Jerusalem to treat with allies like Egypt and

Babylon, whom Isaiah disliked. The passage has no enthusiastic word about Zion, but it speaks the prophet's abiding trust in Jehovah.

(2) Chap. xviii.—Here is a scornful warning for Ethiopia. Has Egypt managed to trouble Assyria and hinder Sennacherib? It shall be but for a day. For far beyond Egypt, far south in Abyssinia, alarm flying south shall paralyse all men. Assyria shall humble Africa utterly. Not a word of safety or promise for Judah comes till the very last sentence. Not even there aught but the prophet's faith that, after all, not Assyria shall be supreme. Ethiopia shall acknowledge God, who is the God of Israel, Lord of all hosts, whose chosen seat is Zion.

Chap. xvii. 12–14. This is apparently a declaration that Assyria too shall suddenly pass away. But it has no word of Zion, scarcely even an allusion to her. Isaiah's heart is checked. The cries of joy in Zion do not leap out now so grandly. A cloud is upon his soul darkening his once precious earthly jewel.

(3) Chap. xix.—A scornful cry against Egypt. Whatever help she may have brought, she shall be utterly undone. Her little gods shall give no help. Civil strife shall unnerve her. Her great river shall fly away in shame; fisher and farmer shall weep for want. Her counsels and counsellors are all foolish, twisting about, always wrong. Judah shall become a trouble to her. David shall actually rule over her.

But Isaiah was the preacher of grace, and grace must bring healing to the wounded, even if these be outside the pale. When at last Egypt becomes Assyria's servant, then both shall bow to Jehovah. With these two servants of the God of hosts Israel shall be the third.

Here is no jubilant exaltation of Zion, nor a cry of exultation in her. The prophet's tone is changed. He is no longer the greatly honoured seer in Zion. He is still, however, even in his pain, the devoted man of Jehovah, who is Lord of hosts, God over all the earth.

The tone of these last few oracles thus seems to confirm the opinion that Isaiah lost repute as a successful predictor at the end of Sennacherib's campaign. The pendulum of favour was swinging away from him and from his faith for a little while. The reaction of Manasseh, of which we have to hear, was the greater manifestation of the disfavour we saw rising so mysteriously in the end of the narrative of Isaiah xxxvii.

As we turn from this description of his oracles, let us sum in brief their course.

1. First, following his call, was a period of denunciation, keen and awful. At its close was sense of failure of that method for conversion.

2. Recalling his first vision in Zion's temple, and God's grace in it to him and his there, although all unclean in life and lips, Isaiah hastens out again to preach that grace of God, ready to touch and teach and heal the worst.

3. He proclaims persons at first as the signs of God's grace, saying comparatively much less of Zion. There is a remarkable succession in the sorts of persons. First it is the infant yet unborn, then the family of the prophet, then a new-born babe in the royal home, heir to all the great endowments of David, and at Ahaz's death it is the new king who follows, springing from the old and wise Nahash-root. But the hope in persons grows at once more ideal and less real in the utterances of chap. xi. at Samaria's fall; for less is said here of the actual human well-known prince, and far, far more of endowments to be given and gotten from the descending and abiding Divine Spirit. At the same time the Zion faith is growing into plainer utterance. Doubtless the disappointing discovery came that persons are not all one hopes from them. Possibly easier times made men less devout, less devoted at the prophet's call. Doubtless also, then as

now, religious enthusiasm was wont to grow cool at least in appearance; most of what purely spiritual impulse could accomplish for the time had been accomplished. Then it is the nature of such feelings and conviction to crystallise and harden. Faith shows its power to resist decay by its grasp of visible tokens, its strong love of them, its adornment of them. They are the visible evidence of life when finer signs fail and do not record our relation to the unseen. So Isaiah's faith in Zion came to foremost utterance, and in event after event his prediction of safety in Zion was proved correct. At last the darkest day of all came. Then Isaiah cried out again his faith in Zion's safety, but rose now back again from that to the highest ideal faith for persons that he ever uttered, "Sinners in Zion shall be forgiven." It was a limited vision indeed, but it was a vision into God's divinest treasure and gift. When after this Isaiah's external hopes seem baffled, and men's hope grows cold, we can be satisfied. He has preached to Zion the very gospel. Better that earth's joys grow dim, and the cross be held of God before his closing eyes. He triumphs still, and shall still triumph.

CHAPTER III.

A SYSTEMATIC VIEW OF ISAIAH'S FAITHS GENETICALLY CONSIDERED

§ 1. *The kernel of Isaiah's character.*

LET us announce at once the conclusion of the matter. The kernel of Isaiah's character is his faith in revelation. Certainly the revelation he believed in was a revelation to himself; and his faith in it was his constant intense sense of a very atmosphere of Divine communications always breathing in upon him. It would be vain to look for theological definitions in his century, and of all the writings in that century his are far too thoroughly busy in persuasion of the people round him to furnish us with leisurely reflections on the nature of the revelations he enjoyed. But if we count as a Divine revelation that which comes to a soul in trouble, and gives it most joyful light on its path, then Isaiah lived in a constant sunshine of such experiences. Most people do count such experiences as their real revelations of God.[1] We have such experience of conversion and of providential leading to-day; the Hebrew prophet's vital air was a sense of such Divine help and illumination. Isaiah overwhelms the reader with the thought that his mind was all on fire with such high fellowship, all his life-purposes were splendidly controlled by

---

[1] From the admirable tract of Professor Herrmann of Marburg, on *Offenbarung* (Giessen, J. Ricker, 1887, p. 65), I take this definition. That tract is indeed a study in dogmatics; but it is a most attractive dogmatical utterance, for it sets in simplest speech the story of the actual Christian experience of most people.

it, and all his speeches planned with a masterly aim and high dignity inspired in him by the consciousness of this marvellous fellowship.

He was essentially the prophet; he was the chief of prophets. This does not mean that he counted it his great business to predict, although he did predict at times; but, in most direct and clear fashion for that age, he professed to tell his people and the world what was the mind of Jehovah, the God of the Hebrews. It is indeed remarkable that chaps. ii. to v., that is, the record of his early sterner work, contain no allusion to himself or to his office. But this is not unnatural; rather may we consider it a truly manly trait that he makes no claim to special professional authority while he is indignantly denouncing immorality. That denunciation can stand on its own merits. And yet he reveals even in this section an instinctive sense that he has an authority men cannot escape. It appears, of course, in his formula, "Jehovah saith;" but it gleams, if possible, more determinedly through the quotation which opens chap. ii. He says in effect, "These words have authority; they hold your reverence. I, Isaiah, plant myself on that foundation, and declare only the clear consequences of that which you admit." What could hold his hearers more inevitably? In other words, this use of a text was a real and powerful appeal to supreme controlling force, to Divine authority. Such is likewise to-day the practical principle underlying the preacher's use of a text. The preacher does not swear by the text—indeed, like Isaiah, he may contradict it. But the hearer's just reverence for the words secures attention for those declarations of the preacher which are logically connected with the text either by their parallel nature or by their contrast. With unfailing certainty does the soul hear God in its own reverent, honest judgments. So is God ever seen in the true soul of man. The true Son of man is Son of God. Such was Isaiah's skilful, ideally homiletic attitude in his most youthful work. He was "The Prophet" from the first.

But with the new, deep sense of the devotion of his God to the Hebrews, as it flashed upon him in his remembrance of the initial gracious vision, there came evidently a new intense consciousness of his personal possession of prophetic mission. At once after the sixth chapter we find him going out with a prophetic badge, that fine symbolic oracle, his boy Shear-Jashubh ("When a remnant returns"), walking by his side. And it is to the king he goes now, as the co-ordinate high officer of Jehovah's people. He is no mere general preacher of God and good; he is of the Divine executive, and has definite demands to bring.

The little son so honoured is guide into an honoured home. Of the many children Isaiah names symbolically, two were his own, we know; and they were held close to the father's heart as part of his dearest self and strength. When one was as yet not born the babe was the father's theme in his counsellings with God and his self-consecration. When the father was living through hours of agony for Jerusalem's safety from Syria, or from the vastly greater enemy, Assyria, he clasped his elder boy's hand or cried aloud the lad's loved name for cheer. There is a pathos altogether unique in old Hebrew records in the words (chap. viii. 18)—

"Behold, I and the children Jehovah hath given me are for
    signs and wonders in Israel:
From Jehovah of hosts, who dwelleth in Mount Zion."

But not pathos alone is here. The man who spoke saw the power of God in himself and in all that was knit about him. The outermost circle of his personality was the circle of his disciples, learning his words and reproducing his faith. "Seal up instructions for my disciples," wrote he, chap. viii. 16. Thus the outermost wave of his influence was very truly himself. Then within these were his beloved, his boys. But inmost was the dear wife of his bosom, and her he calls "The Prophetess." Such a title no other prophet gives his spouse. This is the finest stroke in this great picture of a prophet. All that was of him, with him, in him, was charged of God with revelation. This was truly a high conscious worth. Here was a profound faith in inspiration. The home was a revelation. At the table's head sat such a father and mother, their children nestled near, and down the sides sat the honoured disciples of the high calling. The bread they shared was the revelations of their God.

These revelations to him and round him were messages of supreme help in hours of utter helplessness. They were overwhelming convictions of the arrival of God's opportunity in the actual hours of man's extremity. There was certainly a growth in the reality and joy of this experience. In his earlier days and words, amid despair over the uncleanness of men, faith arose in him that the cleansing which seemed impossible should be accomplished first by a supernatural interposition of awful judgment to burn away bad men, and then by a new creation of men to replace these. But this grasp of a hope was only an infant's lesson compared with the great faith of the later prophecies, those which follow chap. vi., that Jehovah would descend in His love to unclean men, would touch their unclean lips, would cleanse them, and even give into the charge of these new-created souls the dearest, holiest, most glad messages He had to give. One is often struck, when reading Hebrew psalms, with their prevailing mournful opening and their frequent joyful close. The prayer for the peace of God to fill the heart now sadly empty seems in the very hour of prayer to be answered. It is a peculiarity not confined to psalms; it is the recorded fact in all spiritual experience. It is the story of true men; it is the law of the true God. Isaiah's story, his oracles, his experience, and his character written in all these, were pre-eminently an illustration of that story of true men and a symbol of that law of God. He was a sign and a symbol of the Divine, the supernatural, the strangely intervening help, strength, light in utter darkness. This we have seen recorded in his hope declared to hopeless Ahaz (chap. vii.); and again in the faith uttered when Ahaz died (chap. xiv.); then again so brilliant in the gospel preached to the foolish bacchanals (chap. xxviii.). It was splendidly declared in the face of Assyria (chaps. x., xi.), when all human probability allowed but one night's respite to Jerusalem before her utter ruin. And the splendour of this utterance is in its fine spirituality, for mere physical deliverance is but little to the writer's soul. He rushes on, not content until he has announced a great supernatural regeneration of the hearts of the delivered Hebrews (chap. xi. 1 *ff.*). Now let the reader beware who thinks to find the supernatural in the method of regeneration described, or who even thinks that Isaiah's declaration, "Regeneration shall be," is a supernatural rock whereon we may stand and argue thence that therefore regeneration shall be, forasmuch as Isaiah was supernaturally moved when he spoke. Such fancy would be to identify an easy argumentation on our part with those transient visions which overwhelm us, and, wrapping us about in silent solemnity, make us whisper, "Speak, Lord, thy servant heareth thee." No, God's opportunity is not only in the hour of triumph of skilful reason; in man's extremity is God's opportunity. So it is now, as it was in Isaiah's day. The revelation to him was that conviction borne in upon him as he looked on Zion and recalled all his experience there: "God is with us." "Jehovah will not let Zion fall." The whisper came, worked providentially. He trusted; his trust was itself a flame breathed of the great Creator Spirit. He stayed his soul upon that faith; he opened the floodgates of his soul to let it in more and more richly even to utter fulness of the hope; he let that hope pour its glow over all things round him. His thoughts were fired, he saw in imagination the march of Asshur, and in his faith he quickly pictured their crashing fall. He looked on the ruin, he looked on his own helpless countrymen, and in that hour he believed Judah should be made good and strong. His thought beheld at once in readiest form the longed-for healing. He stayed not even for dialectic criticism or for stern experience to test the expectation, but there it stands, fair vision, truth in poetry, undying declaration of the faith of a soul that knew God and said, God can and will make men good.

Likewise glows his sense of God's presence with him in all his argumentation with his people concerning Egyptian help against Assyria (chaps. xxix., xxxii.). Ever realising the darkness that clouds and clogs men, feeling its deadly grip, ever does he rise to proclaim his gospel of trust in the devoted God of Israel. Finally, we may set that wonderful chap. xxxiii., where the interposition is so utterly unexpected by the sinful hypocrites in Zion, that Isaiah mixes powerful sarcasm in his picture of their terror and of the contrasted near salvation, which their evil eyes do not see. Even to them cries Isaiah, Yes, ye do well to be afraid, but look upon Zion. The dwellers shall not even be sick. Ye shall be forgiven your waywardness.

Such brief *resumé*, then, indicates the ground of our definition of the kernel of Isaiah's character. That kernel is his faith in revelation. For the faith is manifest from the first in his tone of certainty; it is manifest in estimate of his own personality and of his home; it is manifested to us in his fearless forecasts of events, and in his brilliant theoretical deductions concerning the ways of God and men drawn from the various known sources, the facts of life, the ways of thought in the time, and a keenly strong imagination. But all these were grasped and intensified and controlled by a soul utterly devoted to Jehovah, and absolutely certain that Jehovah was with him, utterly devoted to him and his, and all-powerful to help. The forecasts and theories were not the revelations; this was rather that love for God, that trust in God, that sense of the love of God, and the present power of God underlying all his forecasts, theories, thoughts, and words, and worked in Isaiah by the disclosure to him of God Himself. This picture of Isaiah will be established as correct as we proceed to more and more minute acquaintance with his thoughts or faiths, and arrange them in ordered sequence.

§ 2. *A scheme of his thinking.*

We turn to the consideration of these thoughts, and here we shall group them in two divisions, thus:—

(A.) More general faiths, the term "faith" being used here in the less strict sense of "religious opinions." This avoids the use of the term "doctrines," which as applied to Isaiah in any way is somewhat misleading. Under this general title stand his faith in—

(1) The overlordship of Jehovah;
(2) The necessity of purification of the earth;
(3) The grace of Jehovah; and
(4) A regeneration of men.

This general division will give a genetic view of all his faiths and a historic account of his whole theological character. Then on this basis we shall seek to formulate—

(B.) The essence of his thinking on the three fundamental questions—

(1) Concerning the nature of God;
(2) Concerning the nature of man; and
(3) Concerning perfect life.

From this we shall proceed to estimate in another chapter Isaiah's place in Hebrew religious history, his advance on what had been before him, the new problems he started and left to be faced by those who followed him, and his whole value as a religious factor in the life of his people and in the life of all men.

§ 3. (A) 1. *His faith in the overlordship of Jehovah.*

(i.) This is an inherited faith; it is an opinion Isaiah holds in common with his time. We have traced its rise and growth from the golden age in the days of David. We have seen that supreme hero of the people become ruler over all the peoples round about his own from Egypt to Euphrates, and we have seen the Hebrews learn to count the God of the conqueror the Lord over the gods of the conquered. So David gave to the people a worthy rank, and for Jehovah he worked out true reverence among men. He was really the man after Jehovah's own heart. We know also how Elijah led the host of Jehovah, small though it might seem, to final struggle with the host of Baal, and in that struggle on Mount Carmel the popular lingering liking for Baal-worship had to bow to the new faith that Jehovah was after all the supreme God.

We have read Amos's unhesitating summons to all peoples to receive from Jehovah what judgment He should adjudge to them. Although Amos makes little of Zion, yet he does once bid all men look to that city, because its God, Jehovah, is about to sound forth thence the doom of Syria, of Philistia, of Phœnicia, of Arabia's tribes, as well as of the Hebrews. Amos's visions have not a very wide horizon, yet he knows of Egypt, and even of Ethiopia, and of distant regions too, far beyond the Syrian north, and over all these he counts Jehovah supreme God.

Hosea's knowledge was greater, and his faith in this overlordship is none the less. He lived in Samaria, and perhaps shared the northern kingdom's jealousy of Zion, yet he exalts Jehovah even more clearly than Amos does. Assyria and Egypt loom largest in his thoughts, for he is a statesman, and knows that these great world powers are the chief engines in the society of the time; but it is just these chief engines that Jehovah controls absolutely. Already the main fact of past story in Hosea's mind is Jehovah's deliverance of the Hebrews from great Egypt. And now God knows all their foolish coquetting with that former slavemaster and with the rival Assyria, and He ordains what scourging or what dishonour the one or the other rival shall contribute to the chastisement and regeneration of His own chosen people Israel.

But stronger than all these statements of Jehovah's supremacy is the implication in the constant lament over the division into two kingdoms. It was David's unification and consolidation of the many Hebrew tribes that made him easily rule many more as subjects far beyond. Thus the unity was the foundation of Jehovah's great glory. Hence the division that came so sadly meant a constant seed of fear, of doubt whether He who did not hold His own in strong unity could nevertheless control all gods, and of trembling lest His people should become slaves again and even He should lose His honour.

Here now entered a remarkable divergence in the advance of faiths. The faith in Jehovah and His supremacy wavered in some, but it grew the stronger in others. Indeed, among a large class of careless or fearful or selfish people, it wavered even to failure, for such is the meaning of the prophet's complaint of much turning to other gods. But all the while there was the nobler class, the godly prophets, the godly men, the indefatigable workmen, whose faith in Jehovah never failed, but rather grew, and grew stronger and purer. We say these were godly men, for their nobility, their goodness, is what we count a Divine product. We say of it, with our ideas of God gained from our Christian faith, that here was true sonship of God, truly godlike character; in their character spoke the supernatural. So we conclude that the advance among the Hebrews towards, if not as yet quite up to, monotheism, was the work of the good men, the godly men, the men with supernaturally inspired true character. This advance was not a national advance, or a natural advance strictly so termed; it was not the work of all the people, or of all the thinkers, or of all the leaders. Rather, when external circumstances tended all the other way, there was another spiritual element in the environment of the souls of these few men that swayed them in this distinctly new and better direction. It was God's opportunity in men's extremity. It seemed a dark hour, but light for the whole future of the world shone in from God.

(ii.) The prophets held fast their faith in the supremacy of Jehovah, but moved away from faith in the worthiness of the people to be the supreme people. It is at this point in the story of faith that we hear the voice of Isaiah breaking in upon the ear.

Isaiah's opinion concerning the supreme government of the nations is first a scornful denial of the hope that the Hebrews are fit to be the chief rulers, and Zion the capital of all. Yet along with this there pervades the whole of the first stern period and its oracles a determined assertion that Jehovah shall be exalted. Alone, indeed, He shall be, and He shall shake the whole earth. Already all the judgments brought on the Hebrews, whether from within or from without, are worked by Jehovah. He is described as certainly coming to dash to ruin all other gods. Isaiah calls them "little gods," of whatsoever national origin they may be.

When he recalls and records his initial vision, as we read in chap. vi., it is his own faith that we learn in the ceaseless confession of the angels, "Jehovah's glory fills all the earth." God's heart is indeed holiness itself, which is devotion and love, and the yearnings of that love centre round one chosen family and pour out on it all blessings; but at the same time His great glory, which is the weight of His Being, overawes and subdues all nations and all things. Prof. Duhm shows, *Theologie der Propheten*, p. 170, that Jehovah's "glory" and His "holiness" are co-ordinate æsthetic attributes of Jehovah; the former the quality He wears towards all nations, the latter the quality He wears towards His own, *i.e.*, His devotion to them. For us the important fact is that Isaiah believed in a supremacy of Jehovah over all things, while at the same time he counted his God's strictly Divine occupation, that is, Jehovah's care and love, as all devoted to the one nation, the Hebrews. Now this opinion of Jehovah stands side by side with the remarkable consciousness that the whole people, and even Isaiah himself, are so utterly unworthy of this devotion; God's approach to them ought to mean death to them all. Yet to Isaiah it has brought life, and to many more it will bring life, because Omnipotence is found to have a new meaning not known before. Overlordship has come to mean a power to restrain retribution and its agents, to prevent the pains that might overtake the unforgiven and the God-forsaken.

It is this aspect of overlordship we see disclosed now. The prophet is "searching what the Spirit within him signifies" "concerning salvation;" and he has plunged down to deeper depth than ever before was sounded in the great heart of God. With joy he pours out henceforth this new conception of Jehovah's supreme power in all his subsequent oracles.

(iii.) A rapid glance will reveal this.

(*a*) The bold offer to Ahaz is not alone a brilliant declaration of Jehovah's omnipotence to rule all signs in the depth beneath or in the height above. It is a declaration of faith in Jehovah's absolute power to help and to heal Ahaz and both the divided kingdoms, foolish, wayward, sinful though they be.

(*b*) The oracle of chap. xiv., 28ff. bids the Philistines of the coast halt in their conclusion that Jehovah's smiting King

Ahaz to death means any unmerciful anger on God's part. No; out of the old David stock that once ruled the nations in the past He is able to raise new rulers to bless His people more than ever. For, while He brings Assyria to devastate Philistia and all the coast-road, He can give shelter from Asshur in Zion even to Philistine refugees. Jehovah controls the world-powers to the saving of the Hebrews.

(c) The sum of the dramatic poem and homely philosophy of chap. xxviii. is that Jehovah controls Asshur, controls Sheol, controls the elements and the fruits of the soil, all with the same excellent working and healing purpose toward His beloved people.

(d) Here follows the magnificent *Te Deum* of chaps. x. and xi., which sings Jehovah's marvellous swaying of Assyria as a father sways a rod of correction, or a woodman sways a pruning axe. And when the loved child is corrected then he shall be filled with all the fulness of the Divine spirit and mind and will. When the forest is pruned then shall Jehovah's own plants grow in beauty and goodness. God will heal the sin-sick children. He can prevent all hurt in Zion. He can cover the sacred soil with knowledge of Jehovah. To such gracious end will the Supreme Ruler work.

(e) The series of oracles from chap. xxix. to chap. xxxii. have a fresh striking feature. Assyria's power and purpose are indeed to be disappointed utterly, as Isaiah had believed before. But new and startling almost to amusement is the prophet's cool estimate of Egypt. Isaiah counts the qualities of the great rival of Assyria, and the citizen of a little hill in Judah laughs with a fairly astounding cynicism at the ancient mistress of the Nile. The height of his assurance seems moreover all the greater when we recollect that in the result he under-estimated what Egypt would do. Egypt was not by any means an insignificant power. We have already seen how the prophet's ultimate loss of reputation as seer was due to his under-estimate of her strength. But his great faith in Jehovah's overlordship pressed forth from his heart a cry of utter contempt for Egypt. Jehovah would save, forgive, heal Judah. Jehovah, the supreme God, could do this. Was Egypt rival oppressor with Assyria! Did any men count her a rival with Jehovah, and a saviour instead of Him! Out upon her, proud Egypt! Out and away with her, useless Egypt! The faith is sublime; and it is faith that Jehovah is the greatest God, although Jehovah's people are the feeblest folk.

(*f*) This assurance rises to a height that men might call fanaticism in the day of actual awful siege by Sennacherib. Then the weirdly inspired man flings at the enemy the shriek and laugh of the daughter of Zion. "O Asshur, mightier than thou art is our God Jehovah! He ruleth thee, and we laugh thee to scorn!" Now enters a new phase of the faith, whose full significance Isaiah did not see, nor did he live to hear its later greater proclamation. His confidence that Zion shall stand scatheless wavers a little. Quick he leaps in his assurance upon another rock that has indeed been looming dimly in the mists of danger. He grasps at a great new possibility, which is indeed a profounder truth than all he has yet known. Zion may fall, but the escaped shall take root again. Jeremiah long afterwards was to understand and proclaim this fully. And now sounds forth grandly the new, richer formula of overlordship—

It is the zeal of Jehovah, Lord of all hosts, that shall perform even this (chap. xxxvii. 32).

(*g*) The jubilant voices of chap. xxxiii. are the fitting hallelujah chorus at the close of this great Isaiah oratorio. The utterance of faith in Jehovah's supremacy is here truly sublime:—

>   Woe to thee, Asshur, spoiler!
>   "O Jehovah, be gracious unto us.
>   At the noise of the tumult the people fled."

> Jehovah is exalted, for He dwelleth on high.
> Now will I rise, saith Jehovah;
> Now will I be exalted;
> Now will I lift myself.
> The sinners in Zion are afraid.
> Look upon Zion, the city of our annual tryst with Him.
> There the glorious Jehovah will be unto us a place of broad rivers and streams,
> Our Euphrates and our Nile.
> But therein shall go no galley with oars, nor gallant ship,
> For Jehovah is king.

(*h*) Finally, if chaps. xxiii., xviii., and xix. are the last words of this man, and from his hour of disappointment and death in darkness, they are verily nevertheless an amen to all his faith in Jehovah, Lord of hosts. They paint the Tyrians and the far-off Ethiopians marshalled by Jehovah's word, and then they close with this striking legend:—

> Blessed be Egypt, my people,
> And Assyria, the work of my hands,
> And Israel my inheritance.
> "This shall be the blessing of Jehovah, God of hosts."

(iv.) As we leave these scenes of Isaiah's faith in the supremacy of Jehovah, let us note how he was in all this interpreting the real need of the nations at the time. If the Hebrews were filled with satisfaction in the thought that David controlled all the kings who touched them, and their God controlled all hosts in earth or in heaven that could do them good or evil, the Assyrians and the Egyptians and the Syrian tribes were seeking eagerly at the same time a similar sense of safety, for this was the meaning of their warring for world-empire. And it was not merely a strife as to which should be the supreme nation, but all we know of any of them tells of the faith of each in his several deity, that his god was fighting for and with the nation. They fought each for the supremacy of his own god. In the hour of victory the victor soldiers might die, but the victor god was supreme. It is vain to say, in depreciation of all religion, that these peoples were ignorant and fanatic; for ignorance is only a relative term, and to acknowledge the fact of fanaticism is to acknowledge one set of religious phenomena. These people were not without some assurance in their souls and of a longing for more of just such assurance; it is the untempered sway of that assurance which is fanaticism. It is vain also to say, in depreciation of all non-Hebrew religions of that age, that those were base religions, and we ought not to seek any light from them on the nature of better religion, and on the nature of the prophet's inspiration. It is the fact that there was in Isaiah's day a common yearning in all souls for some fellowship with unseen forces, spirits we call them, who should control all other powers in earth and heaven, and thus give their human followers safety. Isaiah's faith in the supremacy of Jehovah is the answer of a godlike soul to this universal yearning. We say he was godlike, not because he was a Hebrew, but because his character was good, which is godlike; and we test his character by comparison with the ideal which Christianity has begotten in us to-day. Thus we recognise in Isaiah a Divine seer for his age. He was indeed far above contemporary Hebrews in his wonderful insight into the profounder features of this truth we have just traced. We feel, as we follow him, that it is no wonder his people became ultimately the leaders into pure monotheism and the greatest religious influence in the world. We acknowledge the hand of God unveiling His own purpose and nature in Isaiah's mind and oracles. We discover in this man an answer, from the great God and Cause and Father of all things, to the questioning which He had brought to birth in the souls of all men in all lands in that age. In the unceasing process of education of our race, who are His children, God had moved them by all the influences of their environment to count it necessary, for their very life, to be assured of the absolute supremacy of some one great power in the world, and the favour of that power towards themselves. Isaiah shares that common conviction, and answers it with the firm assertion that the righteous God, Jehovah, the devoted Divine Lover of Israel, is supreme Lord. The seer of a little tribe is the interpreter of the problem of the age.

§ 4. *His faith that the earth must be cleansed.*

The closing declaration of last paragraph, that Jehovah was essentially a righteous God, might be generally acknowledged; but at the same time, no doubt, the usual estimate of the quality of that righteousness is indistinct. It is customary to apologise for the righteousness as something, of necessity, very unlike righteousness to-day. It is supposed that good men like Isaiah could preach the massacre of a whole tribe, its men and its babes, and that they wrote or sang imprecatory psalms. An apologetic for that would certainly be right, but it ought to await the exact tabulation of the crimes and wrongs which Isaiah abhorred and strove to cleanse away from his people.

At the very outset of his work he proclaims a catastrophe that is to fall on the "day of Jehovah." In that day Jehovah will arise and delay no longer. He will cause that His will alone be done. And a terrible day it shall be for the Hebrews, for they have been doing anything but Jehovah's will; their hands and hearts are full of what disgusts Him and what He will destroy. The well-known formula, "In that day," is the dread opening of oracle after oracle of warning. At first these are fierce but general threats of overturning by the hand of Jehovah in His day of visitation. He is now absent or busy otherwise, but then He will visit to inspect, to enforce His will. The conceptions do not seem high. We have learned the poverty of the conception of an absentee Creator of the Universe by our observation of deism. Our knowledge of the inadequate morality of deism makes us hesitate to give our approval of the anger and furious threats of the prophet against the people he condemns. And we hesitate still when later on he drops the general warning of a catastrophe, and proclaims the coming of the Assyrians as the coming of Jehovah's judgment on the Hebrews. Of course it would be a mere superficial criticism of this Isaian reading of Providence to point out that it hurts the good men as much as the evil. The more serious cause for hesitation is his whole theory of Providence; for we have learned from the crucifixion of our Lord the truth of the later doctrine that He whom we too readily "esteem stricken, smitten of God and afflicted," is wounded for our transgressions. "It pleased Jehovah to bruise Him; He hath put Him to grief . . . but the pleasure of Jehovah prospers in His hand." The stricken one may be Jehovah's righteous servant; the cross is not the sign of God's anger with the crucified. Isaiah's doctrine of providence is not indeed on the same level with the high faith that was to come.

We have seen in the former paragraph how he rose to the conception that all things are controlled by one Lord who loves intensely; and that conception would surely sweep away the thought of an absent Lord. It did sweep it away, and brought in the Immanuel-faith, as we shall presently see. But we turn to a test of the prophet's religious worth that is more unerring still when we ask, What were the evils he denounced and strove to cleanse off the earth? What was immorality in Isaiah's eyes; and what were the demands of his moral code? Here we find what makes Isaiah indeed our own brother in heart.

(i.) The moral sense of Isaiah revolts most intensely at carelessness of God's honour. It was not the honour of Deity as such, but Jehovah's honour that was dear to the prophet. The nature of the Absolute had not occupied any one's thoughts so far, and Isaiah does not defend deity in the abstract. So much the better. He knows by experience a Being to whom he bows; he knows the loves of that Being, His haunts, His ways, and His inspirations and thoughts, and he has bowed to that God. He knows that all men round him share at least some of these experiences. They have bowed sometimes because they felt it was right. But they have turned their eyes and ears and thoughts away from all indications of His presence. This Isaiah condemns at first, at last, and always. To have no care for God is to be bad. The early chapters denounce this carelessness in the luxurious. The songs of the vineyard and the outstretched arm in chap. v. denounce it in the selfish. Ahaz's worst deed was his sneer at Jehovah's interest in him. The shocking profanity of the bacchanalian orgies among priests, prophets, and people is the heaviest burden in chap. xxviii. It is hypocrisy that chaps. xxix. to xxxiii. condemn most strongly. With their lips they honour Jehovah, but they have removed their heart far from Him. To Isaiah the heart was the seat of the mind, and his accusation here means that men do not care to know Jehovah's character or His ways. And yet the essence of his regard for Jehovah was not something learned by custom. Isaiah bowed before the inevitable inner voice, "Thou oughtest to do right;" and it was this voice, he said, that must be honoured if a man would be right and good. It is of secondary consequence to discover the original occasion of the appearance in men or in Hebrews of the sense of "ought." Indeed, we cannot think of what we call man as existing without it. Isaiah knew the control of this voice. He counted it righteousness to honour this voice with thoughtful, whole-hearted care; and to dishonour the controlling Divine voice was to him always utterly bad.

(ii.) Second only in severity is his condemnation of vanity. His satire on the showy coquetry of the ladies of Jerusalem is the most striking case of this severity; but it is by no means all of it, it is only the best seen symbol of much more. The homes are showy, and the men are passionately fond of display. The wealthy Israel and the smaller Judah vie with each other in festival dress. It is the spirit of the age. Assyria is at best pictured as never done counting and telling her exploits and her powers; and Isaiah's scorn of Egypt is scorn of big-voiced claims and professions of strength and wealth or performance and purpose.

But why condemn this? Pleasure is not in itself a wrong thing. Isaiah would be the last to teach that. His pleasure in things of beauty beams in all his description of the adornments of the homes and the persons about him, although he is condemning them. His songs tell the same tale; how he knew the delights of love, and the merry joy of the vineyard and of the feast. His interest in them tells that he had taken part in them, and he had done so with keen interest. Why should he then condemn the pleasures round him? Just because he knew the real value of beautiful things he could expose false pretensions to beauty and he could check overestimate of value. Listen to his plain talk to those women, "Ye go ogling with your eyes." We understand the words; we know the parade of lures to win a regard that is not deserved. Isaiah was condemning vanity. He was not condemning pleasure or beauty, but falsehood. These gay folk were telling men to come and enjoy all the precious joy that true womanhood can give; but they told a lie, for true womanhood never thus parades her gifts. The sumptuous householders stored their homes with gold, silver, and gems, and rare paintings relieved their walls. This was a profession of ease, perfect ease, perfect satisfaction with life; but to Isaiah it was falsehood. He was a Hebrew and a man of Zion as well as they, and he was a man of insight as clear as any other; and he was ill at ease, he saw dangers all about him. Their homes might any day be ruined, and it was a time for sternest training for conflict rather than a time for the enervation of luxury. Worse still, while there was danger all round them they were losing their devotion to Jehovah in their easy luxuriance. They were losing there their one national inspiration; they were losing the very soul of their strength; and it was false to say to self and family and fellow-men, "We are very safe and happy." The sin was their vanity. It was the untruth of their life that Isaiah struck and would cleanse away. The same untruth was to him the fault of Assyria's boasting and Egypt's pride. True, he saw it as perhaps they did not, for it was their claim to be stronger than Jehovah that he condemned. But the vanity of men, whether at home or afar, was sin. This prophet is truly upon a high plane morally, for to him dishonour of what is Divine ranks evidently worst among bad things, but linked with it at every point, and only second in badness, is untruth in life, the vanity of men, of women, of nations.

(iii.) Intoxication is wrong. If Isaiah does suggest any relative order in badness, this seems to rank next to what we have seen. While the two evils we have already counted are badness in the root, bad principle, the further evils he condemns are rather badness in the fruit, bad doings. But this evil of intoxication is a double evil; it is poison let into the channels between root and fruit. Isaiah does not say that all use of wine is bad; he knows what good wine is, and calls bad men "wine mixed with water." He knows the beauty of the old prophecy which he quotes in chap. xvi., and here he is at one with the best men of his people, for the same old prophecy is quoted with keen zest by Jeremiah a hundred years later; and that old prophecy laments the possible silencing of the vineyard song and shout. The drying-up of the winepresses on the hillsides of Moab would mean to him the departure of all Moab's gladness. What he does count wrong is quite evident from the two denunciations he hurls against it, first in his earlier stern preaching in chap. v., and later in his severe though kind-souled exposure of the bacchanal orgies just before the fall of Samaria (chap. xxviii.).

In the former the wrongdoing is the restlessness for alcoholic stimulus that steals from the couch at dawn to drink spirits. And all day long, writes Isaiah, such men keep following, following something—"a phantom in a mist, and it's wine that so excites them." Feeble, are they? Unable to control their passion, do you call them? Not so thinks Isaiah, for he tells how they arrange merry feasts, with songs and players all skilful enough, all clear-headed enough; they are very champions, men of power, and all are strong-minded enough to shut out certain things from their thoughts. When we find that it is Jehovah they deliberately shut out of thought, and when we find that they will not take His ways and purposes into account, then we need not hesitate to approve Isaiah's condemnation. What he condemned was strong men's deliberate and violent alcoholic self-excitement, that stifles noble impulses and is practised in order to stifle these. So we have not said Isaiah condemns the use of wine, for he does not, nor have we said he condemns drunkenness, which is a state of death; but he rather condemns men who are strong while they sin. Intoxication is a better name for the conscious self-debasement he strikes at. This is fully borne out by his scorn of the bacchanals in chap. xxviii., who know well the risk they run and the ugliness they put on when they begin their carouse. This second denunciation is only more powerful than the first because it pictures the height many a sinner falls from and the depth of the degradation. Prophets fall so, and priests too, from the most precious functions of teaching God's oracles and ministering to men's peace down to staggering and babbling and filth.

By contrast now we know the moral height to which Isaiah would raise his people. In a word, his command is, Refuse what degrades your soul, your power of thought, imagination, and judgment. Never unfit these to handle the realities of life. Certainly Isaiah's moral level was very high.

(iv.) We need not prove now in detail that he condemned

disregard of fellow-mortals. It is quite true that Hebrews in various ages identified the poor with the good; and when they did not quite identify them they frequently confused them together. This we shall see from time to time, and Isaiah shared in the view. It was no wonder that he did. For the Hebrews were a small, feeble people, and Judah especially was an insignificant, ill-equipped tribe, and like all weak tribes was exposed to risk of robbers, slave-hunters, ruinous and murderous wars; yet at the same time it was the national faith that they were the people Jehovah delighted to bless. It was an easy mistake to count themselves all good, and to identify the poor with the good. Much of Isaiah's condemnation of cruelty is denunciation of foreign cruelty to Hebrews. We might easily, therefore, be led to discount his condemnation of injustice to the poor as largely a national resentment against Assyrian injuries and the like.

But it is certain that Isaiah condemns Hebrew disregard of Hebrew fellow-men, and women and children. He does not speak so much of unchastity as Hosea did, but its plentiful presence disgusted him, and his withering wrath at it is too plain for public use to-day. Again, there was a common wickedness in Judah as well as in Israel which we have almost explained away from our picture of Zion life. Murder was quite common. Christianity has indeed cleansed the earth, for in mediaeval times Rome and Spain and England were probably not so bloody as Jerusalem was in Isaiah's time. They did need a purification of the earth.

One might expect that people and preachers who constantly saw bloody cruelty about them would lack all the finer care that kindly folk learn in gentler days. The daily need to guard their very lives, and anxiety as to that would surely prevent all gentler feelings. But no; in such a day there could live and think and plead such as Isaiah. Doubtless even among wolves there is maternal kindness;

perhaps there is much more. So Isaiah could plead hard in such society for kindness to the orphan and the widow, and to the poor man who needed legal counsel. We grow weary at times of the pursuit of our high ideals; often we smile at the enthusiast who would cheer us on, and who always ends his speech with, "Things do move, after all." But what an enthusiast was Isaiah, who declared with intense unceasing determination to that unchaste, dagger-drawing people, "You must spare the widow and the orphan. Hands off them! The land must be cleansed of all who hurt these, and unjust judges and bribe-takers must be cleansed away from our courts of justice." Isaiah never sounded the revolution's triple-voiced cry, but he was a revolutionist. He demanded fire from God to burn, and wind from God to scour away impure deeds, bloody deeds, unmanliness, all disregard of fellow-mortals.

(v.) Another blot he believes must be cleansed from earth; it is abuse of land tenure. This was long ago, and we cannot look to the methods of that day as a correct guide for the reform of our present land laws. Nevertheless the hope that starts within us at the bare suggestion of any light on the perplexing question is not doomed to entire disappointment. For Isaiah's faith that there can be a righteous law of land, and that all the injustice which prevents this shall be done away, tells certainly at least of an old, old instinct in us to look upon the soil with some such yearning as we feel towards a fellow-being.

Isaiah has not many words directly touching the matter, but they are enough.

> "Woe to you who are grasping house after house,
> And you are linking one broad acre to another as your own
> Till there is no room for a man to stand,
> And ye get you left alone in the midst of the land."

As in some work of Rembrandt, the grim horror of this picture dawns upon you only after you have gazed a while. Then peering out of the darkness the gaunt face of the lone man, lord of all the acres, chatters an awful appeal for help, comfort, brotherhood ere he die, and for burial then.

Although this is the only denunciation of land-wrong that Isaiah has left to us, his followers had nevertheless a keen sense of this very evil. And as we read we find why, for he delights in field and tree, and waving corn and juicy green pasture, ruddy vineyard and pale olive-grove; joy in fellowship with the soil is poured forth in his verses as in few others. To him ownership of land was necessary to life, for a man must have a place whereon to stand. And since the gods were in his view dependent on families of followers for their right to godhead, he who drove away the people from a land destroyed the god of the land. He who evicted Jehovah's people evicted Jehovah; and so the soulless, godless land about his home became a polluted land. We can understand that beyond this there was a still deeper sense of the evil when we remember that all believed then, as Isaiah certainly believed, that Jehovah Himself needed to possess certain portions of soil. He could not act nor live among men otherwise. So families and men must have inalienable rights in the soil, else they die. Therefore land-monopoly is a sin to be cleansed away. We find then that exclusion of men from all share in land-possession was practised, and Isaiah counted it a great wrong. The earth must be cleansed.

(vi.) Finally, he holds that the ritualistic formalism about him is an evil which must be done away. Let us note at the outset that among the few words he writes about such worship is one prediction (chap. xix. 21), that in the ideal days to come the Egyptians shall know Jehovah, and then "they will serve him with slaughtered victim and with gift; they will vow vows, and always fulfil them." So Isaiah recognised a symbolic value in religious feasts and ascetic pledges.

But much fuller reference, and the only other reference he makes to the topic, is in that chapter (chap. i.), of so uncertain date that it is wisely regarded as a summary of all the book, placed as preface, not as a first youthful utterance of his least-considered thoughts, but rather as a well-balanced summary of all his opinions written in his maturest years. There he pictures the people satisfying their religious cravings by feasts where the slaughtered victims are many, and the smoke of much burning fat ascends into God's nostrils, and much blood of oxen and lambs is scattered. But Isaiah thinks Jehovah does not desire this. There is much attendance in sanctuary worship. But Isaiah says decidedly Jehovah has not asked this. They give gifts, they burn incense; they observe religious days weekly, monthly, and they hold religious assemblies. But all this Isaiah counts a pain to the soul of the Unseen Lord. When he scorns those who stretch out their hands to make many prayers we do not argue that he would have nobody ever pray, not even a god-like soul whose cry to God would be as genuine and as right as an infant's cry for its mother. Isaiah certainly thinks of a religious feast as a natural expression of true fellowship with God. Yet he denies any Divine requirement of ritual service at the hands of his fellow-countrymen, and does this in language so strong that we must say Isaiah counted among the bad things that are to be cleansed away all the religion of ritual or law, whether written or unwritten. There is a passage, chap. viii., that seems, in our ordinary English version of it, like an exaltation of some body of law and testimony. But Torah (תּוֹרָה), usually translated "law," means not legal prescriptions or codes, but the "instruction" of some counsellor such as a prophet or a priest; and in the passage in question Isaiah is very plainly speaking of his own instructions to his own disciples. It is quite true, as we have seen, that he is the real founder of the peculiar Jewish faith in Zion as the saving sanctuary, but here he acts as a discoverer of something new, a new hope. Otherwise he is an iconoclast, much like Amos before him. He denounces formal worship, bidding men cease to do this evil and learn to do well. The earth must be cleansed.

In these pictures of the wrongs Isaiah condemned we see the baseness of Hebrew life about him. It is certainly well to be able to check the mistaken impression that Zion was a very moral place. On Isaiah's evidence it is proved to have been sadly filled with godless men and blasphemers, with conceited men and shameless women. It had always too many hard drinkers and debauchees, and very often it became a pandemonium of filthy carousers. Not the peasants only drank too much, but the very leaders, prophets, and priests staggered about at their religious tasks. Consequently there was harlotry, as with us; and, clearly more than with us, murder and violence to the widow, the orphan, and other helpless persons prevailed. There was administrative injustice, and there was disregard of a fine national instinct that every man should own land. Finally, there was much injurious ritual.

Such were the ordinary Hebrews. But in the picture we see more than this. There was a shadow across it. Conscience breathed its secret "Thou shalt not." The voice of Isaiah would have been meaningless had there not been a hidden conscience in every one of those Hebrews echoing the condemnation of the prophet. They knew their deeds were evil. Isaiah's condemnation and his demand for purification tell more than his own opinion; they tell what every good man would then wish to do, and what the conscience of every evil man knew. We have learned not a mere set of opinions acquired by one man; we have learned how the Spirit of God then was "convincing men of sin, and of righteousness, and of judgment." These later words express very accurately much of the constant nature of revelation.

Here we must observe the history of Isaiah's condemnation of sin as it advanced from his first utterances up to his latest. For his temper towards these wrongs varies. His minuter delineations of wicked deeds are in his earlier utterances, as there also stand the fiercest denunciations. That was the work of his younger ministry. It is the high prerogative of youth to feel strongly. It is the high prerogative of youth born anew into godliness to feel keenly the voice of conscience, and to cry at once its loud enthusiastic praise of goodness and indignant scorn of bad deeds. So did Isaiah speed out from his lonely ordination to demand at once utter destruction of all evil deeds and men. His burning word was itself fierce castigation. The conscience awakes to-day at the words. But Isaiah himself felt most keenly the bitter pain of his words; and they were sure to weary him till he rested on deeper truth. In the great advance of his life, when he gained his new insight into grace, he moved forward also to a maturer, calmer, truer condemnation of wrongs. In his later years the definite evils he strikes are rather evil principles than evil deeds. The one sensuous sin which he then singles out clearly for wrath and scorn is intoxication. But just that sin is doubly evil for it means deliberate self-debasement first in preparation for evil deeds, and afterwards the vile condition of the drunkard which it produces. Isaiah attacked that indeed, crying aloud for its cleansing in his later days as well as before. But the most of his later denunciations were against disregard of God and against untruth in life. He condemned then the unfaithfulness that trusted Egypt rather than Jehovah, and this means that his outlook was larger; but at the same time it is in these later chapters that he writes his verdict against the private churl and the hypocrite in Zion. He could see a wider horizon, for he was a larger man; but he could scan individuals now, and more thoroughly than before, for he looked past their lips and hands and discovered evil in their hearts. It was alongside of such keener verdict of guilty, guilty of more than deed, guilty of malice intent, that he rose far above the Amosian way of purification by excision, and far beyond the Hosean theory of seclusion also. How his spirit wrestled with this problem of the method, and how he reached that last wonderful prophecy of cleansing for Zion, "They that dwell there shall be forgiven their iniquity," and what that cleansing of forgiveness meant, we are to trace in the next paragraphs.

§ 5. *His grasp of the grace of God.*

Deeply interesting are the two facts that Isaiah rose to faith in grace, and from his first grasp of it his whole life was one great struggle to understand its depths. So our introductory chapter, "Isaiah and Zion," which made us acquainted with the man's soul and a tale of his life, was simply a story of his discovery of the grace of God. So too all we have seen of him since, as we have walked by his side and watched, has been lit up by this bright faith breaking in on point by point.

Therefore a systematic formulation of the prophet's doctrine of grace ought to be a simple index to the experiences of the man, and to the story that has passed before us. Recall them rapidly.

(*a*) The story of Isaiah and Zion told of his young manhood's strokes for the right, and his cry, "Down with all wrongs, and God save the good." These were the oracles until soon and naturally he failed, as the prophet of judgment must fail to heal. Then came his soul's backward gaze to the day of his own first devotion to Jehovah. The Giver of all thought touched the heart with recollection of His gracious descent to spare, to cleanse, to commission the man who knew his own uncleanness, and to send him forth full of devotion and of speech. Now and to the end Isaiah was the prophet of just such healing and grace. Such favour to the fallen, he declared, should be found in Zion by the dwellers and worshippers there.

(*b*) We have learned also how this conception of Jehovah's character expanded the earlier and less definite conception of His holiness. All the earth was full of His "glory" (כְּבוֹד יְהוָה), and glory was the robe He wore before all peoples. That is, they knew only His great importance; the Hebrew had come to believe that all peoples were bowing to Jehovah's supreme control. To the Hebrew, again, his God exhibited His devotion (קְדֹשׁ יְהוָה). They believed that all Jehovah's affection and energies were devoted to them. But hitherto this had meant simply a great good for the nation as a whole, and more generally still a great good for the nation as naturally worthy of it, and only so long as it was thus worthy. There was little thought of individuals and their value; there was no blessing, and even no life, for the evildoers.

But now Isaiah learnt to believe Jehovah would be devoted also to sinful men in Zion. He had been so graciously devoted to one man of unclean lips that henceforth, said Isaiah, He would forgive, heal, and bless all who dwelt there.

(*c*) We have seen this new vision of God lighten up another of Isaiah's early faiths with a new great glory. We have read how the national faith in Jehovah's overlordship arose and grew. Isaiah had shared it truly, but he came to read in it far more than he dreamed at first. For the great Over-Lord, who could make the Hebrew David king over many tribes beyond the national home lands, was not disobeyed by Egypt, or even by Assyria. These might scourge God's chosen tribe, but they obeyed His command, and they did it to work out His chastening purpose. For Jehovah meant to cause the remnant to return, and Israel to be indeed restored in sure and settled purity and goodness. Jehovah was to prove Over-Lord over sin, for He would forgive it. Over-Lord over all powers of evil, for He would cleanse the unclean men of Zion and make them good. This was the new overlordship; it was the old faith all woven through with the faith in the grace of God.

(*d*) But now let us trace the prophet's struggle to fathom the deep meanings of this grace. And we shall follow this best by watching the successive tokens of this grace which he discovers.

(*a*) First then, when he recalls his initial vision and reads its fresh revelation he grasps at once that estimate of Zion's significance which, as we saw above, pervades all his further oracles. This estimate of Zion colours also all his discoveries of other tokens of the Divine grace, as we shall see. And yet even in the picture given in chapter sixth there is besides Zion another token; Isaiah himself is likewise an exhibition of that grace. It was not Zion alone that was blessed; it was not, after all, the mere place on earth, the sacred spot, or the walls, or the altar, nor was it even the throne, which was "high and lifted up," rather than gracious in its nearness. It was Isaiah who exhibited in person the marks of the love of God, his lips bore henceforth the purity God's cleansing gave; those lips spoke Jehovah's will of God with an utter love for Him which the gracious Divine love had wooed and won. Isaiah's soul lived anew, happy, strong with a new life which God had begotten; Isaiah was a work of grace. He was so in Zion indeed, and he never forgot that.

(β) We turn to a second notable record of his faith in God's grace, and of his recognition of the channels where it flowed. It stands in the words of chap. viii. 10, 16, 17, 18. Here, as before, Zion is the place; but the grace is revealed from a

God who dwells there, and unto persons who dwell there too. "Behold *I and the children whom Jehovah hath given me* are for *signs* and for wonders in Israel from Jehovah of hosts, *who dwelleth in Mount Zion*." This utterance marks his rise from faith in a sanctuary to higher and finer faith in God's love for persons. It is remarkable, and surely not without import, that the prophet declares in an early verse in this chapter, "God is with us" as a people. A foolish people we are, ay, and untrustful towards Him. Yet He is with us, and our wisdom would be to count Him devoted to us. Then a few verses later on, as if he is hardly able to count them all worthy of this oracle and this counsel, he somewhat limits his grasp and his token, and says this teaching must be sealed and treasured up by his pupils as their own. Then once more the limitation proceeds, for even pupils may not all prove true; but in his own soul, whose life he knows, and in the children that are of his own body and moulded by his own character, in all this his real and full self is an unquestionable gift and token of Jehovah's merciful saving love for this people.

(γ) Soon follows in those chapters, so full of mingled oracle and narrative, chaps. vii. to ix., the further stage of effort to understand how Jehovah can be graciously present although the people are not all good. He will dwell upon and in the prince. "Unto us a king is born," who shall be a very Divine person in his heroic strength, in his wisdom, and in his fatherhood of his people. Here is a hope co-ordinate with the prophet's faith in his own personal representation of God, and also in some sense a higher faith than that. Higher it is in so far as the king is in actual touch with the people more fully than the prophet. The serious defect is the frequent want of true godliness in the king.

Isaiah sees this. Thrice over does he prophesy of the king as such a token of God's saving love, and each time does he grow more solicitous for Divine mercy to make the king fit for the task. In chap. ix. we have the first impassioned picture; in chap. xiv., when Ahaz dies, is the belief that even out of death Jehovah can raise living strength, and beside a tomb build refuge for His beloved poor. Then, finally, in chap. xi. is the wonderful realistic representation of Jehovah's regeneration of the prince for the sake of saving all the land and people. It is of great interest to observe here the steady rise of Isaiah far above all faith in the inherent goodness of institutions, or even of men, and his discovery of rest in God alone. All things else, tested one by one, seem to fail, but the character of the invisible Jehovah grows to Isaiah more sufficient, more gracious, more utterly trustworthy in its love.

(δ) Chapter xxxiii. is Isaian, although its present form may not be. (But see Cheyne, Or. of Psalter, 237). Here there are a few words about the king's work and beauty, but they are very few indeed in comparison with the emphatic utterances of the value of Zion, and the safety of all who are found there. Yet this is not strange. The facts concerning the chapter are these. It pictures the failure and sin of men, and their need of forgiveness, health, grace, more emphatically than any previous oracle since chapter sixth. At the same time it proclaims Zion, the great refuge, with what is at first sight a startling exaltation of a mere material instrument as working salvation of every sort. But this proclamation only serves to exalt as the real and only and utter Saviour, not Zion, and not any personage at all, but Jehovah. Isaiah is so absorbed in this thought of Jehovah that he forgets his own personality, does not quote Jehovah in the third person when he begins his oracle, but is a mere channel for Jehovah's personal utterance.

> Hear, ye that are far off,
> What I have done.
> Acknowledge, ye that are near,
> My might.

And in cries of splendid rapture he sings—

> The glorious Jehovah will be unto us our
> Euphrates and our Nile.
>
> . . . .
>
> For Jehovah is our Judge,
> Jehovah is our Lawgiver,
> Jehovah is our King.
> He will save us.
>
> . . .
>
> The inhabitants of Zion shall not say,
> I am sick;
> The people that dwell there
> Shall be forgiven their iniquity.

One is startled indeed by Isaiah's limitation of the area of grace, but by it he seems able after all to concentrate his gaze on the fact of grace and on its cause. Plunging thus into the very centre of the soul of God, he leaves it to later seers and ages to watch the circling waves of that ocean of love. We know by our vision of Jesus the Christ that the ocean is infinite.

§ 6. *His rise to faith in regeneration.*

Ever and anon in what we have seen hitherto there have been unmistakable utterances of a faith in Isaiah's soul that Jehovah must create utterly new life if there is to be any true goodness in the land. Proof is hardly needed here that he does so speak; what will be in place is rather a picture of these utterances in their actual setting in the prophet's story, and in the history of the whole period. Recall then a few features of the time.

(1) In the earlier century, when Elijah fought for the supremacy of Jehovah, there was not much thought of a character in the people as over against the character of Jehovah. The people were prized by the God as a possession

co-ordinate with the land which He possessed as His special country.

(2) When Amos spoke, the conception of Jehovah's character as supremely righteous was rising high and growing profounder than ever before. Necessarily there grew the keen sense that the people of this righteous God must be righteous too. So the cry of Amos was, "Seek good;" and, to obtain a people who are all good, Amos declares Jehovah will cut off all the evil. In one sense this is of course a gospel; it is a prophecy of a clean land. And it is likewise a gospel of salvation, for the land and the good who dwell there are to be saved from the defilement of the bad. But there is no salvation for the bad, and there is no regeneration, no work of God that changes character, and makes a bad man good.

(3) Hosea believed the bad Hebrew could be good. If the bad soul were prisoned away from the wine and whoredom that depraved his mind, then at once with cleared vision he would see the right way and walk in it. The nature of the Hebrew was essentially good; he needed no change, he needed only freedom. Hosea did not preach regeneration.

(4) But Isaiah saw deeper into the evil. There are two remarkable declarations of the need of regeneration and of its certain coming, and one of these he preached amongst his oracles of judgment; the other stands among his oracles of grace. We shall see that either the one prevailing faith or the other, either the supreme faith in judgment or the faith in grace, demands a regenerative work of God, a creative interposition, a supernatural work, a permanent and immanent Divine aid for men.

(*a*) In the earlier period, although Amosian, Isaiah is far more searching than Amos was. If the sinners of the people were all cut off, then should there be no man left in the land. So in the end of chap. iii. stands the dread scene of desolate death. The bereaved city sits upon the ground in speechless woe for her sons. All are gone, just as Amos prophesied; all sinners have died by the sword. The gates are gaping mouths that howl. The misery is only made more real by the peopling of the emptiness with representatives of sorrow; there are seven women to wail, and round one man these seven hunger greedily for spousal love with weak devices to hide their jealousy. Then, says the prophet, if there is to be any more life in Jerusalem, it cannot be the simple fruit of Jerusalem's homes. If the city is to be a garden of flower and fruit again, the trees must be altogether of God's creative planting. Prof. de Lagarde, Semitica I. 8, throws much light on this oracle by telling us how the Hebrew and the Arab distinguished between the crops in cultivated fields, which were man's work, and the herbs, shrubs, trees which grew in the broad untilled lands afar from men's toil. These latter were plants of God; they might be Baal's plants, here they were "Jehovah's shoots." There is another fine illustration of this figure in a passage where we read that Egypt was watered by man's foot, but Canaan was a more blessed land, for there the "eyes of God," which are "the springs of God," the bubbling wells of water which God alone sends forth, are everywhere and always, Deut. viii. 7; xi. 10.

So Isaiah in the hour of absolute desolation and death believes that God will create new souls. They shall all be good souls, and every one registered in the rolls of the living inhabitants of Zion shall be holy, devoted to Jehovah. The prophet carries on his fair creation scene; Jehovah will clothe all souls, all women, and all homes with the garments of goodness, for He will create above each roof the pillar of smoke, grey by day, ruddy by night, that tells of a sacrificial fire and feast on the hearth below.

The land must be full of godly men; and God's hand will create them. This faith in regeneration rose out of Isaiah's doctrine of sternest judgment.

(*b*) But Isaiah learned more of God, and better; he

learned to preach that Jehovah comes down in grace to the unclean, cleanses him and fills him with God's own mind and utterance. This is itself regeneration. No wonder that, when once he had clearly realised this experience, a few years' reflection on it resulted, on a day of intense emotion, in that most splendid outpouring of the faith of his God-filled soul that stands in chap. xi. Professor Duhm has pointed out that this oracle is not opened by the formula, "Thus saith Jehovah," and he suggests that possibly Isaiah hesitated to attribute the grand future of the coming golden age to Jehovah's inspiration. But we must not be moved to accept this theory by the consideration that, were the oracle introduced by this formula, it would be an infallible forecast of the regenerated future; whereas lacking the formula it lacks the infallibility, and we need not perplex ourselves over the difficulty of a lion eating straw. The triviality of the conclusion reveals the triviality of the principle which produced it, and the barrenness of such conceptions of God and of man, which weary our souls with puzzles. Isaiah seems rather to be utterly unconscious here of any separation between himself and Jehovah, and "all taken up with God," he pours out the faith, the conception, the self, that are indeed all God's own. The insertion of the formula would rather signify some consciousness of distinction between the Inspirer and the speaker, and this is here all gone as in many another of the best utterances of the Old Testament, and as in so many of all the words of the New. Isaiah could say, "I live, yet not I, but Jehovah liveth in me." If a theory of infallibility is troubled by this fact, it is troubled. We turn to the story of Isaiah's new faith in regeneration.

He has just described the chastisement of the people by the Assyrian rod. He knows chastisement is not enough; he has learnt, some years ago now, that the rod of judgment fails. There must be regeneration of character in those who remain; but how? Evidently the thought that the Assyrian forest of spears shall be all hewn down recalls to the prophet's memory that very oracle of his which we read in chap. iv. But he does not repeat it now; he mounts from it with the wings of his new faith in grace to the newer, truer vision. Jehovah can descend to sinful souls in Zion; and He who has cut off all the Assyrian forest will hover like the wind in the tops of the Hebrew tree to fill it with Himself and make it all godlike. That tree-top is, to the Oriental thinker, the prince. That monarch shall be filled of God with the Spirit of God, with reverence for Jehovah, with knowledge of all His will; and then by the absolute rule of the prince the people shall all be led righteously. Observe here the beautiful fountain of a new stream of God's truth that was to swell into a great river between Bethlehem and Calvary, and to roll on thence as a river of the water of life through all the ages. Isaiah's first doctrine of regeneration was that of utterly superhuman action; the new is a conception of the spirit of Jehovah working in man, and through man upon man. When five centuries later the collision of the Greek faiths with the Hebrew under Antiochus made awful agony, the resistance of each toward the other was only the instinctive travail of each to bear love toward the other. The Hebrew struggle was begun by Isaiah when he conceived—God moving in Him, as He moves in all such conceiving—that regeneration must be the work of Divine men. Do we wonder that the evident, simple possibility of such a work on the one hand, combined with its inevitable, matchless, godlike outcome on the other, filled Isaiah with a rhapsody of delight, tuned his voice into idyllic melody, and bade him wrestle with what he thought unwilling nature to compel her to aid the universal joy and to forego all her work of pain. Shall the tree-top shake with the wind of God? then the clods of earth too can know Him. All things from the prince to the very soil beneath the feet shall be changed, and even savage beasts shall learn to work together for good in this coming day of regeneration. There shall be no hurt in Zion or in her territory. The rival divisions of the Davidic people shall be one, envying each other no more. The surrounding peoples who bowed beneath David's overlordship shall run to serve the people of Jehovah. Egypt and Assyria shall send home all Hebrews who may be enslaved in them, and the way home shall be safe.

The problem has been raised, Can an evil man become good? In jubilant faith Isaiah begins the long process of solution by his emphatic "Yes," and by his wonderful vision and song of the result. He did not wait for the tests of experience upon his theory, but he ensured their long slow application. His plan raised many a fresh question, and so heralded more and more of the revelations which God vouchsafes to those who ask and think and listen in their souls for the truth. Were Isaiah's picture or his theory a final ordinance of God, then God would have given up His function as Creator of sons unto Himself who should ever learn from their Father's providence and from their communion in spirit with the Father of Spirits. God gave through Isaiah a theory of regeneration which was sure to pass away by awakening others to learn more and more from that Divine inspiration themselves.

The idea grasped by Isaiah in the eleventh chapter is not a momentary thought that soon vanishes. It pervades much of his later oracles, and especially that in chaps. xxix. and xxxii. But there is no further rise; rather is there a more cautious emphasis upon the more purely spiritual phases of the regenerated life. The passages are especially xxix. 18 *ff*, and xxxii. 4, 15 *ff*.

§ 7. (B.) *Isaiah's thought on the three fundamental questions.*

(1) Concerning the nature of God.
(2) Concerning the nature of man.
(3) Concerning perfect life.

We think of theology to-day as a carefully articulated expression of our mental grasp of the facts of religious life. Not every one needs a theology for the purposes of his life; although every one needs a religion, and indeed every one has a religion. But to know another man's religion, and to have true regard for it, and to delineate it, you must think out for yourself and get into clear mental grasp all the facts of his religion—in a word, you must construct the theology of his life. Isaiah was not a theologian; he does not write for us his theology. He was simply a great religious man, a man of intense faith pouring out splendid utterances of that faith. But we may and must trace the groundlines of that faith if we would pourtray the man truly in all his fulness.

(1) First then let us formulate what was to Isaiah "the nature of God." Theology circles round a definition of the central religious fact in a man's life—that is, round a careful expression of what God was to the man; therefore we must collect the *momenta* of Isaiah's thoughts of God, some of them prominent and already described above, others more hidden, the essential framework rather than the apparent features.

(*a*) Isaiah spoke then of a Person Jehovah, and spoke of Him as a Divine Being. He spoke of Him, to be more exact, as one of the Elohim; he meant, so far as the meaning of the word can tell us, that Jehovah was one of the far-outreaching beings. For the words Elohim, Eloăh, El are evidently connected with 'alah = he reached out, he sware (reaching out the hand), whence also 'el = unto, 'elah = pinetree, &c., *ĕlleh* = those, *allon* = oak, &c. The word for "God" is also an intransitive (= outreacher), as its main vowel "i" shows. Professor de Lagarde's careful and repeated discussions of the word throw abundant light on the matter, and are invaluable. (See his *Orientalia*, Göttingen, 1880, ii. p. 3, &c.) Isaiah therefore was conscious of an Unseen Person who "reached out" to him, and to whom instinctively his soul and cry and praying hands reached out.

But this does not lead us far. The profounder fact is that Isaiah felt his own faiths and opinions concerning the nation, its symbolic personages, and himself, also his faiths concerning the destiny of all these, and finally also concerning the duty of nation and self—he felt all these to be the mind of this Divine Jehovah communicated to himself. Jehovah was therefore not "One afar" only, but also a very present Person who created in the prophet's mind faiths and thoughts. So the prophet speaking out these called his own words the word of Jehovah, God of hosts, the Devoted One of Israel.

These words point to the source of this consciousness of God. He obtained this like all his national inheritances, his body and his life, his possessions, speech, knowledge, and traditions, from the people among whom he was born. His religion was no fancy of his own; it was a historic possession. It was conceivable, of course, that such an inheritance might become worn out in time, or be given up, as some inheritances are; it might, on the other hand, be as essential to life as is one's very body, and might also increase constantly in beauty and in preciousness. Certainly to Isaiah his faith in Jehovah was such an inheritance; he needed no proof that Jehovah was. Yet he could increase in knowledge of Him; he could even leave faulty conceptions of Him, and new features of his God's love might burst upon the vision of the wondering prophet.

Isaiah's conception of his God Jehovah was in a sense

parallel to our Christian conception of Christ, who is to us God manifest in the flesh. When we formulate carefully what God is to us, we write down the story of our new birth into life in the kingdom of God wrought in us by our Saviour the Christ; and the narrative of this experience of ours, comprehended as part of the great story of experience that circles round the Cross, is our story of God revealing Himself to create us anew. Our hold on God is an assurance within that we are alive through and in this ever living, present Christ. So Isaiah's faith in God was his assurance of inward communion with the Divine Person whom the Hebrew people had known through the ages as a God devoted to them, called by the name Jehovah.

(*b*) But how did Isaiah conceive of the action of Jehovah upon himself and men, and what was his conception of the concrete form of Jehovah's self-revelation?

(*a*) It is of secondary importance here to know the significance of the vision described in chap. vi., yet that significance is intensely interesting. Evidently the vision took place amid unusual natural phenomena; and this lessens its importance to us, for we wish to know how Jehovah was to be recognised when only ordinary natural phenomena were occurring. Isaiah saw, as he records, a lordly One exalted high upon a throne, and His train skirting about that glorious throne filled all the palace where the Divine throne stood. We understand most of these features; we know what lordly appearance is, and what the singularly exalted throne. But we do not know what the train was of which he speaks. Was it a great sweeping robe, or was it the glorious host of seraph courtiers? The result we reach, if we try to conceive of the scene, is that Isaiah does indeed conceive of God in anthropomorphic manner, but his anthropomorphism is uncertain. He is not strongly realistic; he tends rather towards a more austere, more spiritual conception.

(β) Let us remember that even in the earlier ministry, when we might perhaps look for more anthropomorphisms, we find very few, and fewer of these are strictly tangible features. We read of the paths of Jehovah, and that He standeth to judge; but these are scarcely realisms. When the prophet with fine sympathy grieves at the thought of Jehovah's glorious eyes embittered with pain, and when in anger he draws back the veil and reveals Jehovah's arm outstretched to strike, in these things we have all that is very material in Isaiah's conception of Jehovah's nature.

(γ) But the oracles of the later more gracious period represent God's action in a still more spiritual way. The regeneration of prince and people, and of earth and beasts of earth, and all men and things, is to be worked by the resting of the Spirit of Jehovah upon the prince. The "Spirit of God" we may translate by the "wind of God" if we choose; certainly the moving of this Spirit is represented by the figure of the wind that moves in the leaves of the forest. We hear the sound thereof, we know its presence and its work, but we see it not, nor can we tell whence it cometh and whither it goeth. It is interesting to observe, by the way, how much of the forms of New Testament speech may have been the natural fruit of converse with the voices of the prophets of long before. And as the conception in John iii. was finely spiritual, so was that in Isaiah xi.; largely so was it through the choice of figure for the representation. The hovering figure of the defending Jehovah (chap. xxxi. 5) is of course in significance closely like the figure of the wind; and this bird-figure is likewise used in the New Testament. Throughout these later oracles this level of conception is well maintained. The writer certainly does regard the thunder as the voice of Jehovah, calling it His glorious voice; but again and again he alludes to the monitions of conscience as the Divine voice also (xxx. 21). All the more striking is this allusion when we find the simple husbandman's judgment concerning his daily farm duties described as the very instruction of God, Jehovah of hosts.

(*b*) Here then we have clear light on Isaiah's conception of Jehovah's communication of His oracles to him. As he conceived the brooding Spirit giving to the prince all godliness and knowledge of Jehovah's mind, so we must think did he count all his own knowledge of Jehovah to be the work of that unseen brooding Spirit, and he trusted in Jehovah that He did not mislead him.

(*c*) This leads us at once to the few words necessary here concerning the power of this God Jehovah. We have seen already the full story of the prophet's faith on this matter. Jehovah was the controlling Lord over all hosts and all powers in the world around him, and in the nether world. And this faith was expanding into the larger belief that Jehovah ruled over the causes of sin, and could lift men out of the disease of it back into the healthy condition of the righteous, and He could give them again all the gladdening marks of children of Israel.

The conception of Jehovah as suzerain, or lord paramount over many Divine powers, each in some sense sovereign, was thoroughly a conception of the times. It does not satisfy the philosophy of our day; that is unnecessary. But it arose at once from observation of the customary royalties of that age. Given the profound sense of control by many invisible Persons, and a faith that the Israelite Deity, Jehovah, was the Supreme One over these, we at once appreciate Isaiah's mode of representing these ideas.

(*d*) Here we recall the various æsthetic features in Isaiah's conception of Jehovah. There are, he intimates, certain sensations produced by the knowledge of Jehovah's presence which are akin to our sense of beauty. These tell us, the prophet feels, partly what the æsthetic characteristics of the very Person of Jehovah are, and partly what are the fit characteristics of His environment.

(a) Glory is the ceaseless efflux from Jehovah's Person, of which Isaiah speaks in almost every oracle. The man who is conscious of God's presence feels a radiance as of glorious eyes beaming on him, and the voice of God is glorious, whether it is heard in the thunder or in conscience. This impression of effluent glory was literally a sense of the weight of God. It signifies a sense of the transcendent importance, the exceeding value of Jehovah. We have read how Isaiah felt that this sense filled all the earth; all things were overpowered by the sense of the glory of Jehovah.

But in the beams of that brilliance Isaiah says the Hebrew soul could see a still more wondrous light. Love streamed along those beams. While all others bowed overwhelmed the Israelite could feel that wondrous sense that gives ecstasy to a lover. He was beloved. Jehovah's presence made that impression. Isaiah's greatest task was to sound the unknown depths of this love and proclaim it to his fellows.

(β) But only a certain environment was fit for this great Person. Not always nor everywhere could His presence be felt. His subjective æsthetic quality required an objective æsthetic setting. A very tangible part of this was Zion, according to the clear and eagerly declared mind of Isaiah in his later days. The great glory of Jehovah could be known indeed throughout all the earth, but only in Zion could His devotion reach and enswathe every soul, and there only could this matchless depth of His character be felt. There too the worshipping Israelite could behold and even touch the glorious robe of God, for in the Zion temple the heavenly train could be unfolded to fill that house. There the hosts of His court could assemble and hold high converse on His name. But even they counted His appearance too sacred to behold; utterly satisfied were they that Deity should be invisible. This is a remarkable feature in Isaiah's conception; it borders on appreciation of the invisible nature of God. And it is the more remarkable because the man who has a part in the scene, as representative of beings not yet all pure and perfect, does see a form while the perfect souls forego all sight.

The perfection of these perfect spirits consists in their ceaseless realisation of the love of Jehovah, which is His highest attribute and His essential nature. Such an environment befits this Deity; this is His garment.

The question whether Isaiah counted sacrifices and ritual of any special and considerable degree of elaborateness as the worthy environment of Jehovah has been already discussed. Isaiah lived in an age that loved feastings, meats, and wines, and considered these as religious occasions wherein the Deity took pleasure because they did. Isaiah is a man of his time, and he shares the feeling that such pleasure may be religious; but he does not exalt the custom as the very desirable way to honour Jehovah. He does not prescribe a ritual of worship, either sacrificial or otherwise, he does not hint at any such ritual as well known and worthy; he condemns unsparingly all the Hebrew sacrifices he mentions. Only once does he predict any sort of altar worship; it is to be performed by the Egyptians, as (xix. 21) he says—

Jehovah shall make Himself known to Miçraim,
And let Miçraim know Jehovah in that day;
And let Miçraim serve with sacrificial slaughter and with gift.
Let them vow vows to Jehovah and keep them.

The true attitude Isaiah desires in the people and counts worthy towards God is goodness in thought (chap. xi., &c.), in heart and in speech (chap. xxxii., &c.), in calling (chap. xxxiii., &c.), in home (chap. iv., &c.), and throughout all in trustful love for the ever-present loving Jehovah (chap. viii., &c.). Such is the æsthetic character of Jehovah.

(c) The moral character of Jehovah, as Isaiah conceived it, is inseparably manifest in all His æsthetic features; and it has also appeared in the pictures we have gained of His self-revelation and of His administration of His power. And certainly, as the stream's highest level tells the level of the fountains, so the Isaian conception of the goodness of Jehovah must be a picture of Isaiah's own conscience. What Isaiah thought was right was sure to be what he thought Jehovah's moral nature was. The pictures of Isaiah's own high moral aims, as we have seen them all along our way, are therefore truly also Isaiah's conception of the high purposes of Jehovah. Such then is this prophet's theology proper.

(2) There is an Isaian anthropology. It is simple, elementary in a sense, and unlike ours; yet it exhibits growth, that infallible sign of life.

(*a*) This then we may record of it in the first place, that Isaiah's conception of human nature is a conception in process of development. Our study of details in the matter will make this plain; meanwhile we may remember that *à priori* we must expect Isaiah to be a man of progress, and progress most decided. For essentially he was a receiver of revelation, as we saw. His whole life was one constant listening to the mind of God, ever newly poured forth in him; he was one constant record of that revelation in speech to men. He certainly did not limit the truth of God, and there is no evidence that he had any inherited philosophical system or code of oracles whose ever new light was to be got by simple process of exegesis. No, he expected always to receive Divine visions of truth, and ever and anon to forsake opinions he had earnestly proclaimed to be Divine that he might move forward to grasp others quite different, and proclaim these as the new word from God. He thought in this way on every subject; it was certain that his conception of man would not be crystallised, but organically growing.

(*b*) We turn to the oracles preached, and find that, for the most part, like Hebrews before him, he thought of all Israel as a mass. The possession of Jehovah was "the people as a whole;" there was little thought of the value of an individual. This was perfectly natural. Of course there was individual conscience, but there was not much reflection on its meaning. The reflection which was essential to the prophet's speech circled chiefly round the great Divine conception, a conception that seems to have been more utterly absorbing to a Hebrew than it is to Western minds. So too in the denunciations of chaps. ii. to v., while there is indeed minute description of wrong deeds, these deeds are charged against all Israel as a whole. There is certainly no distinct individualisation of sinners in the repeated formula, "Woe unto them that, . . ." as if there were some who did this evil, and some who did that, and some who did neither. The words do not necessarily carry that meaning. They say simply, "Ho, ye! joining house to house," "Ho, ye! rising early to drink," &c., &c. The descriptions and the woes are addressed to the whole people. It is "my people" that has no knowledge. It is "the inhabitants of Jerusalem" that have disappointed Jehovah. It is "the daughters of Zion" that are haughty. We read, "O house of Jacob, come ye," not "O sinner, come thou." And so we might quote through all the periods.

But especially in a passage like chap. xi., which does single out an individual, the absence of individualism is evident. The prince is indeed to have a direct personal gift of the Divine Spirit to make him of quick understanding and make him rule righteously; but the Spirit is given no further. The individual Hebrew's capacity for such a gift to make him a true subject or citizen is not realised by Isaiah. When the prince is once divinely swayed, then he sways all his subjects by his power and command as one drives a flock of soulless sheep. There must be one central soul, one conscience and will; and this is regnant in one over all, and not even in one of the mass, but in one above them. This kind of solidarity is characteristic throughout the oracles.

Finally, the lack of individualism appears in the plan of salvation by residence in a city, Zion, which is assured of safety for itself and all its inhabitants. These people are treated as a mass, without regard to individual character. Nay, more, even the sinners in Zion, the debauchees (chap. xxviii.), the hypocrites (chap. xxxii.), are in a sense divested of their distinctive character and their desert, and are saved in the mass in this first wonderful effort to conceive of forgiveness and salvation. Thus the loftiest grasp of God's love at this date conceived only of His love for a mass, a people as a whole.

(*c*) And yet very evidently a deeper vision was beginning. The evidence is largely the same as we have just had. There existed already the conviction that at least some one human soul must have individual grace from God if there was to be any righteousness and any salvation. The prince was, in a sense, an individual Hebrew; and his individual function and value were well estimated, even although it were Oriental and despotic. And other individuals were emerging from the dim haze into clear outline and preciousness. The prophet's own value certainly was, as the story of his call shows. But so also were the figures growing distinct that moved about the prophet's personal life, his spouse, his children, who were signs from Jehovah too; and his pupils also were being detached in character from the general mass. So too, on the other hand, wrongdoers were being singled out. For while it was "the people" that were astray and condemned, yet it was "the rulers" who caused this (chap. xxviii. 14), just as good rulers could produce national righteousness. Moreover, in the terrible song of woe and of "the outstretched arm," where "the people" as a whole is condemned, there is also some specification of individuals. The ordinary English versions are ambiguous, as we have seen, and may not be pressed too far. But there is a change beginning in the distinction, chap. v. 23, between "the wicked" and the whole people who "justify the wicked," and between "the righteous" and the whole people, "who take away the righteousness of the righteous from them." There is scarcely need of evidence, for the man who attacks sin must see individual sinners, and the primitive childlike dream of the people as a mass is sure to break down. Isaiah's anthropology, then, was in process of change. His mind was searching ever deeper, and thus did God give to him revelations.

(3) Isaiah had an ideal of perfect life. We might call this his eschatology. It is certainly his "doctrine of the last things," for he always speaks of the ideal as yet to be realised when the golden days shall come. He begins his description of it mostly with the familiar ביום ההוא, "In that day." When that day shall have dawned there shall be no sunset that Isaiah knows; then shall have begun the grand last things. Our Christian thinking bears the impress of Isaiah's mind, and has been so inspired by his faith as to conceive many a time its own ideal of heavenly life in the wondrous forms he spoke. Isaiah's eschatology has moulded ours; his ideal of perfect life is a well-known vision in the treasure-house of our own ideals. Its features here following are therefore somewhat familiar:—

(*a*) It was an old faith our prophet took and wove into it newer, finer features to form his vision of the future. He opened his oracles by quoting from the past, although he was to become and abide prince among Hebrew preachers. He took an old faith in Zion, shook it to the foundation, lest evil might cling to it, and clothing it in the new robe of Jehovah's gracious love for ill-deserving men, he made the Zion temple the centre of his new heavenlike kingdom on earth.

(*b*) The title "his doctrine of last things" seems to grow inappropriate when we find that its central figure is David, the hero of the past. But so it has been in other Utopias; the golden age to come is a return of the golden age that is gone. Of course the secret is, that the ideals of to-day are read into the honoured past when this is so far away that its troubles are forgotten. God smooths away the lines of care from the cheeks of our beloved dead; and He has ordained that we shall magnify the beauty of the far-off past while we think ever less of its pain. So Isaiah glorified the age of David, the long-past days of the foundation of the Hebrew monarchy; and when he would picture the glorious age that he hoped should come, he thought it must be just the glorious David-days come back again. So he sang his vision of the perfect life to be.

(c) We have seen that he felt there must be a very radical change of nature when that new age begins. Men and things must be virtually re-created. Men must be regenerated, and turn to new thoughts and deeds. Here the prophet had struck on a law of life that has proved fundamental; Christianity has exalted it as a very part of the constitution of the kingdom of God among men, and the thinking world in general seems to be adopting a similar theory. But when Isaiah leaped to the conclusion that the nature of all things must be changed as well as human nature, his mind was doubtless moved to this by two considerations. For to him thus far men and other things had seemed to be all of one nature. As we have seen, he had little thought of the value of the individual and of character. If then men and things were of the same sort, and one part of these must be changed, then surely the other part must be changed also. Again, it was to do away the evil that was in the world that the change was necessary; but while men did much of the evil, it seemed to him that the beasts also delighted to hurt and destroy, and the sea and the desert helped to make ever-dreaded slavery a more bitter curse. So Isaiah learned to believe that if true happiness is to come on earth, the very earth herself must become pervaded by the mind of God; her form must here and there be changed, and her forest beasts must put on new nature, her serpents, her bears, and lions must have a new physical organisation. Isaiah did not see—it was left for later prophets to see—ever more clearly that evil has little to do with circumstances, with earth and beasts and death, and sin belongs only to souls. Isaiah's prophecy lay in the hope for some golden age of perfect life, not in the manner of it; and the Perfect Life that came to highest bloom on Calvary was realised through greatest pain.

(*d*) Here we must record how Isaiah's picture of perfect life contains certain other features, of great beauty too, which reveal how a true estimate of the value of character should come about, although it had not yet quite come to Isaiah himself. He tells in chap. iv. how each living soul registered in the Zion city-roll shall be devoted to Jehovah. This is, of course, the mere statement of the high hope; but the next few words tell of another feature of the happy time, whose mention shows in what direction thinking was sure to progress. Every home should be a sanctuary, and every hearth an altar; on every roof should rise the pillar of smoke by day and gleaming light by night that marked the place where a sacred feast was being prepared or enjoyed amid devout praise and prayer, and in faith that Jehovah Himself was a present guest. Along this path of love for home godliness, where womanly purity would be the central fragrance, Hebrew thinkers were certain to rise to consciousness of the value of each individual soul. The man who carried such conceptions of perfect life as Isaiah had was sure to be constantly advancing to deeper truth and to more truth.

(*e*) There is often a fine interlacing of ideas in Isaiah; and this makes the point which we have reached the right place to speak of the agricultural wealth which Isaiah expects shall clothe the coming perfect days. For he gives one of his fairest visions of this in a passage where he emphasises peculiarly woman's share in producing or in delaying it (chap. xxxii. 9-20). And the agricultural prosperity of the coming golden age must be mentioned here for another reason—namely, this, that while Isaiah does predict a radical change of the nature of beasts and the like that do hurt to men, yet he certainly speaks much more of the good things and good times that may come by ordinary wise husbandry. In fact, while he desires all evil agencies to be stopped and turned to good, he desires also all good agencies to be abundantly used. And he has far more to say of this latter than of the former. He is not often a dreamer, but mostly a very practical economist. For quite certainly material joys bulk very largely in his ideal of the highest good. The fact that men to-day are learning to count these material comforts an important part of the gifts of the Gospel suggests an interesting question. When men believe strongly in a very present God, as good men are more generally coming to believe now, and as Isaiah and his fellow Hebrews certainly believed, are they then always more likely to believe in the necessity of material good? A deistic belief in the absence of God from earth and its concerns and us has coloured much of the religious thinking which is just now passing away. The same religious thought has been apt to relegate all true joy to the far-off, unseen, future world; such, at least, has been the creed. And we have been wont to count all the Hebrews materialistic, and to find too much of it even in Isaiah. Are we to become more just to him and to all of them? Are we to say they were wise in hoping for heaven upon earth? Is our real advance beyond them only the discovery that heaven is already upon earth to the Son of man and to His brethren, forasmuch as He said, "The kingdom of heaven is within you"?

(*f*) Isaiah certainly included also what we call spiritual features in his ideal of the good time coming. Of course his picture in chap. xi. of the prince regenerated by the Divine breath brooding upon him, and fitting him to work all good, is a picture of spiritual excellence, although only one individual is supposed to receive it immediately. Later on, however, by the time he wrote chaps. xxix.-xxxii., Isaiah had probably gained larger views. He is not speaking to the prince only when he says—

> Jehovah hath poured over you a sleepy wind,
> And He hath bound fast your eyes.
> And your insight into all things has become like things in a
>   sealed record;
> Give it to one who understandeth records and say—
> "Read this, I pray."
> But he will say, "I cannot; it is sealed."
> Give it to him who understandeth not;
> And he will say, "I cannot read!" (chap. xxix. 10 *ff*.)

> But *in that day*
> The deaf shall hear the things recorded;
> Yea, even blind men out of very mist and darkness shall see.
> Those who are meek-in-Jehovah shall grow in joy;
> And those who sorely feel all human needs shall find that in
>   Israel's Devoted One they may dance for joy (chap.
>   xxix. 18 *f*.).

> Though the Lordly One shall give you trouble to eat and drink
> Yet no more shall your Torah-givers be silenced.
> Yea, your eyes shall see those Torah-givers;
> Yea, your own ears shall hear one saying from behind you.
> "This is the way; walk here!" (chap. xxx. 21).

> The song ye shall have shall be like the night when they pre-
>   pare a feast,
> And delight of mind as when one marcheth by the sound of
>   the flute,
> To come to the mountain of Jehovah, even unto Israel's rock
>   (chap. xxx. 29).

> Lo, when kings rule with firmness, and among princes they
>   work for justice.
> Then each common man shall be a place of hiding from the wind
>   and a shelter-place from rain.
> Yea, like streams of water in Zion,
> And like the cool shadow of rocks in a weary land.
> Then the eyes of those who watch shall not wander,

> And even the ears of those who hear shall grow more attentive.
> Yea, the thoughts of the hasty shall discern knowledge;
> The tongue of the stammerer shall at once speak plain.
> There shall not be said to a churl, "Oh, excellent man."
> And it is not of the cheat they shall say, "Success!"
> For whoso is a churl, churlish shall he talk;
> In all his thoughts he shall do mischief,
> Thinking how to do godless things,
> Talking utterly mistakenly about God.
>
> But when a man is "excellent," he always desires excellent things;
> And he shall endure in the excellent days (chap. xxxii. 1–8).

Without being a literal translation, this is the substantial sense of the words of Isaiah. Beautiful and good indeed they are. And now there is evidence that these finely spiritual words concerning the golden days to come were not merely childlike and unreflecting, but were accompanied all through his later work at least by a wondering effort to understand the matter, to analyse the nature of such spiritual phenomena, to discover the causes of them, and to enlist all men in the Divine work of securing them. We have seen some evidence of this in chap. xi., in the theory of the regeneration of the prince by the brooding Divine spirit; and the date of this passage we know to be not earlier than 720 B.C. Read now the later evidence of it in chap. xxxii., the conclusion of the beautiful passages just above quoted. Their date is, as we saw, about 705 to 700 B.C. The prophet sings of the present imperfect life, and then tells how it can be changed, as he believes:—

> On the vineyard soil of my people's hearts thorns and thistles are luxuriant now;
> For such cover the very houses where delight should be.
> Ah! thou once merry town!
>
> Thou art a delight of roaming asses, a pasture-run for flocks,
> Until there be revealed and blow upon us that spirit that cometh from on high;

Then shall all change; men shall feel all has changed.
Then shall steppe land seem like vine land,
And vine land shall seem like forest;
For then shall judges' writ prevail in farthest steppe,
And steadfast character shall dwell in all vine lands.
The fruit of steadfast character shall be health;
Yea, steadfast service shall cause quiet,
And there shall be security on into unknown time.

In those good days, therefore, knowledge and wise thinking are to come, and the high agent to work their coming must be that spirit-being who comes like the unseen wind from heaven. The work and the character must be spiritual. Isaiah is sure of that, and he is thinking over the problem what all this means. We too are meeting it; and although we know far more than he, there is still far more to learn.

(*g*) Finally, in that day something shall have taken place for all Hebrews which Isaiah calls "forgiveness." Sinners as well as righteous, all who dwell in Zion, shall be forgiven their waywardness. They shall be נְשֻׂא עָוֹן (c. xxxiii. 24). What does this mean?

(*a*) The mere literal sense of the words is, of course, that "twistedness" shall be "eliminated" from all who dwell in Zion. Or, the words being read the other way about, which is more correct, they mean that all the Zion people shall be lifted up out of twistedness and all its works. But what does this mean?

(β) Watching carefully the cries of fear and of faith in the verses just preceding, much is evident. The deliverance preached to the hypocrites in Zion is to set them in the same comfort that the righteous enjoy. These are free, and so all are to be free, from the horrors of invasion, from slaughter, from starvation, from slavery. Like those perched high in rocky fastnesses, with plenty of food beside them, with fresh watersprings near, all shall be able to laugh at the invaders and sit fearless, although the lurid fires of enemies' camps and burning villages gleam and gloom by night and day.

(γ) But the words mean more still; a worse evil is to be lifted away. Utter desolation is felt by the sinner to be the expected and proper outcome of his sin. He chose the premiss clearly, and so clearly chose the conclusion. "Who among us," he cries, "can dwell among everlasting burnings? Only the righteous!" But Isaiah preaches a break between the premiss and the conclusion. "Look upon Zion, the city of God's tryst with us," he says; "look, Jehovah has pledged Himself to do a wondrous thing for all dwellers there. He will save us all." The prophet certainly does not preach that anybody in Zion may do as he likes, good or bad, and God will always coolly annul the law of cause and effect as regards sinners, upholding it only in the case of good men. No, we shall see presently that this is not his mind. But he does say, "Ye have been godless, cruel, greedy, filthy, murderous; but come in here, Jehovah has come down to find us, and to purify us in this sanctuary. Come in, then, and He will work for you all gladness where you expected all evil. You expected evil rightfully; He will give you good."

We say to-day, here is the mystery of forgiveness. Doubtless Isaiah did not appreciate it fully, else he would have seen and said that it might apply to all men equally, out of Zion as in Zion. But he did feel that it was a mysterious gospel. He felt that it needed explanation to persuade men to trust to it, pleasant though it might sound. So he said something more was contained in "forgiveness."

(δ) For it meant further their realisation that Jehovah was their King, their Lawgiver, and their Judge, and that for these reasons He would cause their safety.

Let us remember that the actual facts of religious experience in those days might be largely the same as the facts which we experience now, while the way of looking at those facts was very different. So Isaiah had a controlling conviction of the love of the unseen Lord for him, and this conviction, or vital faith, as we should call it, simply made impossible all fear, and gave a sense of highest pleasure even amid pain and danger. He felt exactly what Paul meant when he wrote, "All things work together for good to them that love God." However, the understanding of this had to depend in each case on each one's understanding of the ideas "God" and "good," and "love" and "all things." Isaiah thought of God as "Jehovah," that one of the heavenly host pledged to care for the Hebrews, and in Isaiah's own experience ready now to purify all Zion worshippers. To be such a worshipper was to cast one's self trustfully upon this Jehovah; it was to realise in an act of confidence, and then in its results, what a Saviour Jehovah was. Isaiah invited sinners to the act of confidence, joyfully sure through his own experience that every trustful one should have the same fearless sense of safety. So, cried he, all who dwell in Zion shall realise what Jehovah is, and this realisation may well be called a lifting away of all waywardness.

(ε) Finally, the sum of all these phases of forgiveness is this, all the people who dwell in Zion shall feel they are full citizens of that city of God. They shall enjoy all the good things flowing from undisturbed fellowship with each other and with their Lord in the home of the great good Divine King. Such was forgiveness in Isaiah's thought. It meant full citizenship in the kingdom of Jehovah; it meant trust in and realisation of Jehovah's love. It meant a break in the sequence of their deserts for their past wrong; it meant safety from all evil. Thus all twistedness was to be lifted away.

If we think the prophet would recognise better nowadays the inevitable sequence of wrong and retribution, folly and failure, cause and effect, let us recollect that the Christian's view of the world with all its pain is that it is all good, and the Cause of it, the God of it, is love; or to use the thought of a really Christian teacher, we find all happiness, although often the happiness is so like pain that we can only tell it from pain by knowing that we choose it rather than all the world beside.[1] Such is present-day Christian philosophy; and Isaiah's oracle concerning forgiveness, while not big enough for all men, was a true prophecy of the greater faith that was to come.

Such then was his whole ideal of perfect life, and happy was the world wherein it was uttered.

[1] Compare "Romola," Epilogue.

CHAPTER IV.

ISAIAH'S PLACE IN HEBREW RELIGIOUS HISTORY.

Our method prevents us from claiming that the following estimate is absolutely final. It is quite possible for us here to register in summary the steps we have seen this prophet take beyond his predecessors Hosea, Amos, and the general body of Hebrews, so far as we have been already able to record their religion. But it is also possible that our progress forward may disclose to us in controverted documents some records which shall clearly tell us more of the period and the people whom we have now been studying. Indeed, this was the hope held out by our method. We were to study the uncontroverted records of the times, those monuments which were the very autographs of the preachers as they sought to persuade their fellow-men. This study of the preachers' religion by analysis of their sermons was to give us understanding of the times which produced the preachers, and to which these men preached. Then we hoped that this study would give skill to detect where some controverted documents most probably arose, and the further picture of these historically located records would fill our picture with many a new and fair feature. Therefore our present description of Isaiah's advance on the religious position which we had noted ere we reached him can tell us only how life grew in the society immediately about Isaiah, and in those parts of it which Amos and Hosea and himself represent.

Isaiah was a prominent man in his society, in Zion and the regions of Judah and among the southern Hebrews. We have seen that he probably caused the rise of this people to the higher literary level of caring to preserve the written words of their leading thinkers. And yet, great as was this service, it was a service to a very small people. Isaiah's immediate area of influence could not extend much beyond the city of Jerusalem. He was known then to the people of a moderately sized town and to the outlying villages and farmer folk in a kingdom only thirty miles square, whose population was not very dense, not 150,000 at the most extravagant estimate (see Professor Socin in Bædeker's "Palestine," Introduction). Our study above of the religion of Hosea must not be supposed to imply that Isaiah's influence acted at once over all the northern sister kingdom; rather does it mean simply that Hosea's influence moulded the southern way of thinking by its affecting at least Isaiah. What advance, then, in the religious thought of the little people in and round Jerusalem is revealed by the advance of Isaiah beyond the writers we have studied before him? Having first examined (I.) this advance, we shall ask (II.) what problems seem raised by Isaiah and left for later solution?

§ 1. *Advance in conception of God.*

(I.) 1. Recall first of all the different conceptions of God. Isaiah has seen more of the lordly Jehovah's character. Amos's revelation was, "Our God is righteous, pure, good." But in this goodness Isaiah has watched new beams of glory kindle. Jehovah is good—yes; but that goodness is now known to be best in its grace and favour to the undeserving. Amos knew the word that means "holy" or "devoted," but he seemed to dislike it and avoid its use, as if it could not be true that Jehovah was devoted to this evil people. Hosea's soul felt the old traditional sound of the word echoing within him, and ventured to hope that herein lay some hidden way of deliverance for the doomed. Isaiah rose from the despair of Amos, above the despairing hope of Hosea, to faith in Jehovah's cleansing of his own unclean lips and life, and then to like faith that this God could love the worst men in Zion and would save them.

Isaiah's advance on Hosea is the point of special interest to us here. Hosea caught eagerly at the hope of salvation, but his oracle was his only declaration of this hope to his fellows. Isaiah went much farther. He planted virtually a firm symbol on the soil to repeat his gospel to all who saw it; for he proclaimed the new quality of the old Zion, and so he made a new Zion. Zion, said he, is and shall be the everlasting symbol of God's saving love. Isaiah saw the need for manifestations of truths to men, and hereby he stepped at once into the front rank of the great seers of our race. No sage, artist, or ruler has done a more needful work than this which Isaiah did.

Here we recall also Isaiah's advance to profounder grasp of the power of God. From the early childlike fancy or faith that everything has its own hidden God within it, the men of Israel had risen already to the belief that all the nations and their separate tribal gods were controlled by their own national God Jehovah. Such was the long stride in unconscious argumentation from faith in a cause for every effect up to faith in one central control over the separate causes of the separate nations. But Isaiah began his keen share in the practical solution of life's problems, and now men heard of greater power in the God Jehovah. He controls more than the nations of earth and visible actions; He is Lord over the powers beyond death. But He is far more powerful still; He can regenerate souls and all the nature of princes, men, beasts, and soil. He has control of the subtle forces in the soul that demand retribution for sin. He can forgive. Although He does not write out in order his philosophy of religion, yet His teaching and grasp imply such a philosophy —implicit indeed, but of a very high order. Of course we

are giving up the dream long common that the attainment
to a conscious monotheism and clear possession of it was of
far earlier date, aboriginal indeed, forgotten repeatedly by
idolaters, but always reasserted by the prophetic men. It is
perhaps sufficient comfort that we are thus laying aside the
unworthy Chinese landscape into which we had forced all
the vivid life of the great Old Testament centuries. When
God creates He causes development: He did so then as now.
So the man Isaiah rises up before us; searching are those
eyes, strained that massive brow, nervous and quick those
speaking lips, firm yet questioning, his tread and grasp of
hand, the whole man a questioner profound, every fibre of
him studious, ever learning, knowing all that all men know
about him, and ever coming to greater knowledge of the
truth. Great Isaiah, peer as searching thinker he of a Plato,
an Aristotle, a Paul, a John, an Origen, Augustine, Abelard,
Thomas, Bacon, Descartes, Spinoza, Kant, Hegel.

§ 2. *Advance in understanding man's nature and value.*

2. Advance has been great in understanding man's nature
and his value. There is no need here for more than a summary, for we have just been examining the details. One
can hardly avoid the impression that society is in a slightly
better state at the end of this period than it was at the
beginning. There is much sin, and it is very bad, but there
is a slightly more hopeful impression left by Isaiah's story of
it than by Hosea's. Of course, Amos's fierce demand that
all sinners must die makes a very dark picture, and yet its
fierceness inclines us all the more to care in judgment. Was
he not, we say, perhaps unduly fierce? And may not society
have been less guilty than his tone suggests? But when we
read the kind-hearted Hosea's tale of his own wife, and hear
him tell of his enduring devotion to her, his patient suffering and his pleadings with her, all of which he regards as

not simply providential but most directly ordered by Jehovah, and when we read of domestic ruin in such a good man's home, we may well be appalled. How many have said this must be a supposed picture only! No wonder they have thought so. But the occasion for such a supposed picture would have been itself very bad. The northern kingdom in Hosea's time must have been strangely wrong. In Isaiah's account the wrongdoings seem at least a little more manly and womanly. Perhaps this was more natural in the sterner, hilly Judah lands than in the more luxuriant, voluptuous plains of Ephraim. Or perhaps the destruction of the fair city Samaria sobered all men a little. In any case, Isaiah either lived in a slightly purer society, or he judged men more gently.

Amos had simply ordered men to "Seek good," naïvely implying conscience and some kind of ability. Perhaps he reflected somewhat philosophically on the matter ere he declared his final sentence that the evil-doers must all die. Perhaps he had concluded that they who did not seek good could not, and therefore were worthless. Not so Hosea, who must have reflected a good deal on the matter. He believed that seclusion, total abstinence, strict denial of alcohol and whoredom, would leave the mind, which to him was the heart, quite pure, ready for good action, and sure to do right. In Hosea's view the real nature of every Hebrew was good. He left Amos far behind. But Isaiah saw more deeply than Hosea, and declared that there must be a change wrought more deeply than a monastic seclusion can work. Isaiah denies entirely Amos's theory that evil men are worthless, but he denies also Hosea's theory that they are naturally good. He says a man may be radically changed; he must be regenerated by the working of the Divine Spirit brooding upon him. And here Isaiah rises beyond that massing of all Hebrews in one sum, or at least in two, which Amos and Hosea had both implied. These former prophets had not

T

handled the case of any single individual; Isaiah thinks at least of the individual case of the prince, of his special character, his special regeneration, and his individual influence. Finally Hosea and Amos had described awfully the evil in man, but had said little of the character of the good; while Isaiah moves on to definite descriptions of the good features of a good man, as we have seen just above (chaps. xxix.–xxxii.).

§ 3. *In estimate of religious relations.*

3. The advance toward definite estimate of the religious relations of the soul is most marked. Amos had condemned all sanctuaries, and had refused to call himself a prophet. He saw these forms filled with wrongdoing, and he struck at both together. But they were not necessarily one, although he so identified them. He identified a man and his sin, and knew no way of separating them, yet his successors found they could be separated; and so also religious forms are not necessarily full of evil. Hosea went back, and naturally, to a love for religious symbols and to a lament for their loss. He longed for religious life, and he knew that it must have some form in which to appear. The position of Amos is thus directly traversed. Isaiah follows Hosea, and carries his doctrine to a much further issue by his faith concerning the Zion sanctuary. We have seen how he implies that this form must be full of life, and the clearest confirmation of this lies in his further negation of Amos's position respecting prophets. For he asserts not only the value of a Zion sanctuary, but also the Divine authority of a professional prophetic body, that body being certainly to his mind full of living devotion to Jehovah, for it consisted of himself, his wife and children, and his disciples, all possessed of and devoted to his own teaching, which he believed to be Jehovah's own mind. Herein, as we have said, Isaiah was consciously asserting a

great principle of life that was to be a main feature in later Hebraism, and was also to lead to the faith in the only true, yet necessary visible sanctuary, which is the person of man.

§ 4. *In comprehension of the future.*

4. Finally, we record the advance in comprehension of the new world of life that was looked for. All believed it must come; each described it, and toiled to hasten its day. But while the way of its attainment was with Amos death and with Hosea slavery, with Isaiah it was creation. We shall see this positive method expand greatly in the ages to follow, until, when once it has moulded the whole popular cosmogony and has fought in great conflict against the keen sword-like subtlety of the Greeks, it merges into the grand utterances of Galilee and Calvary: "The kingdom of God is within you," and "My Father, into Thy hands I commend my Spirit."

§ 5. *The problems he started and left unsettled.*

(II.) What further problems did Isaiah's work lay bare and compel good men speedily to face? Many thoughts must have been suggested by the reading of his oracles in the generations that followed one by one, but there are some questions that must have risen very soon. Certainly we ought to be guided here by the actual historical occurrence of such rise of questions. It would not be just to write history even in this case on *à priori* expectations. But, borrowing a little from evidence which we shall speedily read, we need not go far astray in singling out some questions which Isaiah was sure to start. These questions will rightly complete our picture of Isaiah as he stands in his place in history casting a flood of light around him, backwards from him on the past, and forwards on the seers who were to see still more than he.

§ 6. *His limit of Divine presence and salvation.*

1. First, this question was sure to spring: Why Zion only? Why should Jehovah's grace be limited to dwellers there? Were there not sanctuaries far older and still beloved? Abraham, Jacob, Moses, Joshua, Samuel, David, Elijah—yes, Hosea too—had tasted that grace in sanctuaries in Ephraim, Moab, and the southern desert. Local jealousy would quickly resist the Isaian doctrine. And in all these pleas, stronger or weaker, true sympathy could surely hear the honest whisper of many a soul, "Must Jehovah be so far away from me and my home?" Joyful men as well as troubled spirits everywhere must have God nearer to them. Isaiah's teaching must have made the generation that followed him full of such questioning. We shall see that a reaction followed him at once in the long reign of Manasseh.

§ 7. *His hope for material prosperity.*

2. Another question was sure to arise: Would Zion prevail? We know that Providence did not exempt Zion from invasion and terror; for the Assyrian records of Assurhaddon's and Assur-banipal's taxation of Judah, and Herodotus's story of the Scythian ravages on the Euphrates, and in Palestine and Egypt, confirm the information we get from the books of Kings, Nahum, and Zephaniah, to say nothing of the later trouble in the days of Josiah, Jeremiah, and the enslavement under Babylon. Zion was not providentially spared. But we have learned to believe that such sparing is not the best thing for us, and not what we may expect from Providence. Now, although this later Christian doctrine of Providence must not be read into the thoughts of any men in those days, yet the strength of a Christian doctrine lies in its focussing and gathering into clear vision the thoughts, the instincts, the questionings

which have been seeking clear utterance always in all men. So, although the Christian doctrine that Providence is sure to give us suffering was not understood in those days, yet doubtless many hesitated to accept Isaiah's faith in the immunity of Zion and the certainty of all blessing for her inhabitants. Again, some must have questioned the probability of the fulfilment at any early time of the hopes of change of the very nature of the world out of hurtfulness into helpfulness. Doubtless some sadly feared the visionary day would never be real. These would have in their souls a prophecy as true as Isaiah's—namely, a prophecy of suffering. Isaiah's high hopes would be counted the natural expression in his bright hours of great faith in God's love, and that faith in itself was far more precious than the passing expression of it. But as surely as the pendulum swings and life throbs, so surely would other men speak their expectation of suffering in Zion, and they would speak it with equal trust in God. Isaiah's positive expectation was sure to produce doubt. The hope and the doubt were both part of the life he produced, and together they picture the great soul in his place in history.

§ 8. *Of the expected prince.*

3. One more question, sure to rise, we must name: Would there come a true godlike prince? The Isaian doctrine of regeneration through the prince's absolute sway was certain to awaken questioning. It directed attention to the character of the prince, and brought him into comparison with other men as never before. He ought to be best of all, and the centre of all good men and work. Was he this? If he were not, were there other men who were the real channel of the Divine spiritual re-creation? Here were several problems. One was the whole problem of government; and we shall see how great were the changes in men's

conception of it that soon arose. Another was the greater problem of Divine government and God's relation to the individual character. Ere long this became a chief question among thoughtful men.

Such was Isaiah, the noble heir of great heritages, the truly great seer, thinker, speaker of Divine truth, miner into unfathomed depths of life and of God, bequeathing to the ages great oracles, and, an even better legacy, the thirst for more. Child of his age he was, and its spokesman; its teacher too was he, and fashioner of all his race. Isaiah was a very voice of Jehovah saying, "Let there be light, now and henceforth."

PART IV.

RELIGION IN JUDAH FROM ISAIAH TO JOSIAH. THE RELIGION OF MICAH AND RELATED PROPHETS.

CHAPTER I.

PRELIMINARY.

MICAH was a man of the people in the days when Isaiah was a leader. This secondary man, this Epigon, as the Greeks would call him, is almost as valuable to us as a leading prophet would be, because his words show us whether the faiths of men like Isaiah have or have not become common to the people. The religion of Micah will show us how much the people were changing in the half-century after the days of Amos. For Micah lived in the later days of Isaiah, as we know from two sources. The title of the little book (chap. i. 1) says he prophesied in the days of Jotham, Ahaz, and Hezekiah, kings of Judah; and the book of Jeremiah (chap. xxvi. 17 *ff.*) tells a story of Micah and of what befell him when he proclaimed the words of chap. iii. 12 of his book. This happened, said the people of Jeremiah's time, in the days of Hezekiah. The little book itself tells of Micah's predicting the fall of Samaria; therefore very likely he spoke the words concerning Samaria before 720 B.C., that is to say, in the earliest days of Hezekiah, who probably began his rule in 725. The statement that he prophesied also in Ahaz's days, and even under Jotham, may be quite correct, but being evidently the note of the editor and therefore of later times, it is of less moment. We shall presently see further reason for counting some of the chapters quite post-Isaian.

Let us begin our study of the book with a few preliminary notes. An analysis of the contents will follow. Then we may proceed to construct a picture of the religion set forth in these oracles. And we shall conclude with a brief estimate of the point in history at which we have thus arrived, and a note of its importance in view of the period that is to follow.

§ 1. *A few preliminary notes on the book of Micah.*

(1) It is a controverted book. The points under controversy will presently appear. On the ground of these our rule to avoid controverted documents might exclude it altogether. But this is not necessary, for the controversies refer only to portions of it, and the parts affected are not removed far away from the times of Micah (*circa* 725–700) by any save a very few students. It is very certainly from beginning to end a product of the century between 740 and 640 B.C.

(2) One passage seems certainly not Micah's, namely, chap. iv. 1–4, perhaps even all the verses iv. 1–8. But these words are older than Micah; he doubtless quoted them. For Isaiah quotes them too (Isa. ii. 2–4), less correctly perhaps, repeating them it may be from memory; but he quotes them early in Ahaz's days, while Micah used them in the time of Hezekiah. Such quotation is one proof that Micah is a real man of the time. Isaiah quotes rather as a brilliant master who repeats the well-known words from memory, while Micah carefully copies out the words sacred to his fellows and to him, words sure to evoke reverence and response.

(3) The paragraph iv. 6–v. 1 has a touch of exilic scenery about it. It talks of such chastisement as Ezekiel pictures and Jeremiah foretells in his later years. It does seem for a moment to be unlikely that Micah should talk of an exile to Babylonia, since in his days that land was a mere province of Assyria, sometimes revolting indeed, but always firmly subjugated. And yet why should not Assyria like to people her refractory provinces with slaves from afar? What more likely; and what more natural in Micah's countrymen and himself than fear of such enslavement? The passage is quite like Micah, but probably from his later years in the reign of Manasseh.

(4) Following this paragraph in chap. v. 2–9 is a joyful exhortation to courage even against Assyria. The previous reference to Babylon has led some scholars to treat these Assyrian references as interpolated. But they are thoroughly and organically part of the whole paragraph. The courageous words are quite in the brave tone of Isaiah or of a follower of Isaiah. They might indeed fit the days of Sennacherib, who was not a very successful invader of Canaan, but they would scarcely suit the more terrible days of Sargon just before Sennacherib, or of Assur-haddon just after him. Most likely they belong to Manasseh's reign. The throne seems to be in weak hands, and a royal heir is hoped for who shall be a heroic deliverer. This would certainly fit the times just before Josiah's birth. Here comes to our help singularly enough the story in 2 Chron. xxxiii. 11 of the exile of King Manasseh, Josiah's grandfather, to Babylon by the Assyrian king. Further light is given by Schrader. C. I. O. T. ii. 53. In 650 B.C. Assyria was in peril from an internal revolt. Manasseh appears to have helped the revolters, and was punished by exile to Babylon, but was soon liberated. A prophet might well write first words of fear of exile, and then words of exultation in faith that a coming unborn king of Judah should free his people from all Assyrian troubling. So

these paragraphs may be Micah's, as we have said, but more likely they date from the middle of the seventh century.

(5) The sixth and seventh chapters are very surely from the darker days of Manasseh, or from the time of Amon, more gloomy still. No point in Hezekiah's reign agrees fully with the sense of utter darkness which the prophet speaks. He is in absolute darkness, and knows no source of light save the Lord. Only from beyond man's ken can come help. So we get one of the world's grandest utterances of faith in the supernatural, the unknown, even God. We hear a man of God speak who sees the Invisible.

(6) The later chapters, chaps. v., vi., vii., breathe throughout the spirit we shall find coming in with the Josian reformation, and recorded clearly in the condemnations of Jeremiah as well as in the ordinances of Deuteronomy. The book of Micah is an excellent guide to the times when the influence of the vivid preaching of Isaiah was changing the whole people into the new form-loving people of the days of Josiah and Jeremiah It is a book of the people, and a monument of transition. It closes for us a whole period.

CHAPTER II.

THE ANALYSIS OF MICAH.

AFTER the title, chap. i. ver. 1, comes a first section occupying the first chapter.

Section I. chap. i. verses 1–16.—Picture of the coming of the lordly Jehovah. And its features are these:—

(1) Verses 2–4.—Summons to all things and men to attend Him. As He advances from His home and treads the earth, planting His footsteps on the sacred hill-tops, the hill-sides melt like wax beneath His brightness.

(2) Verse 5.—A summary declaration that Samaria's very existence is sin. Micah shares the opinion of all the prophets that the separation was disastrous.

(3) Verses 6–9.—Samaria's calamity to come as judgment. She shall be utterly desolated.

(4) Verses 10–16.—The effect of this on the whole country. All the regions south of Samaria, and especially west of Jerusalem, and round about Micah's home in the "wine-press possession" (Moresheth-Gath), shall be in dismay, as across them hurry the Samarians flying from their ruined city and the terrible Assyrians who have ruined it. The dramatic vividness almost equals that of Isaiah's famous "march" scene in his eleventh chapter.

The second main section occupies the second chapter and part of the third, thus:—

Section II. chap ii. 1–iii. 3.—The sin Micah sees close about him. This is chiefly his neighbours' cruelty to the poor fugitives as they pass; also the resentment of these cruel neighbours at Micah's reproof. It is understood more clearly in its details, as follows:—

(1) Chap. ii. verses 1, 2.—Woe to plotting, greedy, thieving men.

(2) Verse 3.—A summary of deserved calamity that is sure to come.

(3) Verses 4–6.—The people resent the prophet's interference, and threaten him with expulsion. They would silence his prophesying.

(4) Verse 7.—His astonishment at such practical atheism.

(5) Verses 8–10.—The cruelty practised on the fugitives: stealing of lands, goods, even clothing, and ejectment from any resting-place.

(6) Verse 11.—Superstitious choice to the prophetic office of men who encourage drunkenness and even untruth.

(7) Verses 12, 13.—Parenthetic cry of faith that the sufferers shall yet be restored to comfort.

(8) Chap. iii. verses 1–3.—The deeper wrong. The leaders hate good and love evil, destroying the very flesh and bones of the people.

Such a policy among chiefs and employers rouses the preacher to denunciation. So follows a threatening section.

Section III. chap. iii. 4–iv. 8.—The consequence. What the Controller of Providence will do.

(1) Verses 4–7.—He will close the Divine visions, the fountains of good guidance for life and joy of soul.

(2) Verses 8–11.—Micah feels it might be retorted, "Then how canst thou be inspired?" and he pours out his faith that the Jehovah spirit is with him. He gives evidence of it, for Jehovah who leaves the evildoer must be with him who condemns the wrongdoer.

(3) Verse 12.—Therefore he sounds the alarm, "Zion, for the sake of your evil rulers, shall be plowed as a field." This was preached in Hezekiah's time (see Jer. xxvi. 18). We should scarcely have expected this under a king supposed to

be one of the best, and known to be much under the influence of Isaiah. But Isaiah's condemnation was launched against the evils and evil men in the out-district near the coast, say fifteen to twenty miles from Zion, and the governors there might be vicious even in Hezekiah's reign. The country prophet Micah could easily identify them with the Zion rule, and would conceive their sin bad enough to involve Zion in ruin.

(4) At once, however, he recalls and records again, as Isaiah had done, the great hope all Judah had for Zion. But Micah does this with real hope, which he expresses in his own words in verses 6 and 7, while Isaiah had quoted the words only to show the present hopelessness. (See Isa. ii. 2–4 *ff.*)

We reach now the first passage which may be of later date than Micah. We say it *may* be. It dreads exile to Babylon; perhaps this was in Hezekiah's day, perhaps not until Manasseh's.

Section IV. chaps. iv. 9–v. 9.—Of the people's reception of warnings of exile, their dread and the prophet's hope for future restorations. He cries:—

(1) Chap. iv. 9, 10.—"Lay aside thy fears, O Zion! even from exile, from the Euphrates plains thou shalt return."

(2) Verses 11–13.—"Those who now mock at thee shall be greatly surprised; their ill expectations shall be utterly disappointed. Thou shalt become a conqueror, a hero for Jehovah."

(3) Verses 14 v. 8.—The picture of the times of Israel's new exaltation.

(*a*) Chap. v. 1.—A summary of it. Israel's smiter smitten.

(*b*) Chap. v. 2–9.—The new rule. (*a*) By a Bethlehemite prince, or a Bethephrathite. (Is there a slip of the scribe here, and is בֵּית־אֶפְרָת a mistake for that בֵּית־עָפְרָה in Micah's own district, chap. i. 10, which was troubled? This is less likely, of course, if the passage is not Micah's.)

(β) The prince is yet unborn. (γ) He is to be divinely strong. Here is an echo of Isaiah's forecast of an infant prince (Isa. ix.). (δ) He is to overcome Assyria. Of course, then, the writer, Micah or the later prophet, was thinking of an infant about to be born, and coming to accomplish this invasion before Assyria's final fall, which took place in 606 at the latest. (ε) This elevation of Israel is to be a great surprise, coming mysteriously, like the dew, all unwatched, but wrought of God and inevitable. Here is a fine picture of the supernatural which is natural, orderly, yet Divine, and beyond men's expectation. (ζ) Israel shall be entirely supreme.

But there is at once reaction in the preacher's soul. Such promises awaken the remembrance of the ill-desert of these very people. There must be discipline.

Section V. chap v. 9-14. The discipline that must come.

(1) All the glorious cavalry forces shall be cut off, to humble the nation.

(2) So all the structures for defence.

(3) All sources of counsel except Jehovah must cease.

(4) All who are careless toward Jehovah's honour and ways must feel the wrath of Jehovah and Jehovah's host.

We come thus to the two chapters (vi. vii.) which seem to belong to a period later than the days of Micah, and are certainly much later than Isaiah. In some respects their character is loftier than that of the earlier chapters; it is more reflective, and even more profound. The conception of high argument with Jehovah borders on the loftiest sublimity. The confession of faith in chap. vii., and the reflection on Jehovah's delight in grace, are two of the very finest of Hebrew utterances. In these we seem to be nearing the age that produced such minds as that of Jeremiah, the early psychologist and theologian, and the deeply reflective minds of the Exile.

Section VI. chap. vi.—The conference and controversy

between Jehovah and mankind, especially Israel. It seems singular that the name "Israel" should be used after the fall of Samaria, but perhaps we give the name to-day to the northern kingdom much more exclusively than it was ever given by Hebrews themselves. All Hebrews were children of Israel. Judah was the princely tribe of all Israel in David's and Solomon's days. After the separation the northern kingdom doubtless claimed to be Israel alone, being the larger section; but the southern kingdom was still Israel, with Judah as its princely tribe. After Samaria's ruin the southern people remained the only Israel.

(1) Chap. vi. 1. 2.—Summons to the mountains, which were sanctuaries, abodes of Divine powers, to attend in audience of this high conference.

(2) Verses 3-12.—The dialogue.

(*a*) Verses 3-5.—Jehovah speaks. He recounts His gifts and wonders, all gracious; He names Moses, Aaron, Miriam as leaders of the Exodus. He contrasts Israel's gracelessness with Jehovah's grace; He wonders why they treat Him so.

(*b*) Verses 6, 7.—Israel speaks. They are humble, and ask how they shall set themselves right. By what worship? By sacred feasts? By anointings with oil that shall make the face shine? By gift of children in some way to Jehovah. Such were the ritual customs of the day, strange to us indeed; but only by knowledge of them can we understand those days and their religion.

(*c*) Verses 8-12.—The prophet speaks. He declares Jehovah's answer, setting forth what God demands from all mankind. God asks only "what is good," thus identifying Himself, the Lord of Israel, the Cause of all things, with conscience. "The good" is equivalent to—(a) just deeds; (β) a gracious heart; (γ) a humble soul. This is also supplemented by special mention of—(δ) wisdom in thought; (ϵ) honesty in trade; (ζ) kindness; (η) truthfulness. Thus ends the dialogue, and here is uttered—

(3) Verses 13-16.—Jehovah's judgment. He asserts His control of all past events and calamities. He passes sentence of famine to come; He pronounces this to be the just retribution for their Ahab-like disregard of their own God Jehovah. They are to be a reproach in the eyes of the whole world. Now the preacher breaks out into lamentation.

Section VII. chap. vii.—The prophet's soliloquy, his pain, and faith.

(1) Verses 1-6.—His lament over the demoralisation about him.

(a) Verses 1, 2a.—He is utterly lonely. All the good are gone.

(b) Verses 2b-4.—All others kill, steal, and pervert.

(c) Verses 5. 6.—Not even home confidences survive.

(2) Verses 7-10.—Amid all this the prophet will trust to Jehovah.

(a) Verses 7, 8.—In darkness light can only come from a source that is beyond man. And it will come; Jehovah's character is "Saviour." The soul shall live by the Invisible.

(b) Verse 9.—The darkness about us is deserved, yet it will be righteousness with Him to give us light.

(c) Verse 10.—All who laugh at us shall be surprised.

(3) Verses 11-13.—The day is sure to come for liberation even from the fear of Assyria or of Egypt.

(4) Verses 14-17.—The coming bliss shall be—plenty for all, wondrous ways of sending this to us, our establishment in control of all men.

(5) Verses 18-20.—Tribute of adoration—
   For Jehovah's forgiveness;
   For His gracious character;
   For His faithfulness to all men of faith.

CHAPTER III.

THE RELIGION OF MICAH AND HIS TIMES.

§ 1. *Its general characteristics.*

(1) THE book and its writer, or writers, and readers utter the voice and speak the thoughts of followers of Isaiah of Jerusalem. They make those advances from the ways of the master which are inevitable amongst all pupils, because each pupil has his own individuality. Moreover, the individuality of a soul has in it something creative; each man must add some utterly new living thing to the world. And yet most pupils have a more limited grasp than the master had; they are likely to stand on a lower level.

(*a*) So the Zion faith of Micah is but a derivative compared with the great discovery of Isaiah. The faith is received and held and upheld with no wrestling and convulsion like Isaiah's. Zion's exaltation is sure. There are difficulties before her, but they are now less real and deep, and the preacher faces them less really. Like a child he sings his exuberant assurance, "All is well with Zion." He is not anxious, and need not be; some one else takes the father's care of the children and the home.

(*b*) So the old David-faith is gently implied rather than distinctly prophesied. The name of the hero-king is not mentioned; only the old home of the dynasty is named, uncertainly indeed, in place of any particular king. Apparently the living king was not a beloved personality; possibly also he was jealous, even cruel, and hence the cautious preacher praised only an unborn child of the line. Herein he was following in part a style Isaiah had often chosen, choosing it however in strong faith with no fear of naming or facing a worthless ruler.

(c) The highest faith Isaiah ever proclaimed is caught by the follower, and made his own soul's best jewel, the centre of his thought, the hearthlight where he sits calm and most restful. Forgiveness he knows as no new discovery, but a precious heritage. His sins can be blotted out, as Isaiah declared; all the sins of the Hebrews shall be blotted out, and the remnant shall return. So the beautiful spirit of this follower repeats simply the *credo* of his master. He only adds, as a pupil would, his reflections on this great gift of forgiveness, and his definition of it as he sits gazing upon it in calm joy.

(d) It is evident at once that the arguments of the book are less steady and the course of thought less continuous; the sections are less easy to mark, and the whole style far less masterly than that of Isaiah.

(e) No wonder, we think, after we have read, that people preserved far more of Isaiah's oracles than of these. Even if they be all of one hand, Micah's words cannot have held men as the master's did. Their great value to us lies in their evidence that Isaiah's words won the people to his faith, and wrote upon many hearts a humble faith in Jehovah's forgiveness.

(2) Yet Micah and his co-workers were men of strong mind. They may not be great men, but they who follow master souls are not weaklings

(a) In evidence we look on the very first passages of the book, for there is that grand picture of the descent of the God Jehovah upon the mountain-tops, that melt as hot wax beneath His tread. Finely dramatic too is the story of the fugitives hurrying in misery from the Assyrian invaders, and pausing among brother Hebrews near Micah's home in Gath only to be plundered and hounded further. These literary gems may indeed have been inspired by the training influence of the master who wrote Isaiah ii., x., and xxviii.; none the less had the pupil a powerful pencil. So might we single out other scenes. It is enough to think again of Jehovah's appeal to justice described in chap. vii., where the gods sit as judges in their sacred seats on hoary mountain-tops, and hear the alternate pleadings of Jehovah and the Hebrews, until quickly the scene shifts as by a lightning flash, and Jehovah is on the throne thundering His dread sentence. On flows the same graphic power through every paragraph. The literary student finds rich treasure here.

(*b*) Brave too the prophet was, and that in moments of real danger. No fancied sketch of an attack is that in chapter ii. When he protected the fugitives the thieving Gittites turned on him with gnashing wolves' teeth. It is far too realistic and too probable to be a fiction; such blows as he brings down in chap. iii. on princes, prophets, traders must have been resented. We feel this before we turn to Jeremiah's book and read how they seized this Micah to destroy him in their rage. The story of his fearlessness, his danger, and deliverance lived on for a hundred years, a beacon-light to check the vicious and to cheer the brave. Later on we shall see that this bravery sprang from real spiritual insight and vision of the Invisible.

(*c*) So here we must record the intense vigour of conviction that fills all the utterances of faith and opinion in the book. We need not single out more than three. First stands that assertion of authority, " But truly, as for me, I am full of power by the Spirit of Jehovah, and of justice and of strength, to set before Jacob his transgression, and before Israel his failing." This man claims power to speak the very mind of God. And for this claim he gives not, and feels no need to give, external signs in evidence; he simply feels his sense of God's presence in him, and God's utterance in him of that conscience which no man can silence, and which his soul clearly hears and eagerly obeys. Here is conviction of such strength that it holds a strong man.

The same intense vigour is in the conviction that all shall be well with Zion. It is the faith of Isaiah grasped by his follower. It does not suggest the keen scrutiny that marks a master's decision and opinion, but has rather the exuberance of the pupil's profession of faith; and yet the profession is perfect in its vigour.

Finally, feel the thrill of strength in the faith of chap. vii. 7–9:—

> But as for me, it is on Jehovah I have all my outlook;
> Let me look towards my saving God.
> My God will hear me.
> Let not then mine enemy rejoice over me.
> For have I fallen? I have risen.
> Yea, am I to sit in darkness?
> Jehovah is light for me.

These terse words utter surely a strong faith; scarcely ever has more vigorous conviction uttered its few quiet but sufficient words.

(*d*) Another mark of this writer's strength is his generous depth of feeling. How bountiful his sympathy with those fugitives, women, children, terror-stricken men. And it is a fine patriotism that knows the old classic song of Zion, and quotes it all in full with the correctness that marks a simple but refined man's quotations. Take, however, also as a higher illustration of his feeling, the outburst of amazed hurt of soul, when some think to stop his prophesying:—

> "Not another word of your prophecy,"
> So do they prophesy.
> Say they:
> "None shall prophesy of these things,
> That this prophet fellow may stop his calumny."

The prophet breaks out upon this—

> What a saying is this, O house of Jacob!
> Has Jehovah's spirit ceased?
> Surely not His deeds are these of yours!
> Will not His words give always pleasure?

How fine the sense of indignity done to the generosity of Jehovah, His generosity in speaking with men, and in beneficent results of all that speech. So on the other hand we have the writer's beauty of heart poured out in his positive utterance of his sense of the graciousness of God (chap. vii. 18-20):—

> O where is a deity like Thee?
> O Bearer of the wayward! O Forgetter of wrong!
> He has not kept aflame the fire of His displeasure,
> For One who delights in grace is He.

While many a Hebrew psalm preserved till now does not find use in our devotions, these words of Micah abide among the ritual of our tenderest hours. And there they will abide.

(c) Another strong feature of the book is the movement evident in it towards meditation, and its deeper reflection upon the facts of life, the possessions of the soul, inherited or universal, and the right path for the future. In the little tract are the beginnings of a philosophy of religion. Of course the strongest of all men is the religious leader, and he is but the second who questions and crucially tests the leader's steps. But he would be no leader whose religious work could not stand the questioner's test. That is not religious life which cannot bear philosophical scrutiny and philosophical expression, for philosophy or pure thinking is the clear eye of the soul where all things must be visible if they exist. The eyes of men in Micah's day were beginning to gaze calmly into the depths of life and of God, and this growing hold on truth was growing strength.

Illustration of this reflection we have in the very first verses, where the question stands, "What is Israel's sin?" A fair question indeed, and not merely curious. Further on a page or so begins that great question of all time since, "And what then is inspiration?" This questioner was certainly a father of theology, although Hosea in the more cultured kingdom of the north had led the march a couple of generations earlier. No wonder that Micah was soon followed by that Nestor of religious thought, Jeremiah. Our book moves on to even deeper question and profounder reflection when in chap. vi. we read, "What does our Divine Lord require of men? What is duty?" and the wonderfully analytical answer comes which we must presently consider closely. Then finally (chap. vii. 18) stands the sublime question, "Who is a god like to this God? What are the characters of the gods? What is God?" There is the legend to be written across all philosophy of religion. And the answer speaks out the substance of perfect religion—

"He delighteth in grace."

§ 2. *The mind of these times concerning religious forms.*

As we seek now closer knowledge of the religion of the book, let us observe first that particular attitude which it bears toward external observances. Here two features will be observed.

(1) Thought concerning forms of worship is coming to bulk more largely than hitherto. Amos had been satisfied with brushing sanctuaries aside, as of no importance to the poor seeker after life. Hosea had lamented the danger of losing kings and sacrifices, sacred obelisks, robes, and teraphim, but had scouted the reverence paid to deities that were not gods. Isaiah had followed the way of Amos at first, and then had learned to prize and to preach Zion and the David-dynasty as the place and token of Jehovah's gracious, healing

revelation. Micah's words show, as we have said, that Isaiah's influence has been moulding all minds.

(*a*) The growing importance of forms appears at once in the answer given in the very first verses to the question. "What is the sin of Jacob?" Micah's answer, "Is it not Samaria?" points partly indeed to the great fault of the division into two kingdoms; but the very naming of the city, the place, the external thing as "sin," and then the mention also at once of sanctuaries, "What are the sanctuaries of Judah?" seem to intimate that it is altars outside of Jerusalem which Micah condemns. We may not lay much stress, however, on this passage, for the text of the second query seems uncertain. We are certain, however, that Micah regards a town, Samaria, *i.e.*, a form, as a sin.

(*b*) Again, in the end of his quotation of the old prophecy (iv. 1–5) he sets words which are evidently his own conclusion from the old oracle, and which give an insight into Micah's own mind towards forms. He writes:—

> For all the nations march, each under the banner of his own god;
> We too, then, shall march under the banner of our Divine Jehovah, even through the ages and evermore.

The writer is beginning to compare and contrast the characters of the gods, and the different modes of worship and degrees of trust due to each.

(*c*) More distinct still is the evidence of the lament in chap. v. 10–15 over the apprehended loss of symbols of worship. The words are indeed surprising to us in our day:—

> I will cut off thy horses from thy midst, and destroy thy chariots;
> I will cut off thy land's watch-cities, and all thy sacred obelisks;
> Yea, divinations from thy hands:
> And there shall be no oracle places for thee.
> Yea, I will cut off thy carvings and obelisks from thy midst,

And thou shalt bow no more before thy handiwork.
Yea, I will uproot thy sacred trees from thy midst,
And destroy thy watch-cities.

The loss of obelisks and sacred trees is classed with loss of watch-cities; as the latter were precious, so must have been the former in that day. The prophet has them all in that equal estimate which is essential to fairness of outlook for the future. He can fairly judge them; and he does judge them. All are to go. He laments it; but he believes good is to come of it. He is thinking deeply of the value of forms, and the generation must have been thinking much of them also.

(*d*) We reach now the plainest expression of this mind of the age. The prophet asks for the people, chap. vi. 6 *ff.* :—

In what form am I to make my approach unto Jehovah?
To bend me, shrinking, to the God whose home is so exalted?
Am I to approach amid ascending smoke, amid tribute of many
  yearling calves?
Is Jehovah to delight in thousand rams, in myriad oil-streams?

Isaiah did not write such questionings; his soul was filled with the overwhelming fact of Jehovah's revelation of Himself all round the prophets in the beloved city. He found no place for questions of man's fit ritual. But he ensured the speedy rising of such questions so soon as the reaction of calmness should return, and when men with troubled hearts even in Zion should cry unsatisfied still, "But what must we *do* to be saved?" Isaiah's work ensured this. When a man of great insight utters a high faith, many cling to him and rest because they have hold on what is secure. But when he passes out of sight the timid souls try to stand, for safety, in the spot where the leader would have stood, and in their anxiety they cry, "What is the exact spot where he would stand were he here?" This is the cry for ritual. And when the leader has had his faith all bound up with one loved form, as Isaiah had his, then in later days the deep insight, the vision of the Invisible which the leader had, having faded, the followers see the form chiefly, and try hard to define it exactly, that by such exactness they may ensure their rightness and their safety. Forms there must be if there is to be life, for life lives in forms. Every living thing can live only when in its own form, and to put on the form of something else is to die. Isaiah's life was strong and had its own form, therefore it brought forth new life; and that new life in Micah and his times revealed itself by its construction of forms for itself. The difference between these times and the times of the great master was that the earlier day was less self-conscious, the later day had more consciousness of its own special peculiarity.

(*e*) The most startling fact for us in this questioning is the willingness of the good men of the time to consider the question, "Should they sacrifice their children as sin-offerings?" We do not ask such questions to-day; it is impossible to ask them. We can scarcely understand how they did so then; we are inclined to think the record has been misunderstood, and that surely good men never thought of such a thing. But there the words stand; they did ask the question. Of course the story of Jephthah's sacrifice about the year 1100 B.C. seems natural as we read this question of Micah, written 700–650 B.C.; and that story of Jephthah does not stand quite alone. The conclusion is, that in Micah's day a better thoughtfulness awoke, faced the unhappy popular superstition, and calmly reasoned it away out of respectability. We can trace the outcome of this reasoning. Less than a century later, in 592 B.C., Ezekiel discusses human sacrifice as a form of Jehovah-worship (Ezek. xx. 25 *f.*). He speaks of it as a thing of the past, yet not very far away; he counts it a very bad thing certainly, and yet a practice actually appointed by Jehovah. The appointment was, of course, for the hardness of their hearts, as Jesus said the divorce law was.

Such then is the story of Micah's attainment to knowledge of duty in respect of forms; that is to say, this is the record of the operation of that great Spirit who caused Micah to know these things. In other words still, which are more popular, this is a record of supernatural inspiration of this prophet touching the way of communion with God. If we should say that it was mere human discovery, and not the supernatural work of God, then we should be atheistic. If we should say that God's supernatural inspiration comes only along lines where the mind is not conscious of working out the results, and the mind cannot work out the ways of the Supernatural, then we should be agnostic. If we should go on to say, that when God acts in His distinctively Divine, supernatural way, He does not act through the spirit of man, then we should be materialistic, denying that God is a spirit. From such mistakes we shall be delivered only if we read earnestly the facts that God has set about us in the story of life.

(2) The growing interest in forms which is evident in Micah's exaltation of Zion resulted in a succession of phases in the Zion faith. After Isaiah's eloquence had passed into silence, leaving only the written record of it, a reaction was sure to follow. Later on the counter-reaction was as sure to come. So in Micah we read the careful quotation in chap. v. of the old prophecy which Isaiah too had quoted, but quoted in bitter sorrow only to lay it aside as virtually void for the sin of the nation. He spoke it in quick haste, almost dislike, heeding not if he was sometimes inexact; but by-and-by he found new faith in Zion, and he declared it. That declaration moved all men till Micah lifted up again the old, almost dishonoured prophecy, and quoted it now with utmost care of words

and with happy fulness of contents. So Micah's use of it illustrates the early influence of Isaiah.

But we read of reaction in the days of King Manasseh, Hezekiah's son. Quite sufficient is the record in 2 Kings xxi. 3, "He built again the high places which Hezekiah his father had destroyed."

Again, part of Micah, chaps. iv., v., vi., vii., were very probably written in Manasseh's later days, or in the days of Amon, about the middle of the century. The reaction is passing away; Zion is becoming the best loved sanctuary. So breaks out the pæan-song of the fourth chapter. Zion shall be more than conqueror. By the time chaps. vi. and vii. were penned hope was calmer, less material, but not less firm. The prophet speaks in the name of the hard-pressed city. She sees only danger, hurt on every side; nay, she sees naught, she sits in darkness. Outward eyes see no help for her, yet faith says "She shall be helped." And so the prophet mounts to the higher flight; she shall be helped of Him whom we see not, in ways we know not. "When I, Zion, sit in darkness, then the Lord of hosts, the Invisible, Almighty Jehovah, shall be a light unto me." So the days were drawing near when the great Deuteronomic law of one sanctuary should be applied to the exclusive exaltation of Zion. Soon Zion was to be established by national law as the one only place for worship of Jehovah and enjoyment of His grace and forgiveness.

§ 3. *Their estimate of the soul.*

Let us pass from these records of care for forms to watch the records of his estimate of souls, especially of his own, and of the character of men about him.

(1) And first we ask, What was his idea of the prophet's nature and prerogative? What were Micah's credentials?

We saw Isaiah conscious of the worth of his life-work; but even he did not discuss its nature as Micah does. In our later prophet is manifest the growing reflective character of the advancing age.

(*a*) Regard Micah's picture of the power of the prophet as we read it in chap. iii. You get a conception of it from the story of its effect. Men's actions are moved by it; it holds them, and they never say it is naught. It holds with iron bands, which do not break. Men know the prophetic power helps them, they feel that it sways the currents of life or of death without them and within. So they seek for prophets, and they tremble with satisfaction or with fear when they find them.

(*b*) The prophetic possession, Micah thinks, is similar to the possession of a man by alcohol. It sways him bodily, it carries him on paths peculiar to itself. His utterance is all exalted in tone, in force, in pathos, until the hearers also are excited and swayed in their words and deeds. The two possessions are similar, but just therefore not the same. A man may, and men do take the one for the other, but then they make a sad mistake.

(*c*) Therefore Micah sets up an unfailing test for discriminating the two. The inspiration of the prophet always blesses the needy. It always condemns him who does a hurt to another life for his own sake. It discovers most swiftly those in high places who hurt others, and launches sentence straight at them. Let us put this definition and test into the exact language of to-day. The prophetic *afflatus*, says Micah, is to be known by its ministration to life. If a man's exalted utterance agrees with and helps what is good, then it is true prophetic inspiration. Such must be the evidence of prophecy, says this old Hebrew record.

(*d*) Micah tells us exactly what he means by the sense

of control which such prophets produce. Such an effect, he says, marks the presence of God. "I am full of such power, therefore truly it must be the Spirit of Jehovah that works in me." He argues from Divine results to the Divine presence. This is of God, because it does God's work.

(c) And this conclusion is by no means a scholastic speculation, interesting enough, but without practical significance. On the contrary, Micah's conviction of the presence of God with him turns at once into an assertion of his own right to speak out all his mind, and his rejection of any popular or governmental limitation of this right. Of course we are ready to say here is the inlet for all self-assertion, for mad indvidualism, and for strife to very bitterness. But we must not forget that Micah established the test that was to check this very selfishness. His aim was indeed high and godlike.

It is interesting to note here that the Hebrew mind was characteristically egoistic and self-sufficing. They did indeed for long ages count the nation or clan as the direct personage with which Jehovah had to do, and only in later days did they learn that God has to do with individual souls rather than with organic masses. Only slowly did they become individualistic; but always, both early and late, were they characteristically self-sufficient. The Greek, and we Westerns all, can inhabit the wide world, and make it all fit to be our home by taking on and into our very frame and features something of the nature of our abode. But the Hebrew wanders and sojourns, yet remains unlike his new countrymen, only like to the old, old fathers in the far Eastern home. He asserts for ever the changeless value of his own old distinctive self. And the Hebrew was very religious, and less philosophical; or rather was he very conscious of God, and less interested in men. He needed companionship with the Supreme, as all men do, but he could not think of the Supreme as visible with a frame like his own, yet so divinely valuable as to make his own frame all unworthy in comparison. The Greek could see God visibly; the Hebrew could only commune with God in soul. He could listen to the rise of thought and word in the soul, where only thought and word can rise; then he would arise to utter the new revelation in the profound faith which he expressed by the great prophetic formula, "Thus hath God said." Here then was danger close beside highest blessedness, danger of proceeding even to terrible cruelty in the name of the great Divine Friend. Islam fell into the danger, and has become almost the very incarnation of cruelty. On the other hand, the godly prophet before us, like so many others, spoke out without wavering and without minimising his grand faith in Jehovah's personal companionship and communication; but he exalted that faith to the even loftier height by submitting what he believed God had given him to the test of a law which he knew to be Divine—the law of good.

(2) But what is good? What did these writers include in good character? Their reflective habit does not disappoint us here; they lay hold of this question carefully, and their definition has become famous. It forms the second plea of Jehovah in the finely dramatic trial-scene of chap. v., where Jehovah and the Hebrews are plaintiffs and defendants before the high court of heaven, the seats of the invisible judges being the mountain-top sanctuaries of the gods. When the defendants have asked, "What then is duty?" the answer comes—

> He hath set before thee, O mankind, what is pleasant,
> And what Jehovah seeks from thee.
> Would you know it? It is—
> "To do justice,
> To love grace ever,
> To walk—to bow humbly in thy walk, with thy God."

Here is an analytic definition, whose points show us well how the thoughtful minds of those days worked. Observe these points.

(*a*) The generic words and expressions translated by our words " good " and the like are important. Our ordinary versions say, " He hath showed thee, O man, what is good." This is correct, but the word here used is " good " in the sense of " pleasant," the Latin *amœnus* rather than *bonus*. Those people were eudæmonists. They could indeed think of the " good " in the sense of the " straight " and the " firm," but very generally they thought of what was truly " pleasing " as what was good. They were not so austere as we sometimes fancy them, in our fondness for finding contrasts between them and the Greeks. Are we not tempted to look down on them sometimes as we read their pictures of the ideal age to come, and find it full of vines and fig-trees' shade, cornfields and comely herds? All the more valuable is this definition in Micah that tells us what the reflective thinker counted really " pleasant."

But before we pass to these specific details we must observe that the generic idea " good" is with these men more than the " pleasant;" it is also, " What the Controller requireth." Their ethics were not simple æsthetics; they felt also a control over the soul. They had a sense of obligation. They were aware of a voice within them that meant a Person over against and without their own persons; and that voice held them inevitably. What this voice required, and that which was pleasant or good, were one and the same. Now let us see what this requirement was.

(*b*) The first command is " Do justice " (עֲשׂוֹת מִשְׁפָּט). God requires thee to do justice, and this is the pleasing, good thing. The terms used signify civil justice. It is godly and good to execute the decisions of the courts and of wise, trained, skilled men, who are set to declare equity.

Here is indeed a very high estimate of the ability of true men on the judgment seat to see the true good. It is high faith in God to believe that He makes men of true character sure to speak justice. These men believed that true manliness is the true godliness. Christian faith is that *The Son of Man* is *the Son of God:* their faith was not far behind. To their mind the path of duty was as plain as the decision of the judges who sat by the city gate.

(c) But this was not enough for them, for many of the affairs and relations of life would never come before the judges in those days as they do not now. Therefore there is the second requirement, commonly read, "Love mercy." The terms אַהֲבַת חֶסֶד express more than that. The verb is a frequentative, and so commands a frequent love, an ever-repeated habit, a constant character of love. And the word חֶסֶד is not that mere mercy which the elder theologians defined as "favour to the undeserving," but that grace which those theologians called "favour to the ill-deserving." We have already referred to Prof. W. Robertson Smith's "Prophets of Israel," pp. 160 *f.* and 406 *f.*, where he says of Hosea's use of *chesedh* that it is not mercy, but the Latin *pietas*, or dutiful love, as it shows itself in acts of kindness and loyal affection. It is that affection which Jehovah had towards the Hebrews, which they ought to have toward Him and likewise toward one another. It is the character that delights in unconditioned blessing given to all. It is the ideal higher than is conceived by laws of *meum* and *tuum*. It gives to gladden, saying, It is life to me to give life to thee, so I clasp thee to my heart, O fellow heart. Jesus summed its law and life, its beauty and bliss, in the beatitude, " Blessed are the merciful, for they shall obtain mercy." The prophet had commanded in God's name, " Do justice ; " he adds another command, " Be ever gracious."

(d) He adds one command more. For men bidden to be like God may easily put on pride. Therefore he says, "Walk humbly with thy God." The words he uses, הַצְנֵעַ לֶכֶת עִם־אֱלֹהֶיךָ, are not so common as the former words of command, but they are not obscure. The omission of Jehovah's name is notable. The duty, he says, is a simple duty towards God, whatever we may hold concerning His nature. And he directs that men walk with their God. High fancy this, fancy that was fact to him who could conceive it. The thought arose evidently from the suggestion of the former command. It is the next word that is uncommon. It bids men bow as they walk with God, but the bowing is not in modesty alone, but in the diligence of the workman who bows earnestly to his task. Finally, the very form of the word means that a man await no impulse from without, but himself render the worthy submission of his soul. Here then was a demand for reverent regard for that ever-present, unseen power that controls. Men are bid to watch for every whisper of the voice beside them, bowing in solemn gladness to obey. First stood the command to be a true member in the ordered fellowship of men; next followed the law of godlike regard for all needs, although society know them not; and highest of all is this law, Live in fellowship with God as His devoted child.

(3) These may be called the positive laws of Micah; they speak in the form "Thou shalt." But he has in mind deeds of which he says "Thou shalt not." We could not be sure we knew all the prophet's mind regarding duty if we had only his analytical meditation; that needs to be supplemented by the outbursts of indignation forced from him by wrongs he saw done. Such quick recoil of his soul tells best what his moral nature was. We recall, then—

(a) His condemnation of the unkindness of men in his own district about Moresheth to the fugitives from the calamity in the north. As they came, suffering and feeble and all heart-broken, fleeing to the south, Micah's countrymen robbed them, and then ordered them to move on out of the district with their weariness and wounds.

(b) He denounces slave-trade, where a brother sells his brother. We denounce it too, of course, but it is easy for us to make too little of Micah's condemnation. For we are habitually heedless of the history and the actual condition of those times, and we refuse to believe that some wrongs were common then. But Hebrews between Isaiah's day and Jeremiah's did entrap and sell their own brothers and sisters into slavery. Micah detested this conduct. He saw the duty to regard a brother's or a sister's freedom as equally sacred with one's own.

(c) Micah counted it disastrous and wicked to keep men from possession of land. Personal freedom was not enough; possession of land was necessary to life. There is an expression in chap. ii., 1 ff., which shows this, and which has also much importance for other reasons. He says—

> Ho! vain plotters, who plot evil on their beds,
> When morning dawns they'll off to carry it out,
> Because it is *within their hands' reach*.
> So they covet fields and seize them.

These words, "within their hands' reach" (כִּי יֶשׁ לְאֵל יָדָם) might as well be paraphrased thus, "They take the lands because it belongs to their divine hand," or, "It belongs to their hand as to a deity."[1] Therefore Micah means that the land monopoliser has indeed the power as a god has power, and none can stay his hand. The law may seem

---

[1] *El* (אֵל), the general expression for "deity," means "outreaching one," "He whose touch reaches to us." The conception is like that of the Greeks when they called Apollo or the sun, the Far-shooting One (cf. Ἥλιος, and Homer's adjectives with Apollo). See Prof. de Lagarde, "Orientalia II.," Göttingen, 1880, pp. 3 ff., especially p. 9.

to be on his side; wealth and power may make the man irresistible. Yet he is wrong to take the land, as he would be wrong to take a life were it in his power. Men must not use such power as the gods may use. The verse rings with the cry, fierce and firm, which is the very mind of God, "Legal right may be immoral."

Of course, so long as the people were tribal, their land belonged to the whole people, and to alienate a man from the land was to alienate him from the people. That meant something else, an awful alienation further; it meant casting a man out from the nation's God. Woe to the man who destroyed such ties then! Aye, woe falls where they are cut at any time.

(d) Micah condemns the prince's use of his power, or the teacher's or trader's use of any power and prerogative he possesses for any end other than their true use. With this we may link his condemnation of false excitement to action, as such could be worked by alcohol. And we link here also his stern condemnation of the restraint of any true excitement of the soul to speak. The test of truth was to be rigidly applied; we have seen that the test of such true inspiration was, "Does the word minister to life?" When that was the result, then the word was to be counted the word of the Spirit of Jehovah. And woe be to him who restrained God! Such then were the ethics, general and specific, positive and negative, of the book of Micah.

§ 4. *His fundamental faith.*

What now were the foundations upon which the whole edifice of his religious life rested? Let us ask what were his clear opinions of the sources of his spiritual being.

(1) He had definite conceptions of God. The conception was a growing vision no doubt, but we can watch its

definite lines of growth. What were then Micah's ideas of God's nature and His character?

(a) Jehovah was to him a God among many gods, and was not yet the absolutely lone Deity. He hopes for the fulfilment by-and-by of the old prophecy that the throne where Jehovah has the right to sit shall be chief and highest among all the Divine thrones (chap. iv. 1 *ff.*). It is true that this is only a quotation of an earlier faith, and we may not impute to Micah all the opinions of an earlier writer simply because he quotes a passage from that writer. Moreover, Micah never uses in any other passage the Divine title, "Lord of hosts," which is used in this quoted passage, and which Amos and Isaiah had used so often. Probably, however, this shows that by Micah's time the common people of Judah were beginning to believe less in the divine power of other gods. But they were only beginning. The magnificent trial scene of chap. vi. implies a belief in the existence and dignity of other gods when it summons the mountains which were the seats of the gods to judge in Jehovah's controversy with His people. And finally, the high question of chap. vii. 18, "Who is a God like unto Thee?" speaks to those who may remember the other gods and their character. But the question also exalts Jehovah so utterly far above all others that we say the dark days of divided fears are passing away, and the wonderful hand of God is lifting men up to a new age of peace by giving them the thought that there is but one great Spirit around them with whom they have to do. Here we can see the process of disclosure of God to men in the ages. This is the act of Divine revelation.

(b) Again, the same utterances show us that Micah thinks of the Divine processes and aims as sensuous rather than spiritual. Of course, it may be said, we can hardly think such a distinction now. Whatever seems to be a material process is in reality worked by a spiritual cause. But Micah did think of Jehovah as finding His supreme satisfaction in material events, and as giving to His friends or enemies material rewards and punishments. Thus His own exaltation is to consist in the exaltation of His throne above those of all other gods. So His people are to be comforted by the fruit and the shade of the vine and fig, and by their political emancipation from Assyria. On the other hand, the death the evildoer deserves and brings is to have his loved Zion ploughed like a field, his arsenals plundered, and his sanctuaries ruined. And yet this is not all. Micah yearns to work good character in men, although he does not rise to see or say that such character is the whole of real life. Although he laments outward suffering as the very stroke of God's anger, yet there is in chap. vii. the most keen lament for the lack of good men as the lack of all that is good.

(c) That the prophet is certainly rising to more spiritual apprehension is most evident from his conception of his own inspiration. Micah is convinced of Jehovah's spiritual presence with him, and perfectly happy in the faith that his own opinions are the very mind of God, and have arisen in his soul by God's spiritual operation in him. He founds his spiritual life on direct oneness of his spirit and power and activity with the Spirit of God. His power to speak, to think aloud, to win or to condemn by eloquent speech, his whole personal beneficent activity, is one with the Spirit Jehovah. Alas that a degenerate later Judaism should have ever become our teacher in such fields rather than this Micah.

(d) Micah believed also in the grace of Jehovah that brings forgiveness. Was it any wonder he had so high a conception of Jehovah's gift of His own thought to the prophet? He had learned from Isaiah the faith that their God was utterly devoted to this Hebrew people, giving forgiveness to all men in Zion. Micah does not advance beyond the limitation Isaiah conceived and set. Jehovah would pardon His heritage; for sinners in Zion only there was forgiveness. But limited though the election was, the gift was gracious. It filled the prophet's heart, thought, lips, with a very heaven-like grace, and his words have become the litany of all sin-sick and helpless, or trusting, glad souls—

> Who is a God like unto Thee!
> That pardoneth iniquity!

(c) The highest point reached by the faith recorded in his little book is marked in the words (chap. vii. 7, 8)—

> "As for me, I will look unto Jehovah;
> I will wait for my saving God.
> My God will hear me.
> Rejoice not against me, O mine enemy.
> When I fall I shall arise:
> When I sit in darkness, Jehovah shall be a light unto me."

The man who trusts in God expects—not what he knows, and can declare, or has imaged within his soul—he expects what God only has as yet conceived. It shall come. That is his faith. What it shall be God only can describe. This height of faith is simply true faith. It has been always in all trusting children of God. Hosea spoke it distinctly (chap. xi. 9), "I will not destroy," as ye expect. "I am God and not man." It was the oracle written over the Cross on Calvary—nay, upon the sacred brow so wounded there. It was written there, although it awaited Paul's expression long afterwards in the great formulas of our faith—

> "Now is Christ risen from the dead."

and

> "Eye hath not seen what God hath prepared for them that love Him."

It is the Divine faith of Man through the ages. Here is the essence of our belief in the supernatural. God knows all His thoughts toward us, but ere they are fully revealed to us they seem beyond our possible belief. When once they have clearly come then we understand them and know their exact fitness. For God reveals Himself to men in men's ways; and no man's soul may say, I cannot have this possession. The light of God that was hidden from eternity is made flesh, and dwells among us full of grace and truth; and although it seemed beyond us, it proves to be all ours, perfectly revealed to us. This is God's way, and such is God's word. Micah and his brethren saw God thus by faith, and said—

> *When* I fall, I shall arise;
> When I sit in darkness, the Lord,
> The Lord shall be light unto me.

Truly this man saw God. Such was his vision.

(2) And these faiths came to the prophet in human ways. If they had not, then they would indeed have contradicted their own meaning. But the evidence is plentiful. The prophet was a child of his race. Perhaps his father and mother had Philistine blood in them, for they lived in an old Philistine town and district; yet, if they had, the fact would only set in stronger relief Micah's own nature as that of an inheritor of the traditions of the Hebrews. What love he had for Zion, and for Samaria too! What love for the words of the past prophets, and what draughts of their faith he drank! The later chapters of this book are almost the first of the prophets' words that tell us about Abraham. Isaiah had indeed said in one of his finest passages these words, "Jehovah redeemed Abraham" (Isa. xxix. 22); but here in Micah, chap. vii. 20, the forgiving grace of God is called the grace bound up with Abraham, which by all His

revelations to the fathers from the days of old, Jehovah pledged Himself to give to His people. The story of trials and mercies in those past days is known, and called to the people's mind in chap. vi. 4 *f.*, as they sit in the high court of judgment opposite the Divine plaintiff. He declares He brought them from Egypt under three leaders, Moses, Aaron, and Miriam. He reminds them that a Moabite prince, Balak, had taken counsel with Balaam concerning them, but that Jehovah's unchanging love had wrought safety for them in spite of that conspiracy, and had saved them again in times of need that arose at Shittim and at Gilgal. Micah's own knowledge of God had been taught him by the story of life past and present, his people's and his own. He had seen God's providence, and so he had learned to love Jehovah. Even so would he kindle love for God in his fellows. To him the Divine faiths come by human relations. Micah's theory of life is somewhat parallel to the philosophic faith, "I think, therefore I am." Micah would have said, "I love, therefore I live."

§ 5. *His relation to the Pentateuch.*

It would be of course of much interest to discuss what were Micah's sources of knowledge of the past, with its patriarchs, its Exodus, and its Davidic age. This is not the place for minute examination of the matter. Be it only noted first that the sources of Micah's knowledge must have been the same as the sources of the Pentateuch records, for both come from the same people. And secondly, had the Pentateuch itself been in Micah's hands, he and other prophets would certainly have made far more use of it as a storehouse of religious argument than they did. And finally, if it had existed, and possessed anything like the religious authority which the post-Christian Jews gave it, the prophets, including Micah, would surely have invoked directly its powerful aid. Their failure to do this is evident. If these prophets whom we have studied, in their often hard task of persuasion, could have called in the words and authority and help of "the Book of Moses," why did they not do it? Since they do not, is it not certain that that Book must be subsequent to such prophets? On the other hand, we shall have to ask latter on, when we analyse the Pentateuch, whether it is not clear that since the Book of Moses says so many prophetic things, and sets forth so many prophetic ideas, it must be a product and reflection of the prophetic age, written by later prophets, pupils of the earlier prophets' schools and spirit.

CHAPTER IV.

CONCLUSION.

THESE final words may be few. For it is not necessary to construct here our estimate of Micah's place in the history. We have been estimating that place all through our study of the book bearing his name. This was imperative because of the uncertainty whether the treatise were not a collection of oracles from successive men rather than the utterance of one man. It was best to look on it as a moving series of visions of what God was and what men could comprehend of Him. In these visions one earthly voice followed another, while the great Giver of all the visions unfolded the continuous revelation, giving to each speaker his power, his insight, his faith, and his utterance. Our study of Micah has thus been a study of a movement rather than of a man. We have watched a procession of inspired men to trace in all the presence and speech of the great Inspirer.

The story of external events in those years between Isaiah and Josiah is comparatively of little account, viewed in the light of the spiritual movement, quiet but momentous as it was, through all that time. We saw the chronological outline above in our study of Isaiah; and occasional notes as we have proceeded have supplemented this. The sum in brief is that the Hebrews became more than ever the vassals of the now brilliant and most powerful Assyrian emperors. The prince Manasseh resisted, but in vain; and he was punished by imprisonment in Assyria for a time.

Zion proved not to be endowed with that immunity from harm which Isaiah had proclaimed. While his noble faith grasped and declared the great fact of God's love for men, he was not gifted with exact foresight of external events. It is not surprising that students of political events count the history of Israel a little thing and barren and uninteresting.

But the religious story of that half century, 700 to 650 B.C., is like the story of a silent night, wherein earth's forces work their secret creations. All living things that had lain down weary, or folded their leaves before the darkness, seem in the light of morn to have been all night long in close and ceaseless contact with vital currents. Sleep, quiet, rest, have made all things ready for the new day with its new joys, and tasks, and conflicts. So it was in Manasseh's times. Beyond the records that we have read in the book of Micah we know almost nothing of the period, save that Manasseh led a reaction against the Zion-doctrine of Isaiah. The king cared for the older sanctuaries. His action was, perhaps, that hesitation to advance which ensures wisest advance after all. His was a quietly thoughtful time; the prince was perhaps a truer servant of Jehovah than has been supposed. The length of his reign, and the fact of his restoration by Assyria from prison to government help us to believe that he and his people did not a little valuable work. They fill the closing ranks in the line of march which we have watched for a hundred and fifty years from the time of Amos and Hosea, through the brilliant age of Isaiah, and the period of quiet beauty and reflection mirrored in the book of Micah.

And now we have reached the eve of events of great moment. As we enter a second period we shall have to chronicle a political and external story more momentous than any that has been recorded above. These outer experiences, again, will be found to be the occasion of notable spiritual advance, enlargement of interest, deepening of character, great sharpening of insight into the realities of God and of life. Thus it will be found that we are now about to enter on days of rich self-revelation of God in men and to mankind.

The experiences which we have already traced will be found to have grown more powerful in moulding the people as the generations travelled onward. The knowledge of God and of good, of man's nature and duty and happiness which the Hebrews received ever more and more through the ages which we have studied, was a thing of great beauty in itself. It was a gracious gift to the men who received it step by step along their own career. But God blest more than these men in illuminating them, and He blest more than the generations wherein they lived. He was all along making ready a people who should give birth by His creative power to souls able to face times and needs such as their fathers had never known. The political developments of national life just ahead of the point we have reached were about to demand deeper thought and greater power than those of Isaiah even. And the way has been prepared for these. As the hour arrives, and the need unfolds, we shall find the "vision" and the men ready, the minds and the truths there together. For not only is it true that the vision grows fuller with the growing years, but it is the fact here as elsewhere that "God fulfils Himself" through many minds "in many ways."

INDEX.

(A.) NAMES AND SUBJECTS.

AARON, 328.
Abraham, 327.
Abyssinia, 224.
Accad, 184.
Advance in Amos, 70, 76.
—— Hosea's, 144 ff.
—— Isaiah's, 168 ff., 261 ff., 286 ff.
—— in Micah, 309 f., 323 ff., 330.
Æsthetic marks, 164.
—— idea of Jehovah, Isaiah's, 269.
Africa, 209, 211, 224.
Age of rapid growth of conscience, 145.
Agriculture, 205, 218.
Ahab, 185.
Ahaz, 51, 166, 169, 193, 196, 199 f., 225.
—— death of, 194, 238.
—— dirge over, 202.
Aim of prophets, 54.
Alexander, 21.
Alliteration, 202.
Altar, 167, 271.
Alva, 212.
Amaziah, 39, 48 f., 68 f.
Ammon, 187.
Amon, 189, 298.
Amos, 19 f., 27, 35 ff., 57, 144, 156, 221.
—— the period of, 49.
—— the antecedents of, 56.
—— his argumentation, 70.
—— his conception of man, 76.
—— his idea of conscience, 70.
—— his estimate of himself, 69, 83.
—— his fellowship with God, 67.

Amos, the man, 41.
—— his revelation, 66 f.
—— his idea of righteousness, 71.
—— scene of his preaching, 44.
—— very human, 67.
—— view of Divine control, 85.
—— wrestling with God, 68.
Amosian judgment, 79.
—— penalty, 31.
Amoz, 156.
Analysis of the Pentateuch, 3.
—— of Amos, 35 ff.
—— of Hosea, 105 ff.
—— of Isaiah, 181 ff.
—— of Micah, 299 ff.
Anathoth, 155, 176.
Angels, 157.
Antecedents of Amos, 56.
Anthropology of Amos, 76.
—— of Hosea, 129.
—— of Isaiah, 233, 272.
—— Isaiah's advance in, 272.
Anthropomorphism of Amos, 85.
—— of Hosea, 137.
—— of Isaiah, 267 f.
—— in Micah, 306, 324 f.
Antiochus, 21.
Apocalypse, 210.
Arabia, 194, 210.
Aramaic, 164, 210.
Ararat, 186.
Area of Judæa, 286.
Ariel, 177, 213.
Aristotle, 59.
Arnold, M., 150, 160, 190.
Arpad, 188.

INDEX.

Art, history of, 8.
Ashdod, 188, 211 *f.*, 219.
Asia, 209.
Asshur, 178.
Assurbanipal, 189.
Assurdaan III., 186.
Assurhaddon, 189, 297.
Assyria, 59, 115, 126, 129, 135, 170, 176.
Assyrian canon, 182 *ff.*
—— empire, 50.
—— march, 208.
—— suzerainty, 211.
Assyro-Babylonian language, 184.
Atonement, 80.
—— Amos's view of, 80, 83.
—— Hosea's view of, 141 *f.*
—— Isaiah's view of, 170, 254 *ff.*
Authority of Jesus, 14.
Autograph records, 16 *f.*
Azariah, 186.

BAAL, 75, 134.
Babylon, 183, 223 *f.*
Babylonian empire, 50.
—— exile, 223.
Bacchanalians, 175, 209.
Balaam, 328.
Balak, 328.
Bashan, 221.
Beauty in Micah, 309.
Beersheba, 38, 153.
Benhadad, 185.
Bethel, 38, 109, 125.
Beth-ephrath, 301.
Beth-haccarem, 46.
Bethlehem, 46, 301.
Bissell, Professor, 36.
Bloodthirst among Hebrews, 248.
Book of Moses, 329.
Briggs, Professor, 36.

CÆSAR, 59.
Cairo, 112.
Calf-god, 107.
Call of Amos, 39, 48.
—— of Hosea, 116.
—— of Isaiah, 158, 162.
—— of Micah, 3 o. 307.
Calvary, 49, 326.
Calvin, *Institutes* of, 25.

Carchemish, 188.
Carelessness towards God's honour, 243.
Carmel, 46, 221, 234.
Carpenter, Professor, 36.
Casdim. 184.
Cave, Professor, 36.
Ceremonial holiness, 162.
Chaldæa, 218.
Chaldæans, 184.
Change in animal nature, 276.
Cheyne, Professor, vii. *f.*, 36, 196, 206, 258.
Child-oracle, 200.
Christ, 101, 131, 183, 267, 320, 326.
Christian teacher, a guide for, xi.
Christological questions, x.
Chronicles, 22, 64.
Chronology, 90, 184.
Classification of inspirations, 31.
Cleansing of earth, must be, 242.
Coliseum, 8.
Commission of Amos, 69.
—— of Isaiah, 158.
—— of Micah, 315.
Compilers, 160.
Confirmation of historical study by analysis of Pentateuch, 9.
Conjugal love, 127, 129.
Consciousness of duty, 145.
Conservative faith, 15.
Constructive account of Hebrew religion, vii.
Controversy, 17.
Controverted book, Micah, 296.
Counsels for analysis, 23.
Court of justice, scene in Micah, 307, 318.
Covenant, 102-130.
Creation, Isaiah's theory of the coming of the golden age, 291.
Credentials of a prophet, 48, 315.
Cromwell, 46.
Crucifixion, 163.
Cruelty among Hebrews, 72, 248, 307.
Cuneiform inscriptions, 182, 185, 297.
Curtiss, Professor, 36.
Cush, 211.
Cyprus, 219.
Cyrus, 223.

INDEX. 335

Damascus, 112, 169, 185, 188.
Daphne, 214.
Date of Deuteronomy, 27.
David, 58, 62, 213, 224, 234.
David-age, 47, 56, 144.
David-faith, 56 *f.*, 305.
David-heir, 200, 203.
David-revelation, 58, 60 *ff.*, 64 *f.*
Day of Jehovah, 39, 87, 242.
Debauchees, 167, 204.
Delitzsch, Professor, 27, 36.
Deliverer-Torah, 24 *ff.*
Deuteronomy, 25, 27, 29, 109, 298.
Devoted One, 141 *f.*, 147, 173.
Devotees, 164.
Dialogue in Amos, 37.
Dirge in Isaiah, 198.
Divine character, 147.
—— control in Amos, 62 *ff.*, 85 *ff.*
—— control in Hosea, 94.
—— control in Isaiah, 234 *ff.*
—— control in Micah, 319, 324.
—— guidance in critical work, 14.
Division of kingdoms, in Isaiah, 235.
Dramatic scene, 204, 208, 306.
Driver, Professor, vii. *f.*, 36, 181, 206, 211.
Drunkenness, 127 *f.*, 204, 246.
Duhm, Professor, ix., 36, 163 *f.*, 189, 202, 237, 262.
Duncker, Professor, 189.

Earthquake, 197, 199.
Eclipses, 183 *f.*, 186.
Eden, 109.
Editors of Pentateuch, 31.
Edom, 186 *ff.*, 194, 210.
Egoism among Hebrews, 317.
Egypt, 115, 126, 129, 141, 194 *f.*, 211, 213, 234, 238, 271, 328.
Eighth century B.C., 21.
Elam, 184.
Elect, 25.
Eliakim, 210.
Elijah, 20, 55, 113, 144, 151, 185, 234, 250.
Elohist, 27, 29.
Enthusiasm of Isaiah, 249.
Ephod, 103, 148.
Ephraim, 111, 133, 154 *f.*
Eponym canon, 91, 185 *f.*

Era, Victorian, 183.
Eschatology, 89, 209, 275.
Esdu-Sarabe, 186.
Ethiopia, 189, 224, 234.
Euphrates, 50, 59, 155, 182, 185, 234.
Ewald, 196.
Exile, 19, 28, 61, 162.
Exodus, 28, 97, 109, 132, 135.
Eyes of God, 261.
Ezekiel, 19, 57, 63, 155, 313.
Ezra, 21.

Faith of prophets, 53.
Fanaticism, 241.
Fate watchword, 205, 208.
Fatherhood of God, 132.
Feebleness of Hebrews, 248.
First Christian century, 12.
Flux in conceptions of Amos, 76.
Follower of Isaiah, Micah, 305.
Forgery supposed, 23.
Forgiveness, 149, 162, 220, 222, 232, 281 *ff.*, 325 *f.*
Formal observances in Hosea, 148.
—— observances in Isaiah, 271.
—— observances in Micah, 310 *f.*
Fotheringham, Rev. J., xii.

Genesis, 3, 29.
Geological controversies, 8.
Gilgal, 38, 109, 153, 328.
Gittites, 307.
Glory of Jehovah, 236, 270.
God, Hebrew consciousness of, 317.
—— Amos's idea of, 85.
—— Hosea's idea of, 134.
—— Isaiah's idea of, 265.
—— Micah's idea of, 323.
Gods besides Jehovah, 324.
Golden age, 40, 95, 100, 209, 217, 263.
Good, definition of, 88, 318.
Gozan, 186.
Grace, Isaiah himself a symbol of, 256.
—— of Jehovah, 139, 149, 233, 254, 256, 270, 325.
—— in Zion, 165, 172 *ff.*, 256, 326.
Greece, 50, 59, 179.
Green, Rev. J. R., 45.
Growth in Amos, 76 *ff.*
—— in Isaiah's anthropology, 288.

Growth in Isaiah's new faith, 173.
—— in Isaiah's conception of God, 286.
Guthe, Professor. 36, 102, 122, 175. 187 ƒ., 193, 202, 206 ƒ.

HABAKKUK, 63.
Haggai, 63.
Hamath, 185, 188, 211.
Handel, 20.
Harem-rule, 169.
Haupt, Professor, x.
Hazael, 185.
Heart, the organ of knowledge, 125.
Hebrew language, 113.
Hebron, 153.
Hermann, Professor, x., 227.
Herodotus, 182, 223.
Hezekiah, 28, 51, 174, 176 ƒ., 187, 193, 201, 210.
Hiddeqel, 186.
Historical books of the Bible, 7.
History of prophets is history of the people, 20.
Holiness, 75, 161, 164, 237.
Holy days, 201.
Holy hill, 164.
Home of Amos, 46.
—— Hosea's, 111.
—— Isaiah's, 229.
—— Isaiah's own picture of, 277.
—— Micah's, 327.
—— sanctuary, 198.
Homiletic method, 121.
Hosea, 19, 57, 63, 90 ƒ.
—— his advance, 146.
—— central characteristic of, 122.
—— his doctrine of knowledge, 138.
—— his knowledge of history, 118.
—— his home and sorrow, 92, 111, 118.
—— his rank, 114.
—— his reasoning, 117.
—— his sympathy, 124.
—— the text of the book, 91.
Hoshea, 116, 187.
Human sacrifice, 313.
Husbands, Hosea's ideal, 148.

"IMITATION of Christ," 80.
Immanuel, 165, 172 ƒ.
Immanuel-faith, 243.

Improvement in character about Isaiah, 288.
Individuals, Amos's estimate of, 78.
—— Hosea's estimate of, 130 ƒ.
—— Isaiah's estimate of, 273.
Infallible authority, 11, 43.
Infallible person, 12.
Inspiration, 31.
—— of Amos, 42, 66.
—— of Micah, 307.
Intoxication, 127 ƒ., 246.
Introduction to Old Testament, Driver, 181, 206.
Isaiah, 19, 57, 60, 144, 150 ƒ.
—— a token of grace himself, 256.
—— his anthropology, 233, 272.
—— his disciples, 229.
—— his experience in Zion, 155.
—— genetic view of his faiths, 227 ƒƒ.
—— his idea of the golden age, 276.
—— growth of his new faith, 173.
—— his home, 229.
—— material blessing, his desire for, 278.
—— the hour of his change, 168.
—— the prophet, essentially, 228.
—— the religion of, 150 ƒƒ.
—— scheme of his ideas, 233.
—— his theology, 233, 265.
—— universal need interpreted by him, 241.
—— view of Israel as a whole, 272.
Islam, 318.

JACHIN and Boaz, 103.
Jahweh, 36.
Jebusites, 153.
Jehoahaz, 187.
Jehovah, covenant name and its meaning, 125
Jehovah's glory, 236 ƒ., 270.
—— grace, 215.
—— of hosts, 62 ƒƒ.
—— more than man, 140.
Jehovah-plants, 261.
Jehovah supreme lord, 64.
Jehovist, 27, 29.
Jehu, 185.
Jephthah, 313.
Jeremiah, 19, 57, 60 ƒ., 102, 146, 153, 155, 162.

INDEX. 337

Jeroboam II., 51, 145 f., 186, 202.
Jerusalem, 46 f., 59, 152.
Jesus, 12 ff., 85, 125, 133, 163.
Jezreel, 112.
Jonah, 202.
Joshua, 25, 60, 63.
Josiah, 28 f., 162, 177, 297.
Josian reformation, 27.
Jotham, 166.
Judæa, 59, 285.
Judaism, 26.
Judges, 60, 63.

KAUTZSCH, Professor, 36.
Kernel of Hosea's being, 122.
—— of Isaiah's character, 227.
Kings, 60.
Knowledge, Hosea's view of, 147.
Kuenen, Professor, 36.

LAGARDE, Professor, x., 36, 92, 261, 266, 322.
Land tenure in Isaiah, 249, 280.
—— in Micah, 322.
Last things, Isaiah's doctrine of 276.
Law, meaning of, 23, 149.
Law of Moses, 23 f.
Leavened bread, 27.
Lebanon, 145, 176, 185, 221.
Levant, the, 50, 113, 145, 212.
Leviticus, 27, 29.
Limit of God's presence, Isaiah's view of, 292.
Linguistic features of Pentateuch, 10.
Lion, the figure, &c., 178, 209, 214, 217.
Literary criticism in first century, 13.
Literary questions concerning Amos, 35.
Lord of hosts, 125, 144.
Love of Jehovah, 270.

MALACHI, 61, 63.
Man, Amos's conception of, 76 ff.
—— Hosea's estimate of, 99, 123 ff.
—— Isaiah's estimate of, 272 ff.
Manasseh, 189, 225, 297, 315, 331.
Manifestations of God, 149.

Marriage, 147.
Material prosperity, Amos's view, 40, 77.
—— ——, Hosea's view, 137.
—— ——, Isaiah's view, 292.
Meade, Professor, 36.
Mediterranean, 59.
Menahem, 186 f.
Men of the Spirit, 128.
Merodach-Baladan, 188, 195, 212, 218, 223.
Method of study, 3, 5.
Micah, 19, 57, 63, 295 ff.
—— analysis of, 299 ff.
—— a controverted book, 296.
—— a follower of Isaiah, 305.
—— his place in history, 330.
—— religion of, its ethics, psychology, theology, 295 ff.
—— his relation to the Pentateuch, 328 f.
Military skill of David, 153.
Mind, its seat the heart, Hosea thought, 125.
Ministers, demand of, viii.
Miriam, 209, 328.
Missionary outlook of prophets, 21.
Mizpeh, 38, 153.
Moab, 28, 73, 187 f., 246.
—— fall of, 194, 202 f.
—— lament for, 202.
Moloch, 216.
Monastic garment, 164.
Monasticism, 80.
Monogamist, Hosea a, 134.
Monotheism, advance towards, 236.
Moral character of Jehovah in Isaiah, 271.
Moral height of Amos, 75.
—— of Hosea, 136 f.
—— of Isaiah, 247.
Moresheth-Gath, 299.
Moses, 25, 132, 328.
Moses-Torah, 1, 24, 132.
Mottoes of Isaiah, 191 ff.

NAHASH-DAVID, 31, 202, 225.
Nahum, 63.
Napoleon, 212.
Narrative books of Old Testament, 1.

Y

Nation, not individuals, dealt with by Amos, 77.
—— by Hosea, 129.
National God, Hosea's, 94.
Need of Amos now, 41.
New Testament, 13, 25.
Nile, 145, 209, 238.
Nineteenth century, 13.

OBELISKS, 103, 148, 312.
Olympiads, 155, 183.
Omnipotence of Jehovah, 237.
Omniscience, 210.
Omri, 185 *f.*
Oracles of grace, Isaiah's, 199.
—— of judgment, Isaiah's, 196.
Overlordship of Jehovah in Amos, 36, 62 *f.*, 65, 70.
—— —— in Hosea, 95, 135.
—— —— in Isaiah, 233 *f.*
—— —— in Micah, 324.
—— expansion of idea of, 237.

PAIN, Isaiah's estimate of, 283.
Paraphrases of Isaiah's oracles, 196 *ff.*
Parent birds, 178.
Park, Professor, x.
Patriarchs, 132.
Paul, 26, 109.
Pekah, 186 *f.*
Pekahiah, 186.
Pentateuch, 1 *ff.*, 23, 29, 63.
—— analysis of, 22, 27.
—— counsels for analyst of, 23.
—— Micah's relation to, 328.
—— narrative in, 30 *f.*
—— not its own standard, 7.
People of God, 131.
Perfection, Isaiah's doctrine of, 233, 277 *ff.*
Persian Gulf, 184.
Persian empire, 50.
Persons, Amos's estimate of, 78 *ff.*
—— Hosea's estimate of, 129 *ff.*
—— Isaiah's estimate of, 210, 257, 272 *ff.*
Perspective in study of Hebrew religion, 150.
Pestilence in Assyrian army, 222.
Phases of Zion faith, 314.

Phelps, Professor, x.
Philistine blood, 327.
—— coast, 112.
Philistines, 145, 174, 186 *f.*, 211.
Philological tests in analysis of Pentateuch, 10.
Philosophy, beginning in Hosea, 149.
Phul, 186.
Pillar of fire, 261.
Pillars, Divine symbols, 103, 148, 312.
Plato, 59.
Pleasure, Isaiah's view of, 245.
Plottings with Egypt, 213.
Poetry in Pentateuch, 30.
Political knowledge of Amos, 62 *f.*
—— —— of Hosea, 96.
—— —— of Isaiah, 170, 175, 225.
Polygamy, 134.
Power of Jehovah, 269.
—— of prophets, 52, 316.
Practical ministry, 121.
Pre-Davidic faith, 151.
Present Christ, 13.
Prince, Isaiah's ideal, 257, 274, 293.
Problems left unsolved, 87 *f.*, 148, 291.
Process of inspiration, 56.
Progress of thought, Amos, 69, 76 *ff.*
—— —— Hosea, 131.
—— —— Isaiah, 151 *ff.*, 199, 237, 253 *ff.*, 256 *ff.*
—— —— Micah, 330.
Prophetess, Isaiah's wife the, 230.
Prophets before Amos, 156.
Prophets' theme, method, and aim, 52 *ff.*
Proverbs, 92.
Providence, Isaiah's theory of, 243.
Psalms, 64.
Ptolemaic canon, 184.
Purity of Hosea, 133.

RAIN-GIVER, 216.
Raphia, 188, 212.
Reflecting spirit in Micah, 309.
Regeneration in Amos, 78.
—— in Hosea, 148.
—— in Isaiah, 233, 238, 259, 276, 278, 283.
—— in Micah, 328.
Rehoboam, 95.
Religious aim, 3.

Religious test in analysis of Pentateuch, 11.
Rembrandt, 250.
Renan, Professor, 36, 59.
ezin, 186 f.
Results of analysis, 23 ff.
Revelation, 10.
—— in Amos, 70, 81.
—— in Hosea, 119, 128.
—— in Isaiah, 230, 267.
—— in Micah, 314.
Rhetoric, Isaiah's, 212.
Riehm, Professor, 36.
Righteousness, Amos's demand for, 71.
—— Hosea's demand for, 98.
—— Isaiah's ideal of, 242 ff.
—— Micah's ideal of, 318 ff.
Ritual, 30, 149, 250, 271.
Rock-caves, 197.
Rome, 50 f., 59, 183.
Russia, 145.

SACRED trees, 312.
Sacrifice, 149, 167, 198, 251, 312.
Sacrilege, 73.
Salman-assur, 174, 185 ff., 201, 211.
Salvation by faith, and by works, 25.
—— Amos's way of, 78.
—— Hosea's way of, 100, 147.
—— Isaiah's way of, 168 ff., 254 ff.
—— Micah's way of, 325 f.
Samaria, 44, 47, 111, 169, 174, 193 f., 201, 311.
Samuel, 60, 82, 153.
Sanctuaries, Amos's theory, 82.
—— Hosea's theory, 149.
—— Isaiah's theory, 150 ff., 270.
Sargon, 174, 187, 194, 210 f., 218, 297.
Schrader, Professor, 182, 185, 223, 297.
Scientific accuracy in analysis, 11.
Scythians, 145, 169.
Self-estimate of Amos, 69.
—— of Hosea, 139.
—— of Isaiah, 256 f.
—— of Micah, 315 f.
Sennacherib, 177, 188, 195, 206, 211, f., 222, 225, 297.
Sensuality, 74.
Seveh, 188.

Seventh century B.C., 21.
Sharon, 221.
Shear-Jacob, 208.
Shear-jashubh, 160, 166, 170, 200, 208, 229.
Shebna, 210.
Sheol, 40, 87, 175, 198, 205.
Shiloh, 153.
Shittim, 328.
Sicily, 186.
Sidon, 186.
Sieges of Jerusalem, 209, 220.
Signs from God, 170.
Sin, Amos's estimate of, 80.
—— Hosea's estimate of, 103, 147.
—— Isaiah's estimate of, 253.
—— Micah's estimate of, 321 f.
Sistine Madonna, 8.
Sivan, the month, 186.
Sixth century B.C., 21.
Slave-trade among Hebrews, 72.
Smend, Professor, 36.
Smith, G., 91, 182, 185.
Smith, Rev. G. A., 170.
Smith, Professor W. R., 36, 90, 122, 133, 144, 163, 187, 320.
Smythe, Professor, x.
So, king of Egypt, 188.
Socin, Professor, 286.
Soil of Palestine sacred, 81, 129.
Solomon, 103, 154, 156.
Son of God, 132 f.
Spirit of Christ, 12.
Spiritual process in regeneration, Isaiah, 278.
Stade, Professor, 36.
Story of the past in Hosea, 101.
—— —— in Isaiah, 156.
—— —— in Micah, 327 ff.
Strong drink, 198.
Students, work and results of, viii. ff., xii.
Suez, 59.
Sumir, 184.
Supernatural, 314. 327.
Symbols, 103, 126, 148, 256, 311.
Syria, 145, 169, 186, 199 f., 210.
Systematic theology, 120.

TALISMAN of fate, 175, 205, 208.
Tanis, 214.

Tartary, 145.
Tekoa, 46.
Temple, 154, 157.
Teraphim, 148.
Test of analysis, 6 *ff.*, 16 *ff.*
Test of prophetic authority, 316.
Theological problem, 3.
Theology, Amos's, 85 *ff.*
—— Hosea's, 99, 134.
—— Isaiah's, 233, 265 *ff.*
—— Micah's, 323 *ff.*
Theophany, 159, 161.
Tiglath-pil-assur, 169, 186, 201.
Tigris, 50, 155, 179, 185, 209.
Tirhakah, 189.
Tithes, 27.
Tophet, 216.
Torah, 24, 132.
Torah-givers, 135, 279.
Traders, 145.
Tribal conscience, 70.
Tryst, 180, 221.
Turanian, 184.
Twistedness, 281 *ff.*
Tyre, 154, 186, 195 *f.*, 218 *f.*

UNCHASTITY among Hebrews, 92, 248.
Uncleanness of non-Hebrew lands, 95, 129.
Unification of Hebrews, 59, 209.
Universal rule, Isaiah's hope of, 236.
Unsatisfactory methods, 7.
Uzziah, 28, 51, 145, 156 *f.*, 166, 186.

VANITY, sin of, 244 *f.*
Vineyard, song of, &c., 167, 198.
Vintage-feasting, 203.

WARWICK, Sir Philip, 45.
Watchwords of Isaiah, 191 *ff.*
Water-tanks, 209.
Wellhausen, Professor, 36.
Whitehouse, Professor, 36, 182.
Wife of Isaiah, 230.
Wine, 125, 246, 316.
Witch of Endor, 58.
Woman, estimate of, in Amos, 74 *f.*
—— ——, in Hosea, 118, 127, 134.
—— ——, in Isaiah, 245, 277.
—— ——, in Micah, 322.
Word becoming flesh, 171.
Word of God, 13.
World-monarchies, 61.
Wrestling of Amos, 66, 68 *f.*
Writing prophet, the first, 71.
Wrongs around Amos, 72 *ff.*
—— around Hosea, 124, 126 *f.*, 135 *f.*
—— around Isaiah, 243 *ff.*
—— around Micah, 321 *ff.*

ZADOKITES, 155.
Zeal of Jehovah, 239.
Zechariah, 63.
Zephaniah, 63.
Zion, 19, 150 *ff.*, 196.
Zion-doctrine, 222.
Zion-faith, Micah, 305.
Zion in Isaiah's early discourses, 166.
Zion's disappointments, 293.

(B.) HEBREW AND GREEK WORDS.

(1) Hebrew Words.

כְּבוֹד יְהוָה 255	בְּרִיתִי 106	אָדָם 124
כָּלָה וְנֶחֱרָצָה 205	הוֹשֵׁעַ 99	אֲדָמָה 124
מַאֲמִין 203	הַמַּאֲמִין לֹא יָחִישׁ 203	אַהֲבַת חֶסֶד 320
מֹשֶׁה 24, 132	הַצֶּנֵעַ 321	אִישׁ 106
לֶכֶת עִם אֱלוֹהֶיךָ 321	חֲכָמִים 142	אִישִׁי 94, 130, 135
נֹשֵׂא עָוֹן 281	חֶסֶד 106, 122, 125	אֵל 322
עִמָּנוּ־אֵל 191, 193	139, 320	בֵּית־אֶפְרָת 301
עֲשׂוֹת מִשְׁפָּט 319	טוֹב 86, 106	בֵּית־עַפְרָה 301
צְבָאוֹת 63	יְהוָה 63, 190	בֶּן־בָּקָר 133
קֹדֶשׁ 161, 255	יוֹם הַהוּא 275	בֶּן־מָוֶת 133
קָדוֹשׁ 190	יָרָה 24	בֶּן־נְבִיאִים 133
שְׁאָר יָשׁוּב 190, 192	יָחִישׁ 203	בְּנֵי־עַמּוֹן 133
תּוֹרָה 24, 132, 251	יִשְׂרָאֵל 190	בַּעֲלִי 134
תּוֹדָתִי 107	כִּי יֵשׁ לְאֵל יָדָם 322	בְּעָלִים 93, 94
	כְּאָדָם 106, 130	בְּרִית 122

(2) Hebrew Words Transliterated.

'Alah, 265.
'Allon, 266.
Baal, 134.
Chesedh, 125, 139, 320.
'El, 191, 265.
'Elah, 265.
'Elleh, 266.
'Eloah, 265.
'Elohim, 74, 85, 191, 265.
Hithqaddesh, 164.
K'Adham, 130.
Maççeboth, 103, 148.
Miçraim, 211, 271.
Moreh, 135.
Mosheh, 25.
Q-D-Sh, 161, 163; 164.
Qadhesh, 164.
Qaddesh, 164.

Qaddishin, 164.
Qadhosh, 75, 163.
Qudhsh, 164.
Rehoboth, 45, 156.
Shechinah, 148.

(3) Greek Words.

Ἥλιος, 322.
Κανὼν βασιλέων, 184.
Nomos, 25.
πολυμερῶς καὶ πολιτρόπως, viii.

(4) Other Foreign Words.

Foedus, &c., 102.
Odium theologicum, 48.
Offenbarung, 227.
Pietas, 320.
Theologie der Propheten, ix., 122, 237.
Zukunftsbild des Jesaias, 175, 187.

Just Published. In One Volume, Crown 8vo, Price 3s. 6d.

NATURAL THEOLOGY.

THE GIFFORD LECTURES

DELIVERED BEFORE THE UNIVERSITY OF EDINBURGH IN 1891.

BY PROFESSOR SIR G. G. STOKES, BART., M.P.

"The Gifford Lectures are an important contribution to the controversy between belief and unbelief."—*The Times.*

"The tone of the whole is eminently candid, charitable, and Christian."—*British Weekly.*

"Will command and must receive the most respectful attention."—*Anti-Jacobin.*

"As useful as it is interesting."—*Observer.*

"A valuable contribution to the literature of their subject."—*The Scotsman.*

"Valuable as well as interesting to all classes of readers."—*Manchester Courier.*

"Its treatment is simple and scholarly."—*Bradford Observer.*

"The subject is dealt with in a comprehensive and masterly way."—*Northern Whig.*

"He has addressed himself to a highly difficult task with breadth and care."—*Newcastle Leader.*

"Practical, substantial, and fresh, and has an unfailing common sense."—*Aberdeen Journal.*

"We welcome with delight this volume of Gifford Lectures."—*Dundee Courier.*

"Dogmatism is absent, and the lectures deserve to be widely read."—*Evening News and Post.*

"The book will supply a complete answer to many questions which thoughtful men are asking themselves to-day, and it should be in the hands of all who wish to meet some of the scientific objections to the Christian faith."—*Yorkshire Post.*

LONDON AND EDINBURGH:

ADAM & CHARLES BLACK.

Just Published.
In One Volume, Crown 8vo.
Price 6s.

PAGANISM
AND
CHRISTIANITY

BY

J. A. FARRER.

The Presbyterian:
"This is a remarkable book."

The Scotsman:
"Mr. Farrer has brought together many passages of great worth and beauty from the pages of the ancient philosophers."

Publishers' Circular:
"Mr. Farrer's book will be found highly attractive."

Liverpool Mercury:
"A bold, scholarly contrast of Paganism as exhibited in the best thought of Greece and Rome with Christianity in its orthodox form. Will surprise many a reader by the curious evidence presented."

Newcastle Chronicle:
"He has therefore endeavoured to put the case of pre-Christian Paganism in its best and truest light, and to meet and controvert a legion of writers who have been wont to misrepresent the state of the older world."

LONDON AND EDINBURGH:
ADAM & CHARLES BLACK.

Just Published. In One Volume, Crown 8vo, Price 5s.

SKETCH OF THE HISTORY

OF

ISRAEL AND JUDAH.

BY

J. WELLHAUSEN,

PROFESSOR AT MARBURG.

THIRD EDITION.

"The sketch is in every way admirable."—*The Scotsman.*

"This work exhibits the vigorous cautious writing of an earnest scholarly thinker."—*Liverpool Mercury.*

"A useful contribution to a subject of ever-increasing interest."—*Newcastle Leader.*

"This learned and able work."—*Newcastle Chronicle.*

"It admirably epitomises the subject, and exhibits on almost every page evidences of Professor Wellhausen's profound study."—*Publishers' Circular.*

"A carefully prepared and comprehensive history of great value to students."—*Manchester Courier.*

"This work is one of the chief formative influences in the attitude which scholars are assuming with regard to the Old Testament."—*Dundee Advertiser.*

"It is invaluable as a guide to the secular history of the people of the Old Testament."—*Observer.*

"It will be instructive alike to the biblical scholar and the general reader."—*Glasgow Citizen.*

LONDON AND EDINBURGH:

ADAM & CHARLES BLACK.

Just Published.

In One Volume, Crown 8vo.

Price 3s. 6d.

THE CHURCH

OF

SCOTLAND.

A SKETCH OF ITS HISTORY.

BY THE

REV. PEARSON M'ADAM MUIR,

MINISTER OF MORNINGSIDE, EDINBURGH.

NEW EDITION, WITH NOTES AND INDEX.

The Scotsman:
" Likely to be of permanent value."

LONDON AND EDINBURGH:
ADAM & CHARLES BLACK.

In Two Volumes. Demy 8vo.

Price 24s.

LIVES

OF

THE FATHERS.

Sketches of Church History in Biography.

BY

FREDERICK W. FARRAR, D.D., F.R.S.,

LATE FELLOW OF TRINITY COLLEGE, CAMBRIDGE;
ARCHDEACON OF WESTMINSTER; CHAPLAIN IN ORDINARY TO THE QUEEN.

"The history of the Church is represented in certain respects by the history of her great men."
—Bishop Wordsworth.

LONDON AND EDINBURGH:
ADAM & CHARLES BLACK.

WORKS

BY THE LATE

ALEXANDER RALEIGH, D.D.

QUIET RESTING PLACES,
And other Sermons. Twelfth Edition. Crown 8vo, 5s.

FROM DAWN TO THE PERFECT DAY.
Crown 8vo, 5s.

THE LITTLE SANCTUARY.
Third Edition. Crown 8vo, 4s. 6d.

THE BOOK OF ESTHER;
Its Practical Lessons and Dramatic Scenes. Fcap. 8vo, 4s. 6d.

THE WAY TO THE CITY,
And other Sermons. Second Edition. Crown 8vo, 5s.

REST FROM CARE AND SORROW.
Fcap. 8vo, 3s. 6d.

THOUGHTS for the WEARY and SORROWFUL.
Second Edition. 3s. 6d.

THE STORY OF JONAH.
Fcap. 8vo, 4s. 6d.

By MRS. RALEIGH.

RECORDS of the LIFE of the late Dr. RALEIGH.
Fcap. 8vo, 3s. 6d.

STUDIES IN THE UNSEEN.
Second Edition. Fcap. 8vo, 3s. 6d.

LONDON AND EDINBURGH:
ADAM & CHARLES BLACK.

In One Volume, Demy 8vo.

Price 10s. 6d.

UNBELIEF IN THE EIGHTEENTH CENTURY
(CUNNINGHAM LECTURES FOR 1880.)
By JOHN CAIRNS, D.D.

In One Volume, Medium 8vo.   Illustrated with 336 Woodcuts.

Price 10s. 6d.

KITTO'S POPULAR CYCLOPÆDIA OF BIBLICAL LITERATURE.

In One Volume, Fcap. 8vo.

Price 3s.

CHURCH STUDENT'S MANUAL.

Also, in One Volume, 18mo.

Price 1s. 4d.

BOOK OF COMMON PRAYER.
ITS HISTORY AND PRINCIPLES.
By Bishop BROMBY.

LONDON AND EDINBURGH:
ADAM & CHARLES BLACK.

THE
ENCYCLOPÆDIA
BRITANNICA

A Dictionary

OF

Arts, Sciences, and General Literature.

In Twenty-four Volumes of about 850 pages each, and Index.

Illustrated with Plates, Coloured Maps, and Wood Engravings.

Price in Cloth extra, gilt top, £37; and in Half-Morocco or Half-Russia, £45, 6s.; also to be had in Tree Calf.

Separate Volumes, 30s. in Cloth, or 36s. in Half-Russia.

Detailed Prospectuses giving a selection of the principal contents of the Volumes and other particulars, with specimen pages, may be obtained on application to the Publishers.

LONDON AND EDINBURGH:

ADAM & CHARLES BLACK.

www.ingramcontent.com/pod-product-compliance
Lightning Source LLC
Chambersburg PA
CBHW020228240426
43672CB00006B/450